The Qwarriors

A CONSERVATION TALE

Linda Vaughn Fitch

Linda Vaughn Fitch

For my sons Lyle and Bruce Andrews
who spent childhood summers exploring the quarry.

Linda Vaughn Fitch

"Here is your country. Cherish these natural wonders, cherish the natural resources, cherish the history and romance as a sacred heritage, for your children and your children's children."
Theodore Roosevelt

Linda Vaughn Fitch

TABLE OF CONTENTS

Linda Vaughn Fitch

Preface

HOW DO YOU TELL A STORY?

In this case it happened that one day I sat down and started typing on my Mac. A plastic bin by my desk contained documents detailing a legal battle on a small island on Lake Champlain in Vermont—which began in August 1995 and ended on December 30, 1998. An eco-battle. Fought, for the most part, by ordinary citizens and coordinated by a trembling pacifist. That would have been me. Over time we began to call it the Quarry War.

I wanted to tell this story for years, but it had become a "black hole" in my mind. Wikipedia puts it well: "A black hole is a region of space-time from which nothing, not even light, can escape." That's pretty much what this story, for eighteen years, was for me: a body of information and emotion so compacted in my mind that no light (well how about words) could escape.

There was so much information, so much emotion related to an intense three years during which we tried to stop an impending quarry operation (yes, right in our backyards) that I couldn't imagine where to start. Or indeed how to continue after a start. But finally, after some eighteen years of hemming and hawing and many false starts, I decided to begin a process of stringing together documents and emails and letters from the three year space of time during which this story unfolded. I looked into old files on my computer. They were written from 1995 to 1998 in obsolete applications such as "Write Now" which, when I tried to open, produced the message "There is no application set to open this document." Thanks a lot, Steve Jobs!

But then I found that I could drag the ancient file (maybe I could call it a "fossil file" which would be very appropriate to this story) to an application in my dock called "Text File." There, magically, it often opened to reveal partially garbled, partially coherent text, along with paragraphs and even pages of strange hieroglyphics (I must ask my adult computer wizard sons what these are). But amidst these technological runes was enough text to copy and paste into updated word processing applications and to remind me of the content of the documents: letters, affidavits, testimony, rebuttal testimony and journal entries in which were described the issues of a citizen fought environmental battle.

I did that transliteration for four weeks in 2012. Transliteration! Here's Wikipedia again: "Transliteration is a subset of the science of hermeneutics. It is a form of translation, and is the practice of converting a text from one script into another." So after four weeks of "converting texts from one script into another," they were now pretty much organized, dated, labeled, and in place. It seemed, as I looked at this long chain of documents that these would be the bones of the story. I knew I must somehow flesh out these bones; create the context, depict the characters, and share the emotions which colored the story: the fear, the anger, the sense of futility--balanced with the learning, the love, the magic, and the creation of community.

It took another two years. Critical stuff was missing. Though many emails were saved, the emails of Joe Bivins, chief hero (among several) of our saga, had tragically and mysteriously disappeared from my computer when the eco-battle ended in 1998. And then, in 2012, I started sorting through boxes of printed materials. In a box that my mother--who passed away in 2008--had stored in her apartment I found, bless her old fashioned heart, that she had printed out virtually all of the emails that I had sent to her between 1995 and 1998. Hard copies! Who does that? I guess you do it if you came of age in the bygone era of paper, pen and ink and then managed, in your elder years, to tiptoe courageously if timidly into the age of the computer. So, thanks to my 94 year old mother, now I had some, if not all, of Joe's emails.

There were other reasons why it was hard to write.

I am NOT a confrontational person. And throughout the "quarry war" I was never confrontational in the sense of expressing anger, insults, or even anything that would mildly resemble aggression. The only way I knew how to fight, the only way I was temperamentally capable of fighting was through the written word, through building alliances with lots and lots of people and through feeling that this needed to be some kind of spiritual journey that would benefit everyone. Would I have gone through with it had I known the effort and the anguish it would entail? I don't know. I think I would have been too horrified and frightened. On the other hand, would we even be willing to go through life itself, if we knew the hard times and the horrors that every life journey presents? Along with the possibilities for joy and for beauty?

Another difficulty I had in writing an account of the Quarry War, I eventually decided, was because during those three years I had to hold back so much. Because I tried so hard to take the high ground, to follow some kind of spiritual path, I repressed some of the truth. Some of my truth. My emotional truth. Always, I tried to understand the other side: the environment versus the jobs issue; the local "heritage of quarrying" issue; the local pride issue; the "guys not wanting to be shown up by this effete, flatlander woman" issue. I tried and tried to repress my own fear and anger, to see the guys in "white light," as "vulnerable human beings," and then later when I tried to write about it, the writing came out as careful and tight as the hundreds of pages of testimony which we had to submit to the Environmental Board, to the Waste Management Office, to the Wetlands Office, to the Water Resources Board of Vermont. Three years of typing "carefully thought through" stuff. It felt as though the emotionally honest woman was—writing-wise at least—five feet under with daisies growing on her grave.

Sometimes, I thought, it would be easier just to write the story as a screen play for, say, a movie with lots of visual shots. It would be wonderful in this movie to see beaver gliding through the water of Big Pond in the old quarry; there could be muskrat, mink, foxes, deer...maybe there's a shot of children exploring Turtle Pond...a recording of sounds, the humming, chirping, splashing, croaking. Or maybe it needs to start much much earlier...

1. Beginnings

"I do not believe that any man can adequately appreciate the world of to-day unless he has some knowledge of--a little more than a slight knowledge, some feeling for and of--the history of the world of the past."
Theodore Roosevelt

IT WAS WARM. VERY WARM. The wind blew, waves beat against white sand and stretching beyond the beach was the warm brown of earth. A few scant growings of lichen, of mosses perhaps, but no other green of vegetation. No sea gulls circling above searching the blue waters for a gleam of fish. No fish. No signs of life. The only sounds were those of the surf and wind whistling through the sand and soil of dry land.

Beneath the blue of sea however was movement. There were mounds on the ocean floor built of small branching fronds; there were cabbage shaped colonies of tiny polyps--feeding on microscopic plankton which surfed the swirling waters. On the ocean floors arthropods crawled, seeing with newly invented calcite eyes. Most of life lived in the salty waters of the vast oceans that covered Planet Earth.

This was an ancient sea, known in later eons as the Iapetus Ocean, ancestor of the mighty Atlantic which would form some millions of years in the future. Four hundred and eighty-million years ago this Iapetus Ocean was inhabited by creatures who had recently (some 50 million years before) begun to develop hard shells or exoskeletons of calcium carbonate. These hard shells served as protection in the predator/prey relationships which had evolved over the years since the great proliferation of life forms which had occurred some 100 million years before that--the famous Cambrian explosion.

As these new armor bearing creatures died, their calcium carbonate remains piled up creating mounds rising up from the ocean floor. Other animals found that these mounds provided places in which to shelter, to feed, to thrive. Formed on the shallow continental shelves of nearby land, the mounds provided protection against the turbulent wave action from the open ocean. These protected areas were lagoons. Flooded by sunlight, they were quiet, warm places. Over time more animals and more plants sought these beneficent, shallow water habitats.

The mound communities grew larger, ever growing population centers with ever more diverse citizenry. The carbonate layers of shells and exoskeletons of the dead were cemeteries which gradually lithified or turned to rock. This rock would eventually be known as limestone which in turn became platforms for the formation of more mounds. Growing ever larger and more complex, they became the first true reefs--complex cities--the first to appear in the long 4.6 billion year history of Earth. "They were the first tentative attempts of life to work in a multi-species community, to build features that would evolve into such massive structures as the modern-day Great Barrier Reef," wrote one scientist some millions of years later.[1] Located south of the equator in the area of current Zimbabwe, they eventually extended to a length of a thousand miles.

Earth's surface is ever shifting through the process of tectonic plate movement whereby great landmasses and their adjacent continental shelves travel about Earth's surface at the rate of several centimeters a year. And so it was that our reefs, the continental shelf on which they formed, and the adjacent landmass that would eventually become North America went on a long journey. Departing from the equator and the location of present day Africa, they traveled, inch by inch, merging with and rifting from, other landmasses year by year until, some 480 million years later, they became part of a region far to the north and the west of where it began. The region was eventually named North America by a species which, after about two hundred thousand years of its existence on Earth, began to call itself "Homo sapiens." Remnants of the reef stretched a thousand miles from places called Newfoundland, Quebec, Vermont and Tennessee.

Some of it ended up as the limestone bedrock of a seemingly unlikely island in the middle of a lake. It was Lake Champlain, a great freshwater lake located between the states of New York and Vermont. The island was called Isle La Motte. Eventually it was claimed by an entity called the "State of Vermont."

2. An Early Evening
"There can be nothing in the world more beautiful than the Yosemite, the groves of giant sequoias and redwoods, the Canyon of the Colorado, the Canyon of the Yellowstone, the Three Tetons; and our people should see to it that they are preserved for their children and their children's children forever, with their majestic beauty all unmarred."
Theodore Roosevelt, Outdoor Pastimes of an American Hunter 1905

August 8, 1995
IT WAS EARLY EVENING on Isle La Motte, the northernmost island on the Vermont side of Lake Champlain. The setting sun colored Lake Champlain with an unlikely palette...peach, purple, tinges of orange. I had driven down the gravel road along the west shore of our little island, turned into the grassy driveway of Fisk Farm and parked the car next to our now, partially renovated barn. The silence of the evening offered a clear soundscape...the squawk of the great, blue heron stretching his wings to soar home from a day of minnow fishing, the occasional rhythmic hoot of the barred owl, the beginning murmur of the tree frogs.

As I opened the car door an appalling sound suddenly cut through the evening quiet. It was coming from the direction of the old quarry next to our family summer home. Lawn mower? Chain saw? Too loud. I walked past our house, followed by my stalwart mini-poodle, Shasta. We crossed the back lawn, and then clambered through tangles of black raspberry (known as "black caps" by the locals), sumac, old stands of lilac and a forgotten apple tree.

Coming out from the underbrush to a flat rock Shasta and I peered over the edge of the cliff down into the Fisk Quarry below and the pond which had formed in the past eighty years. Three turtles dove into the water from a sun warmed rock. In the distance on a dry section of the rock quarry floor just beyond the pond was a man with some kind of equipment, breaking up rock. My heart started to pound.

We made our way back through the tangle of brush, I left Shasta in the house, crossed the lawn to the garage, dragged my bicycle out to the driveway, then cycled down the gravel road to what had once been the main quarry entrance. I passed the point of land, once site of the great quarry dock from which loads of stone were loaded onto boats throughout the nineteenth century. It was the dock onto which Vice President Roosevelt stepped from the elegant yacht Elfreda in 1901 and was escorted the short distance to Fisk Farm and the crowds that awaited his arrival. I made my way through shrubs, trees and black raspberry bushes and emerged into a clear space where a man was operating what I later learned was a bobcat jackhammer. His equipment was in the process of efficiently breaking up rock. As I approached he turned off his machine and climbed off his seat.

"Hello," said I, my high heeled sandals clicking on the quarry floor. "What's going on?"

"Big quarry operation going to start up here," he said, leaning against his equipment. He told me that a big company had bought the quarry and had all the permits in hand to start quarrying. He said that he owned the equipment and that a lot of work was going to be done here.

I hesitantly observed that it was seven thirty in the evening.

"Hey, no problem! Most days we'll be starting around six in the morning and ending at four in the afternoon."

"But it's quite loud," I said. "What about the neighbors? Everybody around here loves the peace and quiet. Six in the morning is pretty early," I said, too distressed to think of anything else to say.

"Wish I could sleep past six."

"And it certainly would threaten the value of the properties in the area."

"The man who bought the quarry? He put a lot of money into it." He climbed back into his cab.

Some years later I had to laugh as I thought back on my parting rejoinder: "Well there must be a win win solution here somewhere."

Win win solutions! The hopeful remark from a flower child of the sixties. He must have been laughing as I bicycled back to the house. I was shaking. At some point later there was some news article in which I was depicted as striding up and confronting this guy with his equipment. "They had words," said the article.

"They had words!" The writer was trying to describe me as this feisty, tough, feminist woman striding in to protect our new little business, a B&B at our family summer home, Fisk Farm. Far from "having words," I was a real wimp. The phrase "win win solution" actually came out of my mouth. It's a nice idea maybe, the portrayal of me as a strong, courageous woman, but it just wasn't true. I was absolutely terrified. And I was not terrified for fear of losing my business or for any economic reasons whatsoever. I was terrified by the possibility of losing the serenity and the beauty which had brought my family and all who lived along the west shore of Isle La Motte here in the first place.

Isle La Motte is a small island just seven miles long and two miles wide on the Vermont side of Lake Champlain, northernmost in the chain known as the Champlain Islands. In the year 2000 the population was listed at 488; in summer the number swells to several thousand. There is a country store, a tiny library, an elementary school, an apple orchard, several campgrounds, a marina, several churches--Protestant and Catholic--and the famous St. Anne's Shrine where, in the 1600s, a fort was built by the French.

There are a number of stone houses built from the limestone quarries, a key island industry throughout the 1800s and the early 1900s. In modern times the island has been connected to the mainland by a causeway and summer homes have risen along shoreline once regarded as useless land, fit only for the watering of the cows.

It is thought that the island was a gathering place for local Native American tribes who, it has been said, preferred to live permanently on the mainland some distance from the lake, fearing the possibility of attack by warring neighbor tribes.

The first European to venture onto Lake Champlain and indeed to set foot on the island was Samuel de Champlain who, in 1609, made his historic voyage down the Richelieu River from the newly founded city of Quebec. He had formed an alliance with the native Montganais, Algonkaian, and Hurons to fight their enemies, the Iroquois. In early July he and his Native American allies paddled south from the river out into the broad, blue expanse of what he duly named "Lake Champlain."

In the early 1900s Isle La Motte resident, Arthur Hill, made a detailed study of Champlain's journals. He wrote:

> "In the extreme N.W. corner of Vermont guarding the entrance to Lake Champlain lies Isle La Motte. This is the island where Champlain landed on 2 July 1609 and where he camped that night and the next night and which he describes as 'Three leagues long covered with most beautiful pines that I have ever seen...in it [the lake] are many beautiful low islands covered with very fine woods and meadows with much wild fowl and animals to hunt, such as stags, fallow deer, fawns, roebucks, bears, and other kinds of animals which come from the mainland to these islands. We caught there a great many of them. There are also many beavers, both in that river and in several small streams which fall into it. This region although pleasant is not inhabited by Indians, on account of their wars; for they withdraw from the rivers as far as they can into the interior, in order not to be easily surprised.' "[2]

Champlain paved the way for French exploration and settlement in the New World. First came the fur trappers, then the Catholic priests to convert native tribes. Forts were built to protect French interests in Canada and what is now Vermont. The first of these, Fort St. Anne, was built in 1666 on Isle La Motte in the northwest corner of the island. The French found that the bedrock of the southern part of the island was limestone and they dug it out of the ground, burning it and mixing it with water to make the mortar needed to construct the log fort. That was the first human use, by Europeans at least, of the limestone which underlay the southern third of the island. With the 1759 defeat of the French by the British in the French and Indian War, both Canada and Vermont became British territory. Records show that lime kilns on Isle La Motte used by the French were later operated by the British as early as 1760.[3]

European settlers came in the late 1700s to Isle La Motte from Connecticut, Massachusetts, New York. The island would have been covered with hardwoods and pines, with simple rutted roads like narrow trails through the forest. Life was rugged for the earliest settlers. An early history of the island recounted "the hardships and sufferings" of one Abram Knap "who was compelled in order to subsist a large family, to use the buds and tender leaves of the bass wood tree to form a mucilage for nourishment, and from the bark fibre to make a sort of cloth for covering and wearing apparel."[4]

Another early settler was Ichabod Ebenezer Fisk, who arrived in 1788 with his wife and family. He bought land on the southwest shore of Isle La Motte and it is believed that the first structure that he built was the small cottage of stone that still stands, just north of the area from which the French got their limestone for mortar as they built their fort in 1666.[5]

In 1803 Ichabod's son, Samuel, built a large house of the same limestone.[6] The quarry from which Samuel carved out the stone for the house became known as the Fisk Quarry.

Four generations of the Fisk Family prospered from their quarrying business. It was the mainstay of the family finances as well as a major contributor to the island economy. In the latter years of the nineteenth century, the Fisk estate became a showplace, famous throughout the north country. Money from the quarry went into the construction of a great horse barn with box stalls for twelve horses and space for several carriages. Attached to the horse barn was a cow barn and an ice house--the latter built of stone. There were flagstone walks, hollyhock gardens, peonies, roses, a goldfish pond, a deer park. The Fisks owned several hundred acres, including the surrounding fields and sites along the shore where shacks for the quarry workers were built. In 1860 the Fisks constructed a company store and post office to serve the village of Fisk.

Fascinating though the history is, it is the poetry which brings us here year after year: the sheer beauty of early morning mists rising off the lake, gulls riding on the wind, sunsets which set the lake on fire or the moon rising so that as one islander said to me, "We set off to do some fishin' the other night. The moon was full and it seemed like the lake was paved with gold. For a few minutes there I felt like I was a millionaire."

I was introduced to the island in 1963 by Peter Andrews whom I had met while he was a mathematics graduate student at Princeton University. I was a Junior at Barnard College in New York City to which I traveled back and forth from my family home in Princeton, New Jersey, just an hour's train ride to the south of the city. Though Peter's family were residents of Tenafly, New Jersey, ancestors on his mother's side were early Hills and Scotts who had settled on Isle La Motte in the early 1800s.

My parents had originally come east from the sand hills of northwestern Nebraska. Ranch country. After emigrating to New York City and getting his Ph.D. in Economics, my father eventually worked in New York City government and delighted in saying that he was the only public official in New York City who could rope and tie a calf. Peter's father also worked in the big city, commuting from the suburban town of Tenafly, New Jersey. In summer the family always returned to the island.

In June of 1963, just six months after we met, Peter brought me to Isle La Motte to visit his family's ancestral home—now the family summer home. It was a brick house in the center of the village, built in 1845. I loved the horse-hair furniture, the chiming of the old clocks, the smell of newly baked bread, the oval framed portraits of ancestral Hills and Scotts, the overwhelming atmosphere of an earlier century. One year later, Peter and I married and moved to Pittsburgh, Pennsylvania where Peter was appointed assistant professor of mathematics at Carnegie Mellon University. Part of our summers were spent with Peter's parents on Isle La Motte.

Disaster struck my own family when, three years after our marriage, my 23 year old brother Devin, a graduate student at Princeton, my gentle, brilliant, guitar playing brother—took his own life. From such a blow you never really recover. Somehow and over time you try to rebuild your lives. Your souls. We all thought it would be helpful for my family to spend summers on Isle La Motte. Mother and I made several trips to the island in search of a small, simple cottage on the lakeshore but never found quite the right place.

During a visit in 1970 to my husband's family home, Peter and I saw that the old Fisk property had come on the market. "Historic Property for Sale" proclaimed a hand painted sign nailed to a tree. I didn't know its history at that time, but later I learned that over the years, the once grand property had changed greatly. Of the several hundred acres once owned by four generations of the Fisk family, most of the land had been sold off. Three acres of lawn shaded by black locust trees remained. The beautiful stone house built in 1803 and once visited by presidents was a pile of fire destructed stone in a cellar hole overgrown with tiger lilies and roses. One wing still stood, a two story stone shell. The once elegant horse barn, now guarded by a moat of nettles and used for the storage of hay, had been sold off to the Hall family who came to the island in the early 1800s and whose descendants continue to run the last remaining orchard. The small stone cottage, built by Ichabod and Samuel was intact. The company store and post office had been remodeled in the late 1920s by the heirs of the last Fisk and now served as the Main House. Paint was peeling, and the front porch was sagging but the whole place, we thought, looked somehow magical.

My parents drove up from their home in Princeton, New Jersey to take a look. Dad looked past the peeling paint of the buildings toward a sheltered cove in which to moor a boat which he, Nebraska born and bred, had always dreamed of. Peter the mathematician saw a lawn for games of croquet and plenty of room to spread out his mathematics papers. I saw fields of golden rod, milkweed and wild blackberries stretching out behind the house. It was odd that our family name, Fitch, was so similar to the name Fisk.

"That old place?" said Peter's mother, my mother-in-law who, born in 1900, had known it in its glory. But Peter bargained, the owners agreed, and my parents purchased the property for a song. We all felt that it could be a place to heal. A place where family and friends could come for respite. Restoration. Community.

Our first summer on the island was in 1971. Our son, Lyle, was a toddler and son, Bruce, was a month old. From then on we came to the island every summer. The boys grew up diving for my father's mooring blocks, climbing the walls of the old quarry adjoining our property, and bike riding to their paternal grandmother's house in the middle of the village, where they learned manners and how to split wood into six-inch lengths for the stove. My mother, a pianist and my first piano teacher, organized family music. During our island summers she would often practice early in the morning before my children got up.

"I like the piano, Nana," said ten year old Bruce once. "Hearing the piano in the morning is like having a nice alarm clock."

"You're saying the right things, Bruce. Playing the piano in the morning is good setting up exercises for my fingers."

Though Peter and I separated in 1981, he and I and our respective families continued to play croquet, to swim, to enjoy cookouts and picnics together. For all of us, our homes on the island welcomed and gave sustenance to the extended family.

Over the years, it has been common for certain residents on Isle la Motte to experience a knock on the door, followed by a request from some rugged though often bespectacled character asking for permission to walk on the land. They are geologists, usually from some university, and they are looking for fossils. They often came to our house asking to walk across our lawn to the quarry cliffs in back of our house. My parents in particular often mentioned the name of one Charles (Chuck) Ratté, who was Vermont State Geologist at the time. He also taught classes and frequently visited Isle La Motte bringing students on field trips. My father in particular was fascinated by the fossils and often accompanied Dr. Ratté on these field trips.

In those days I did not have much interest in geology or, indeed in any science. This despite, or perhaps because, of growing up in a household in which dinner conversations between my father and his physicist brother, my Uncle Val, were often sprinkled with such terms as "leptons," "quarks," and the most elementary of particles. I would sit silently--feeling that science would forever be beyond my ken. In college I chose to major in history with big doses of literature and an ongoing interest in making music. My instruments were flute and piano. Later I picked up guitar. I had been required to take two science courses in college and chose geology in which I earned a resounding C. (The other was physical anthropology which netted me the slightly more respectable grade of B.)

In 1989 a particularly prestigious group visited the island to study the fossils. This was the International Association of Geologists. It was led by a Dr. Charlotte Mehrtens, Professor of Geology at the University of Vermont along with Dr. Charles Ratté. My parents, Lyle and Violet Fitch, trailed along. Photos show my parents bending over the rocks with a group of geologists from many countries, Dr. Mehrtens peering at a particularly significant squiggle, representing some form of ancient marine life, through a hand lens. Little did I know then how important both Dr. Mehrtens and Dr. Ratté would become in my life.

Early in July of 1995 I received a phone call from Charles Ratté. I remembered his name from conversations with my parents who had always been delighted to see him. Over the phone he asked if he could bring a group of adult students from the University of Vermont to view fossils in the quarry from a vantage point on our property. I agreed and asked if I could accompany the group to hear his lecture.

He came on a Tuesday. It was July 11. Dr. Ratté was accompanied by six University of Vermont students (elementary school teachers). I walked with the group across the back lawn to the quarry cliff to hear his lecture from a lookout point on the rock walls above the old quarry.

I must say that I could hardly understand a word of the lecture, my freshman geology course notwithstanding. After the lecture the students explored the cliffs while I sat on sun warmed rocks with Dr. Ratté or "Chuck" as he asked to be called. He told me more about the quarry and this time he used words that I could understand. He said that because of the quarry's unique geological features, it has been studied by numerous geologists from universities around the country. "The limestone in this quarry is part of a geological treasure called the Chazy Reef," said Chuck. "It was formed about 480 million years ago at a time which we geologists call the Ordovician Period." I remembered that from my geology course. Geological periods: Cambrian, Ordovician, Silurian, Devonian, Carboniferous, Permian....Despite my grade of "C" the words still rolled out of my mind and onto my tongue. It is the oldest biologically diverse fossil reef in the history of life on Earth I was to discover.

I learned that part of the reef can be seen in the Fisk Quarry which is why geologists come so frequently to visit and study. But actually, the bedrock of the entire southern third of Isle La Motte consists of this reef. Chuck pointed out the most famous fossils, outlined as large white forms in the quarry walls directly opposite from where we were sitting. "Those are 'stromatoporoids,' " he said, "and this particular genus is called 'stromatacerium lamottenses.' "

I learned that they were a colonial animal, long extinct but possibly related to the sponge of today. "This is not a coral reef," said Chuck. "Corals became the predominant reef builders many millions of years later."

I found out that these reefs had been formed by the calcium carbonate remains of organisms other than coral. Stromatoporoids, sponges, algae, gastropods, crinoids... "This place and a couple of other reef sites on Isle La Motte are pretty famous. They really should be protected for scientific and educational purposes," said Chuck.

I jumped on that. I told him that I had for a long time dreamed of the Fisk Quarry as a bird sanctuary. Earlier that spring, a young ornithologist - Dan Froelich - had come to visit us on Isle La Motte over the Memorial Day weekend. A former music student of my mother in Princeton, he was working on a federal project to identify birdlife on the top of Mt. Mansfield, and came to visit us over the long weekend. During that time he had spent time in the

Fisk Quarry and in the course of a single hour, had identified 42 different species of birds.

Chuck liked the idea of a preserve, both for geology and birds. "Who owns it," I wondered. I could imagine that some company might be happy to donate this old, abandoned quarry site for a preserve to, say, some.nonprofit organization. Chuck suggested that we might pursue the issue. A preserve! What a wonderful dream!

The Fisk Quarry

Stromatoporoids in the QuarryWalls

3. Permit

"Defenders of the short-sighted men who in their greed and selfishness will,
if permitted, rob our country of half its charm by their reckless extermination
of all useful and beautiful wild things."
Theodore Roosevelt

The 1800s

THE AMERICAN WILDERNESS. In the early nineteenth century there was a romantic view of the great untouched forests and landscapes of the new world. Poets and philosophers wrote about it. They were European writers including Coleridge and Kant; they were American writers such as Emerson and Thoreau; they were artists--like Thomas Cole and the Hudson River Valley painters in the East, and George Catlin in the West. They viewed nature, the wilderness, and the inhabitants of the wild places, through a spiritual lens. To experience nature was restorative, healing, offering the possibility of communion with God.

At the same time, forests across the continent were being destroyed, indiscriminate hunting had decimated wildlife; some species such as the buffalo and the passenger pigeon had gone extinct. As in the rest of the country, decimation of the land also ravaged Vermont. Forests were cut down, wood was burned for potash and railroad fuel, land was cleared for farming, for sheep grazing. The land was for human use. Today. There was no thought for the future. In 1810 most of Vermont was covered with forests; in 1860 it was 80 percent deforested.

August 8, 1995

It was growing darker. I picked up my bicycle and pedaled frantically back up the gravel road, crossing to the lawn to our house. I went right to the telephone and called Chuck Ratté to tell him about the jackhammer. The impending quarry operation.

Chuck's first question was, "Do they have an Act 250 Permit?"

"A what?"

"An Act 250 Permit." Chuck said that it was Vermont's Land Use Legislation and that it might just turn out that the company would need a permit. "You should call the Act 250 Coordinator of District Six tomorrow. That would be your Act 250 District. Let's see, I probably have a phone number somewhere around here."

Act 250. I was to learn more about this land use law.

It was 1969 and Vermont Governor Deane Davis, a Republican, was concerned that Vermont was being besieged by developers motivated solely by profit. The character and values, the natural beauty of Vermont, he felt, were being threatened. He asked one Arthur Gibb, a Republican in the House and later to become a Senator, to look into the issue. Arthur Gibb, lover of nature and the environment, was known to campaign in his district by bicycle. Strong controls were needed on this issue, he felt, but what form should they take? His Commission developed legislation called "Act 250" which set forth ten criteria by which all development in the state of Vermont would be reviewed. It was passed in 1970 by the Vermont legislature.[7]

When I finally put down the phone my hands were shaking. My friends--Merrill, Carol and Jim who were living with me that summer--crowded around with questions.

Early the next day, sounds in the quarry started in earnest. The roar of machinery filled the air. As we peered over the edge of the quarry cliff in back of our house, we saw below trucks, groups of men, several bobcat jackhammers. Despite the August heat Carol and Jim helped to close all the windows against the noise. It was impossible to block out the incessant sound of jack hammering on the rocks. I worked up my courage and dialed the number scribbled on a scrap of paper the night before.

"Good morning, Geoffrey Greene speaking." Far from sounding like a cold bureaucrat such as one might find in the state offices of New Jersey, the Act 250 Coordinator of District Six seemed pleasant and approachable over the phone as I told him what was going on next to our house.

"I was told that they might need a permit," I said hesitantly. He asked me to get the name and number of the contact person of the company which had bought the quarry. "The Town Clerk's office will have that information," said Mr. Greene.

"I guess I can get that information at the Isle La Motte Town Clerk's office when it opens on Thursday."

"I would suggest that you take pictures," he said. "I'll come over to take a look."

There's something about living in a place where remnants of its early history surround you; a place which is written about, where old photos, deeds, diaries, and documents still remain, where stone structures built two centuries ago still stand, and where living persons knew and remembered many of the leading characters of legendary times gone by. Ichabod Ebenezer—the first Fisk to settle on Isle La Motte was succeeded by his son Samuel who married Polly Scott in 1804. Polly Scott. (The Scott name also appears on the Hill side of my husband's family when Cornelia Scott married Henry Hill in 1852.) Samuel and Polly's son, Hiram, was born in 1818 and eventually took over the family business from his father. Hiram's son, Nelson, was born on August 5, 1854. Nelson Fisk.

By that time the Isle La Motte landscape was no longer covered by deep forest. One visitor wrote, "After crossing the ferry from Alburgh Point to the north end of the Island, we first drove down to the quarries of Messrs Fisk and Hill, which lie near its southern extremity. The drive through the length of the Island, being some five or six miles, we found very pleasant as we passed over the smooth road, and enjoyed the beautiful lake scenery upon every hand; also the rich fields of grain and grass, and the almost continuous orchards laden with fruit. There is hardly an acre of waste land upon the Island; the farms for the most part are highly cultivated and farm residences improved by planting out shade trees about them, and along the highway. These, with the groves of wood and timber left for domestic use, and the apparent thrift and independence of the inhabitants, make the Isle-La-Motte, a charming little spot—it is the gem of the Lake."[8]

Four years after the birth of Nelson Fisk, the son of another wealthy family was born, this one in New York City on October 27 in 1858. The name of that child was Theodore Roosevelt. Years later, on September 6, 1901, the two men met on the grounds of the Fisk estate where Theodore, as Vice President, was an honored guest for a few hours. Events transpired on that day which were to change the course of American history and continue to be remembered in vivid detail on Isle La Motte to this day.

Young Nelson went to Eastman Business College in New York to prepare for managing the family quarry business. He also ran the store and post office, housed in a simple frame building just a few steps away from the big stone house. It served the quarry workers as well as other island residents. Today, entries in the leather bound store books written in the ornamental Spencerian script of the time, are hard to read. But by looking closely one sees that on a day in the 1890s Mrs. Pickard bought a pair of rubbers for a dollar sixty-five, Mrs. Westcott bought a pie for eighteen cents, chocolate for sixteen cents and vanilla for ten cents, and Mrs. Tupper bought soap for two cents and silk for thirty cents. In 1880, when he was twenty-six, Nelson Fisk married the charming Elizabeth Hubbell from across the lake in Chazy, New York. It was the same year in which young Theodore Roosevelt, age twenty-one, married his beloved first wife, Alice.

Isle La Motte's village center is an entity so small that people often drive through without noticing that it is a village. It was "built by original settlers and their successors during the nineteenth and early twentieth centuries, with Victorian era homes and Greek Revival-style buildings forming the New England character of the village. The Town Hall, a Greek Revival-style wood-framed building with white painted clapboards, looks much as it did in 1891 when it was constructed."9 Next door is the one room library built of limestone from the local quarries. A cannon planted on the front lawn, was formerly situated on a cannon mount in front of the Fisk mansion. Two stone columns once situated in front of the Fisk's home, now flank the front doors of the little library.

On the Thursday after my phone conversation with Geoffrey Greene, I drove to the village and spoke to the Town Clerk. I learned that on the previous February 5, 1995, a Vermont company (hereafter referred to as CMC) had bought both the Goodsell Quarry on the east shore of Isle La Motte and the Fisk Quarry on the west shore from the international corporation, Omya. The price for the two quarries was $90,000. The purchaser's address was Proctor, VT. No name of a contact person was listed. She did not know of any permit that CMC had received. When I got home the Town Clerk called to say that Geoffrey Green had just stopped in at the Town Hall and was on his way down to see the quarry and to talk with me.

A knock on the door was Mr. Green on the front porch. An amiable, youngish man with red blonde hair, he told me that he had talked that morning by phone to the president of CMC.

"He told me that that though quarrying was planned, he didn't know of any work being done in the Fisk Quarry at this time. I've set up a meeting with him in two weeks after I get back from vacation. I need to find out what their plans are, what the scope of the work will be, and whether the Act 250 has jurisdiction in this case. Can you show me where they've been working?"

Together we walked down the road to the quarry entrance, through the dense vegetation which lined the little path into the old quarry excavation, coming to a shallow rectangular pit which had been carved out of the quarry floor in the past two days.

"Hmmm," was Mr. Green's comment. "Well, I've told the company president that no work should take place in the quarry until I meet with him and find out what their plans are. After that I'll send an advisory opinion to CMC and we'll go from there. In the meantime, until I meet with him I'll be surprised if work resumes, but if it does, call one of these numbers. And take photographs. Keep careful records of everything that occurs."

As we were leaving an older man, dark of hair and clad in jeans and a plaid work shirt, appeared at the quarry entrance. He introduced himself saying he was the foreman of the quarry. Mr. Green identified himself and explained why he had come. There was no welcoming smile here. The man looked suspicious.

The old Fisk Quarry was one of a number of quarries on Isle La Motte which, during the nineteenth and early twentieth centuries, were a mainstay of the island economy. The stone was marketed as black and grey marble and shipped all over the country to such prestigious locations as Radio City Music Hall and the National Gallery of Art. Throughout the nineteenth century the Isle La Motte quarries supplied this stone for buildings and bridges all over the United States and into Canada. Their names reflected their early owners: Fisk, Goodsell, Fleury, Clark, Ford, Hill, Scott and Wait.[10] Photos show the Fisk Quarry in the old days: great blocks of stone jumbled about, cranes heaving those blocks into the air, quarry workers with caps pulled over their eyes, posing on a block of stone for picture taking. A railroad track ran from the quarry across the road to Fisk's dock where boats pulled up and loaded Isle La Motte products: barrels of apples, shipments of ice, cargos of stone.

The Fisk Quarry in the early 1900s.

French Canadians came to Isle La Motte in the nineteenth century to farm and to work in the Isle La Motte quarries. They had a long history, both as farmers and workers, in the island quarries. The beautiful black and grey stone to be found on the island was unique; historically there was a good market for it. The lake made transportation relatively inexpensive and easy. To this day "Radio Black" is a byword among local year-round residents for the glamour, the excellence, the fame of stone from the Isle La Motte quarries.

When most of the island quarries grew silent around the turn of the century, memories of stone cutting were still strong—contributing to many islanders their sense of history. Their identity.

The quarries! There was a time when Isle La Motte was prosperous. The quarry industry helped to make it so. Small wonder, on that day in the quarry, that we were eyed with suspicion.

Friday dawned and to our great relief the quarry was quiet. The peaceful weekend stretched over Monday. On Tuesday, August 15, Carol, Jim, Merrill and I had gathered for breakfast around the table in the dining room, a serene and sun filled room, when the sound of machinery started up. Sound blasted through the windows. Operations had begun again. Geoffrey Green had said to take pictures.

"I can't do it," I said. My state of mind called for crawling under the covers and putting a pillow over my head."

"Jim and I will go," said Carol.

"Right," said Jim getting up from the breakfast table. "We'll be the Secret Service. We serve secretly. You probably didn't know that about us, did you."

"Oh Jim!" said Carol, his wife. They headed out into the August morning armed with cameras and binoculars. I called the number that Geoffrey Green had given me to use if quarrying continued; it was the office of the Vermont Land Use Attorney. I talked on the phone to a woman, name unknown, and explained the situation. She said she would pass the information along. She wanted to know how to find the quarry on Isle La Motte and if it would be obvious, once one was there, where the activity was being done.

"It will be very obvious indeed. I think you can probably hear the noise through the telephone," I said.

All day long the sounds of banging, of trucks, sifted through the closed windows and doors until 4:00 in the afternoon. At that point a welcome peace descended on the neighborhood. In the early evening I rode my bicycle down the road to visit the neighbors. Carl Williams, just south of the quarry, was outraged. I pedaled further down the road to find Elva Garanther, Neil and Elaine Hanna, Ross and Phyllis Firth. All had heard the noise. All were concerned.

In previous years the neighbors south of the quarry had established an organization called South Shore Associates. I hadn't known of the association but was delighted to hear that there was one.

"Time to start up South Shore Associates," said Ross Firth. "I love a fight." We agreed to call a meeting.

4. Dreams
"It is true of the Nation, as of the individual,
that the greatest doer must also be a great dreamer."
Theodore Roosevelt, Berkeley, CA. 1911

1880s

AFTER THEY WERE MARRIED Elizabeth and Nelson Fisk lived in the big stone house built in 1802 by Nelson's grandfather, Samuel. The young bride, came from the distinguished Hubbell family in Chazy, New York. She had ancestors who had served in the Revolution and the War of 1812. Having spent her childhood in Chazy, she now lived across the lake from her family. It was a long distance to travel in warm weather, a twenty-five mile trip by horseback or horse and carriage along rough dirt roads and primitive ferry boats. In winter, though, you could travel straight across the ice, a distance of perhaps two miles.

Young Elizabeth loved beauty in all forms. She planted flower gardens around her elegant new home. Flagstone walks were lined with plantings of peonies which bloomed in June—pink, white, and red. The blooming time of her colorful and exuberant hollyhocks was July.

The Fisks spent time in New York where Elizabeth was inspired by the Arts and Crafts Movement, an international design philosophy that developed in the last half of the nineteenth century and into the twentieth. The movement advocated traditional craftsmanship; it shared with the poets, philosophers and artists of the earlier Romantic movement a reaction against what was perceived to be the destructive impact of the industrial revolution. Elizabeth Fisk took a course at the Pratt Institute School of Art and Design in Brooklyn, NY

On Isle La Motte Elizabeth became interested in the old looms stored in the attics of many island homes and began to explore the craft of weaving. As she became proficient she developed new methods of weaving. She created a studio in the attic of the big stone house and trained other Isle La Motte women in the art which she had perfected. Her linens, like her gardens and her home, were inspirations of color and design.[11]

Many decades later, though the beautiful stone house had burned in 1923, hollyhocks still bloomed, peonies continued to frame the stone walkways, a living legacy of Elizabeth Fisk's creativity and love of beauty. I was inspired by her legacy and thought of her as I staked hollyhocks, during the summer months, using an old hand hewn wooden mallet that I imagined she had once used.

The Fisk Home: Early 1900s.

People frequently drove by slowly looking at the remains of the old mansion. Often they stopped. They took pictures. If we were sitting on the front porch of the former old store and postoffice, now our Main House, a few courageous ones would come up to ask questions. Sometimes, as we sat on the porch, my mother and I felt that we should be wearing elegant nineteenth century costumes. Or at least big garden hats.

> "I first came to Fisk Farm needing a respite from some personal challenges in my life. What I found was home in the deepest sense of the word. This place has a soul. It's a refuge for people needing some beauty and serenity in their lives. I want to come back every summer to my heart's home."

This was written by my friend, Carol, actress, poet, artist, who traveled from New Jersey to visit me in Isle La Motte during the summer of 1992. The picturesque quality of historic Fisk Farm inspired both of us.

"Wouldn't it be great," one of us said in 1992 as we took our daily five mile walkabout on the roads of Isle La Motte "to do something in the ruins of the old stone mansion. We could make them beautiful." We imagined cleaning out the first floor of the still standing wing, for many years called "the Workshop." Put in a wood stove maybe. We imagined antique crocks filled with goldenrod, Queen Anne's Lace, glowing against the old stone. Maybe a tea room. A place where people could come for tea and pastries."

"A Tea Garden," said Carol. "Look at art, hear music. Chamber music. Folk music. Jazz. Elizabethan madrigals. Poetry."

"And the barn. I've always wanted to restore the barn," I said. "It's falling apart but its really beautiful. Of course we don't own it." As we walked down the road past the apple trees in Hall's Orchard I continued, "I've also thought of a B&B. I've thought how wonderful it would be to have hand made quilts on the beds, the rooms freshly painted, the window sills refinished. I'm not good at that stuff but they say if you keep dreaming..."

"What do you visualize for the front bedroom?" she asked. "Green? It's green now, but could be wonderful with a fresh coat of paint. Let's go to Swanton and see if we can find fabric." I learned that along with her other gifts Carol was a quilt maker, a craftsperson, with skills in creating, restoring, spaces.

During the next two summers we worked to translate dreams into action. Two visionary woman friends, we grappled with reality which we wore on our bodies and in our hair in the form of wallpaper paste, green latex paint for the bedroom, teal blue enamel for the bathroom, and occasional splashes of polyurethane as we refinished pine window sills. Glazing compound. Carol designed and made quilts for the low ceilinged front bedrooms, checked out flea markets for mirrors to hang over the 1920s sinks that Dr. Whitcomb had installed in the bedrooms. I learned how to wield a sander and got George the electrician to install new light fixtures.

"I'm glad I've found someone as obsessive as I am," said Carol, her mouth full of pins, sitting at a sewing machine at the dining room table making new slipcovers for cushions for old wicker furniture on the front porch.

"My goodness," my mother said at one point coming in from the garden. "Carol, I had no idea you could make slipcovers! To say nothing of those beautiful quilts!"

"I need two husky women to help me load the lawnmower into the trunk of the car," my father said, entering the dining room and glancing at the slipcovers. "Husky?" Carol said. "Well strong maybe. Creative definitely. But husky?"

Carol had definitely become a member of the family.

But the Barn? Even Carol, with all her skills, had not a clue as to how the old barn could be brought back to life. To restore the Horse and Carriage Barn, built during the glorious Fisk era seemed the most impossible dream. When my family arrived in 1971 to spend our first summer the barn was a great wooden structure hovering on the north side of the grass driveway, boundary line between our property and Hall land. The Hall brothers had bought most of the Fisk land in the 1930s when the estate of Elizabeth Fisk was finally settled after her death in 1927.

For years the once elegant barn stood like a lost soul. Holes in the roof opened the structure to wind, rain and snow; great hand hewn beams were rotting. Every summer I fought my way through the chaos of nettles and grapevine which guarded the barn like a moat and squeezed through a narrow slit offered by the sagging doors into the barn. The front room which once housed carriages was filled with old farm machinery. There was a wooden shanty once used for ice fishing. Stalls of past horses still stood, wooden stanchions carefully carved into graceful curves, great box stalls with iron bars. It was hard to walk into. Dangerous holes in the floor were hidden by ancient hay; prehistoric horse manure was two feet deep and solid as concrete. But in spite of all I marveled at the beauty of the barn, worried over its deterioration, and dreamed, not only of restoring it but of having concerts with music soaring into the rafters of its cathedral-like loft, art and craft shows in the 12 horse stalls, perhaps a community square dance.

I didn't own it. I didn't know what this barn needed for its own healing. Each year there was a bit more roof blown off. Every year I saw a little more rotten wood, floor boards crumbling, a hole in the wall becoming larger. The floor in the loft was covered with hay. What holes were widening beneath the hay?

Over the years I invited many people in to see the barn. Maybe someone would have an idea of how to bring it back to life. Perhaps there would be an inexpensive way to buy it. To revive it. I led each visitor through nettles and raspberry prickers and high grasses laced with thorns. Many saw the grace, the careful handiwork, and were enthralled. Others shook their heads. "Don't know what you would do with it." "It's too far gone." "Might as well torch it."

In the fall of 1993 I invited an architect who specializes in barn restoration to come and look. "It's very special," he said. "I have not seen the kind of mix of detailing and texturing on buildings in Vermont and the Northeast that exist here. The window details, the moldings, the directional changes in the clapboard sidings...it is clearly done by someone who cared and knew about design. There are many interior details that are hard to characterize, the feeders for the stalls, the grill details on the stalls, the curved stanchion dividers, the archways in the central section of the barn."

How much to restore it?

"Oh, maybe a hundred maybe a hundred fifty-thousand dollars." He may as well have said a million.

During that winter--on Christmas Eve in fact--I discovered a lump in my breast. "Cancer," said the surgeon after the biopsy in early January of 1994. It was a wake up call. I decided that it was caused by the stress of working in a very challenging situation in Trenton, New Jersey just south of my home in Princeton. I promptly resigned and underwent a course of chemo and radiation. At dawn on July 1 of 1994 I headed north in the direction of Vermont. Mists rose off grass, thin moon shone through cloud and the birds were as excited as I by the new morning and the prospect of going to my heart's home. I determined that my life from then on would be "hands-on," no computer, no community organizing. My work from here on in would "smell like apples." And then there was the Barn! The dream persisted.

On a weekend in early July I met Merrill Hemond, a builder who, having re-stored his own Victorian house in the village, was working on another historic house across the road from his. Carol and I invited him for a glass of wine on the porch and, as with all visitors, to see the barn. Unlike everyone else he looked around and said, "Plenty of good wood here. You can have this barn if you want."

"How much would it cost?" I asked, thinking about the hundred and fifty-thousand dollar price tag mentioned the previous fall. He said that he would take some measurements and get back to me.

In a few weeks, Merrill gave me a price for the barn--materials and labor--that was so unreasonably low that I knew I could actually afford it. But there was a small detail. I didn't own the barn. I would have to buy it. How do you buy a barn in such disrepair that most people are ready to burn it down? What do you offer? After weeks of thinking it came to me. I knew that Mina Hall was owner of the barn. Her son Allen who now worked the orchard and the adjoining fields, had talked about selling conservation easements for some of his family's land. Land formerly owned by the Fisks.

"They're paying around $1,000 an acre for easements on some land," I heard him say earlier in the summer.

What if I were to offer to buy ten acres and ask him to throw the barn in? Finally I worked up my courage and proposed the idea to Allen and his mother, Mina. They agreed.

"Oh wonderful!" said Carol.

"Great!" said Merrill.

In September I signed a purchase and sales agreement for ten acres of land and the barn. Thrown in as an extra. The land was bounded to the east and north by Hall fields, on the west side by our original three acres and on the south side by quarry land. As soon as I had signed, I rushed home and my son Lyle and I walked around the barn. I touched the clapboards, the foundations built of quarried stone, took in the smell of ancient horses in the piles of hay, hearing the beating of pigeon wings as they fluttered in and out of the wide open windows. The closing took place soon after.

On one weekend in September friends came up from New Jersey to help clean the barn and clear some of the surrounding land. Carol came with her husband Jim, a theater director who taught drama at Princeton High School. Merrill, born and bred on a small farm in the hills of central Vermont, stayed away, scornful and doubtful that a bunch of intellectuals from New Jersey could accomplish anything worthwhile.

"A bunch of wussies," he said on a Friday afternoon, climbing into his truck and driving away.

But our city slicker friends plunged into the work with a will.

"The beautiful thing about this," said Carol, pitchfork in hand, "is that there are many jobs to do. There's a job for everyone. There's light stuff to carry if you're not strong and heavy stuff..."

"Light stuff to carry if you're not strong," said Jim. "That's me!"

"You're strong, honey."

Jim the theatre director spoke in a fake Italian accent. "That's-a me. Strong man. I'm-a strong man."

Halfway through the morning we took a cider break, sitting on a pile of 8 x 8 beams which Merrill had ordered. "What kind of wood is that?" asked Carol.

"Hemlock," I said having been present when Merrill called in the order to his favorite saw mill, "Lussiers," in Enosburg Falls.

"I've heard of hemlock," Jim said.

"The death of Socrates," said Lyle. "Plato wrote about it."

"Right, Socrates!" said Jim. "They made him eat a cord of hemlock. He didn't die of hemlock. He died of the splinters. Not many people know that. They clean up history."

It was a wonder that we got anything done. But by the end of the week-end the two feet of concrete manure had been chipped out, hay swept away, and miscellaneous debris taken to the burn pile. For Merrill's benefit we put up a sign: "This barn cleaned by the N.J. Wussies."

With the barn cleared and clean, Merrill started a first phase of repairs. Assisted by Lyle, he jacked up the barn, replaced rotted sills with new hemlock beams, and, using old techniques of his Vermont carpenter grandfather and father, coaxed the barn into a state of structural stability. Many people in the community got involved with the process. Folks lent tools. When our chainsaw died, I found another chainsaw along with cans of gas and oil on the front porch. By early November the barn was standing straight with sills replaced, "new" old hand hewn beams and plates installed and the roof patched.

We invited people to take a look.

Mina Hall was amazed. "It almost looks the way I remember it...without the hay of course."

Someone else said, "It seems like people are more interested in tearing things down than saving the wonderful old buildings. Now our children will be able to play here just like we did and they'll know what happened here."

The barn was standing straight, thanks to Merrill's building skills. Little did we know of another set of skills that were bred into his bones: his deep love and understanding of the natural world. Little did we know that the combination of these two sets of knowledge would be crucial in the years of struggle that lay ahead.

Carl Williams called to confirm that a meeting of the South Shore Associates would take place at 4 p.m. the following day at his house. These were neighbors south of the quarry. With a few exceptions, my family had never gotten to know them very well. This was to change.

The first cottage just south of the quarry on the lakeside of the road belonged to Carl Williams and his wife. Carl, his wife and their two children, Mary Jane and Jeffrey, had begun coming to Isle La Motte for vacations in the early 1940s. During their first summers on Isle La Motte, the Williams had rented a small cottage on the east shore of Isle La Motte and sometimes would visit the nearby Goodsell Quarry, generally known as the last working quarry on the island.

In 1957 Carl purchased land from Raymond Hall who owned the orchards along the Main Road as well as a great deal of land purchased by his father and uncles from the Fisk estate. The Williams built a house on West Shore Road in 1958, within a stone's throw of the Fisk Quarry. Carl Williams was tall and burly; a powerful man. He was warm, loving and was endowed with a temper as well. If it came to a fight, you definitely wanted him on your side. His daughter Mary Jane was married to Dave Tiedgen; both were tall, warm-hearted with a passion for the wildlife in the quarry; their daughter Mindy had grown up learning to love nature in the quarry and was now sharing this love with her son.

Across the road from the Williams/Tiedgen home was a small white cottage belonging to the Masalek clan. Old John Masalek had bought land in 1944 from the Halls and built the cottage. An avid fisherman he had, according to legend, spent hours in the quarry catching minnows for bait. He handed down the property to four cousins, including one Joe Bajorski who played an important part in the saga about to unfold.

Tiny Elva Grant lived next door to the Masalek clan. Her father, Ralph Grant, had bought land from the Halls in 1954 and built a cottage in the following year. She could be spotted regularly in her yard, wearing sneakers or rubber boots, trowel or shovel in hand--spading, planting, transplanting, clipping, cheerfully surrounded by the riotous colors of her flower gardens.

Neil Hanna and his wife Elaine lived just down the road. Neil had grown up on a farm in Canada, went to agricultural school and then, switching careers, became a successful dentist in Montreal. He and Elaine began visiting their friends, the Grants in the mid 50s (Elaine and Elva had gone to school together) and in 1965 bought land--again from the Halls--and built a house in 1966. Like all the neighbors, Neil's heart belonged to the island. He would take visitors on tours of his gardens--veritable art works of broccoli, peas, beans, corn, tomatoes, potatoes. Flowers. He would demonstrate the grafting of fruit trees; he baked bread, set up bee hives (Hanna's Honey), and in the fall, regularly made the world's best apple pies. He was also a woodworker and once described himself as an "old guitar maker."

Ross and Phyllis Firth came in 1963. A former school principal, Ross now spent his retirement years growing spectacular varieties and colors of iris, playing the bass fiddle, organizing family sing-alongs, and looking out for his many grandchildren who spent summers on the island.

We were to meet in the Williams' cottage. Located just next to the quarry, their home was perched on the rocky shore of the lake with an expansive view of the water. The living room was crowded with neighbors. Concerned. Frightened even. We all wanted news. Facts. What was happening? What could we do? We settled down in the comfortable chairs of Carl Williams' living room, fortified by coffee.

It was early evening, the sun just beginning to color the western sky. Carl put down his cup. "Ross and I went by the quarry on Tuesday and talked to this guy who was running the jackhammer. From what he says it seems that the quarrying project is supposed to be pretty big. There's supposed to be rock under the fields clear back to the extent of the 20 acres which this company purchased last February. He also told us that they spent the entire winter getting permits from the Act 250 Board to do this work."

Ross spoke up. "We told him that there was no permit and furthermore there isn't supposed to be any activity in the quarry at all, until there is an Advisory Opinion from the District Coordinator, Geoff Green. The fellow seemed surprised. He said that he had met the previous Wednesday with the company president who said nothing about any of that. Of course this would have been the day before Green had spoken with the guy. The president I mean."

"What a tragedy, eh?" said Elva. "All the years I have been here, from the 1950s to now it has been such a quiet neighborhood. The quarry has been a quiet peaceful place. Remember, Elaine, how we would take walks in the quarry and pick flowers?"

"I called my daughter, Mary Jane," said Carl Williams. "She's coming back from Michigan next week to spend the rest of August. I told her that some outfit was working in the quarry without permits. I said that they're making a big racket and that the neighbors are getting together to discuss it and try to figure out what to do. She was pretty shocked to hear that the quarry had been bought. Right out from under our noses it looks like."

I learned that the South Shore Associates had been formed a few years previously to maintain the character of the neighborhood.

"We actually tried to buy the quarry a few years ago," Ross told me, "but Omya, the big company that owned the quarry at that time, refused to separate it from the point of land across the road from the quarry where the old quarry dock used to be. They wanted 350,000 dollars for the entire parcel. South Shore Associates thought that was too high. But now? Seems to me that South Shore Associates should reconstitute itself and try to do something about this new company which just bought the quarry."

"Sounds good to me," said Neil.

Ross Firth agreed to be president. I volunteered to be secretary. "I love a good fight," Ross said again. I was relieved to hear him say that. I am not a fighter. Put this on the shoulders of an aggressive, competent male.

Two weeks passed. We guessed that Geoffrey Green had communicated the "no work" message to the company. The quarry was quiet but though Ross had said he was happy to carry on the fight, it felt as though a dark and uncertain future hung over our heads.

It was nearing the end of August, the roses faded, the last hollyhock blossoms clinging to their brown stalks; many days were grey and mellow with gusts of wind from the southland, the final stretch of summer. Carol and Jim had packed up, tied their bicycles onto their car, and headed south to New Jersey and back to their jobs. I would miss my friends. I would miss their support. Fortunately Merrill would be around.

In early September the telephone rang. It was Geoffrey Green. He had met with the president of CMC on August 29.

"I told him that in order to determine whether this project would need an Act 250 Permit, he would need to submit in writing the scope of work which the company is planning to do."

So the next move belonged to CMC. Our job was to wait.

The Barn: Before and After

5. The Ordinary Citizen From Hell

"Our duty to the whole, including the unborn generations, bids us restrain an unprincipled present-day minority from wasting the heritage of these unborn generations. The movement for the conservation of wild life and the longer movement for the conservation of all our natural resources are essentially democratic in spirit, purpose, and method."
Theodore Roosevelt, 'A Book-Lover's Holidays in the Open' 1916

1800s

THE ENVIRONMENTAL MOVEMENT IN AMERICA is often described as beginning with the work of George Perkins Marsh. He was a Vermonter, born in 1801 in Woodstock. Lawyer, diplomat and businessman, Marsh had grown up on a farm and learned to understand and love the land. Marsh the traveler observed the devastation of land around the Mediterranean and in Europe, previously lush and fertile areas where man had for too long, in his opinion, deforested and abused the land. He wrote,

> "There are parts of Asia Minor, of Northern Africa, of Greece, and even of Alpine Europe where ....causes set in action by man have brought the face of the earth to a desolation almost as complete as that of the moon....though they are known to have been covered with luxuriant woods, verdant pastures, and fertile meadows..."
> 12

From early childhood Marsh had seen first hand that Vermont was now being ill used in the same way. In a speech in 1847 to the Agricultural Society of Rutland County, he decried the deforestation of Vermont "leaving rains and melting snows to flow swiftly over smooth ground...to fill every ravine with a torrent, and convert every river into an ocean, transforming smiling meadows into broad wastes of shingle and gravel and pebbles, deserts in summer and seas in autumn and spring."

In 1862 he began to write what was to be an enduring contribution to the American environmental movement. The book *Man and Nature* was an in-depth analysis of the negative impacts of humans upon the land: the soils, the water, the air, the habitat. He emphasized the importance of trees as a reservoir for water, protection for soils, prevention of erosion and floods, and--perhaps--even affecting climate. *Man and Nature* was one of the first books in which nature was looked at from a holistic, ecological perspective. Published in 1864, it soon became popular with scholars and the public alike. Marsh, known to some as the father of American conservation, died in 1882. It was just two years after the marriages in 1880 of those two young men, Theodore Roosevelt and Nelson Fisk.

In that same year of 1882, Nelson Fisk at the age of twenty-eight, became involved with politics, elected first to serve in the Vermont State Legislature and then in the Vermont Senate. The year before, Theodore Roosevelt, twenty-three and just a year out of Harvard, entered the political arena by joining the New York Assembly. The youngest member ever of the Assembly, he upset leading lights in the political realm by exposing corruption in high places and pleading for fairness for the average man.

August 1995

In the weeks after the neighborhood meeting I felt that we were floundering, lost in the woods without a guide. None of us were experts. We had an organization but no knowledge of how to proceed. We had no idea that help was coming. From a rather odd source.

Toward the end of August, a car stopped on the road in front of our house. A tall man in blue jeans and red T shirt walked up one of the old flagstone walks--half buried in the grass- and said, with a quizzical look through wire rimmed glasses, "You must be special people to be allowed to live in this special place." This was our first meeting with Randy Koch. How can you resist such an opening?

It turned out that Randy's wife and mother were in the car and needed a rest stop--an amenity quite lacking on our island at the time except in private homes and behind bushes. We invited them in of course and as the women visited the "facilities," Randy and I stood on the lawn looking out at the lake. It turned out that he and his wife lived in southern Vermont and were touring Randy's mother around the state.

"This is paradise," Randy said. I agreed that it was, but that there was a problem in paradise. When I mentioned the words quarry, mining, and Act 250, Randy perked right up. "There's someone you should meet." Randy explained that he was a member of a statewide group called Citizens Participation Network (CPN) whose goal was to preserve the right of citizens concerned about development projects to participate in the Act 250 process.

"But definitely the guy you really want to meet is Joe Bivins. He's the chief guru and founder of CPN, but he's also one of the state's foremost authorities on Act 250. He's not a lawyer but he's presented arguments in front of the Vermont Supreme Court. The guy shows up in his flannel shirts and suspenders lugging his files in recycled cardboard wine boxes. He won a case before the Vermont Supreme Court giving him the right to represent an advocate's group in landfill hearings a couple of years ago. He has a really strong sense of right and wrong and is passionate about the environment. You might want to come to one of our meetings. The members might be able to give your group some advice. Stephanie Kaplan for instance. She's a top notch environmental lawyer who's passionate about this stuff. And you would meet Joe."

In the days following my conversation with Randy, we learned more about Joe Bivins. Along with founding Citizen Participation Network, Joe was musical, playing recorder and trumpet. He had lived in Africa. He taught African culture as a volunteer teacher in the Thetford schools. And, as an ordinary citizen, he had so vigorously fought the legal battle against a contaminated landfill in Thetford, Vermont that an opponent called him 'the ordinary citizen from hell.'

"That's a real badge of honor for him," Randy told me.

Summer 1994

During the summer of 1994, all had not been well with my father. As I finished up the last of my chemotherapy treatments, commuting back and forth between New Jersey and Vermont, my mother reported evidence of my father's failing memory—inability to recall things that had happened recently, a constant losing of his wallet, credit cards, and other possessions. And a growing confusion. She wondered whether this could be the early stage of a progressive dementia such as Alzheimer's. In November my mother told him that Thanksgiving would be in a week. She was startled when he said that he thought that Thanksgiving had been the previous week. Along with this mental failing was a growing unsteadiness of gait.

"He does a lot of reading, fortunately," she said, "though it is difficult to know what he retains. He enjoys seeing people, though he is quiet and does not keep up his end in conversation particularly. We have family dinners with music afterwards which he enjoys very much."

She began to plan a move from their home in Princeton to a retirement community in a nearby town. They would not be able to spend much of their usual summer in Vermont. Indeed, it was becoming clear that with my father's failing health, my parents were not going to be able to continue to manage the complicated property which was Fisk Farm. Could we even keep it? I learned that even before this, they had talked with one another, wondering if the time had come to sell Fisk Farm. The boys are engaged with their owlives," they said to each other. "It's expensive. And Linda won't be able to manage it by herself."

Sell Fisk Farm? I was determined. That was not an option. It was financially difficult to keep and maintain the place. Perhaps it was time for our idea of a B&B to come to fruition.

Summer 1995

Without my parents on hand, my sons recently graduated from college and involved in their own lives, the running of Fisk Farm required, I felt, community. Extended family. Carol and Jim came to spend the summer. Merrill, who had made peace with the New Jersey Wussies, decided to rent his house in the village for a while and came to live with us for the summer as well. There was plenty of room and plenty of work for all.

By this time the barn had been partially restored and in addition to our B&B idea, Carol pursued the idea of serving tea. "We could have tea gardens on Sunday afternoons that would be open to the public." She had mentioned this before.

"What's a tea garden?" I asked again.

"We could serve tea in the ruins. And pastries. People can sit on the lawn. It will give people a chance to explore the place, to hear the history. To see the barn. And it will give us a chance to meet a lot of interesting people. This will be my project for the summer."

During July, Carol and Jim rounded up a number of eccentric little tables, and sanded and painted them with white enamel. Carol visited every yard sale, every auction, and every second hand furniture store around, coming back with motley collections of china tea cups, glass plates, and odd pieces of silverware. We both scrubbed down the first floor of the still standing wing of the old Fisk mansion, a stone shell inhabited for years by spiders, mice, bats, and other critters.

Merrill and I wondered what we could do in the not yet fully restored barn? "An art show. We could have an art show," I said.

"We probably could. There's plenty of good wall space," said Merrill.

By the beginning of August the baking was done, lawn mowed, flyers distributed, and tea cups arranged on what had once been the old wooden counter in Nelson Fisk's store, long since moved into the stone ruins. We hung the first art show in the partly restored horse and carriage barn. Two days before the event we stumbled across a couple who were performers of Irish folk music. We signed them up to come and sing on Sunday afternoon. By August 1 of 1995, chocolate raspberry cake, almond torte, scones and an array of tiny cucumber sandwiches were resplendent under little net coverings on the first floor of the "ruins" (formerly the grand house of the Fisk estate). It was Carol's creation, with her husband Jim and myself hard by as her coworkers, a vision made real. Carol and I, both, ragged and worn in body if not in spirit, dressed in elegant skirts and hats, waited for the first customers, waited, in fact, for an audience.

Somehow, despite torrents of rain in the morning, the afternoon event was blessed by sunshine and turned into a great success. People stopped by to see the art which we had hung in the barn and then walked over to the ruins of the old Fisk mansion where we served tea, tea sandwiches and pastries for small donations which went toward the restoration of the barn. Visitors sat on the lawn at small tables overlooking the lake and enjoyed their tea, their lemonade, scones, chocolate, carrot and cheese cakes and tea sandwiches.

There were the three women from Arizona, delighted to happen upon this quaint local event. There was the visitor from Paris, France who sat in a wicker chair drinking tea for two hours, families with toddlers who played croquet on the lawn, and local residents. One woman who had lived on the island all her life said she was delighted to see the old things being restored and cherished. "It's like an old fashioned lawn party," she said.

"Wow," Jim said later. "This was great! I never thought, when I was much younger, that any kind of tea ceremony would be important and centering in my life. In fact I would have laughed and pulled the ring on another can of beer."

"Not too bad," said Merrill, proud that his Barn restoration had become an art gallery.

Ten days later we heard the jackhammering in the quarry.

September 1995

We hadn't heard anything from the quarry company. Toward the end of September I called Geoffrey Green and asked him about the status of things. He told me that CMC had not yet filed a document with him. He intimated that one of them had said that perhaps they would wait several weeks until members of the South Shore Association left the island for the winter.

But in October a letter arrived. It was addressed to South Shore Associates and was a copy of a letter written by the quarry company's lawyer to Geoffrey Green. After the usual formalities the letter stated:

> "My client proposes to continue removing stone from the quarry, the precise amount is difficult to gauge. As you can tell from the correspondence from CMC, the activity at the quarry fluctuates with the demand you have for the particular stone at the site. My client's company estimates that in a good year they would be hauling out on average 4-5 truckloads per week. These would be tractor-trailer type trucks moving about 20 tons a piece. Some of the stone will be fabricated on

site, that is made into smaller chunks by means of a hydraulic splitter, while the balance will be essentially blocks sawed and removed in one piece and trucked off site. Again, the size will depend upon the type of stone needed by the customer.

At this point the marble company would anticipate doing no blasting. My client tells me that new techniques have been developed by means of a cement poured in joints or holes which expand and cause the marble slabs to split apart.

The days of operation would be in the spring through fall months, with limited or no operation during the winter months. The hours of operation would be solely during daylight hours."

Tractor trailer trucks on our quiet little road? Hydraulic splitters...big machinery...loud noises? Letters suggesting that there had been activity in the quarry for years? Activity at the quarry? What activity? What were they talking about?

My main sense was of helplessness. How could one fight against this? How could I fight? I'm not a fighting person. I felt defeated from the beginning. I felt helpless but not so helpless that I couldn't use the telephone. The person who answered the call was Joe Bivins in Thetford Vermont.

The tenor voice on the phone sounded both amused and confident. "Randy mentioned your case. So I know something about it. Here's the deal. Act 250 says that a commercial enterprise begun after 1970 needs an Act 250 Permit. If the enterprise was begun before 1970 it's grandfathered unless there is an issue of substantial change. In other words, is what they are planning to do in the quarry now, substantially different from what they've been doing there in the past?"

"Heavens yes," I said. "At least in the way their lawyer describes it. Hydraulic splitters! Trucks!"

"So in order to be exempt from Act 250, the company needs to prove that quarrying has continued from pre-1970 to the present day and that their plans involve no substantial change from what has been going on right along."

"What is 'substantial change?' " I asked.

"Well, in one case it was found that substantial change could amount to as much as--or as little--as 10 percent."

"What do we do?"

"You need to write a letter to the District Commissioner stating your case. Don't worry. I'll help you."

I called Ross who gave me the go ahead. Then Joe and I began work on a response letter, working initially for an hour and a half by phone. As we talked I realized I was getting the benefit of one of the sharpest minds I had ever encountered. For several days Joe and I continued to draft a letter to Geoffrey Green, communicating frequently by telephone.

Finally the letter, essentially composed by Joe, was completed to Joe's satisfaction. Among the arguments he had dictated to me were the following: "The proposed mining operation, if instituted, will have a deleterious impact of serious proportions on neighbors who live near the quarry."

He talked about possible impacts of large tractor trailer trucks on the roads, safety issues, the disruption of trucks on "areas where young children play, where people gather for cookouts, swimming and reunions, a quiet rural area where people are attracted by natural beauty, the recreational use of Lake Champlain, and peace and quiet."

"What will happen," he wrote, "to the surrounding lands, the woods and the fields? What about deforestation? Erosion? What about ground water? What about its geologic significance? The quarry has rare fossils and is frequently visited by geologists and geology students. If preserved and maintained, these sites could provide continued opportunities for education and research and they are, without doubt, the oldest, preserved history on the island. In light of our above-stated concerns, The South Shore Associates earnestly requests that the Act 250 process be invoked vis a vis the Fisk Quarry, to the end that a constructive solution be found which is in the best interests of the long term public good."

I showed the letter to Ross. He was impressed. "Who is this guy?" he asked. He agreed that I should sign it and send it on to Geoffrey Green.

As I look back on Joe's letter some years later, I am struck by how early the lines were drawn, how early he had spelled out the issues which would constitute the heart of our case for the next three years. I was grateful for Joe's help in defining the issues. In retrospect I am very grateful that I did not see into the future, did not see what a hard and heartbreaking road we had in front of us.

Mary Jane Tiedgen, her husband Dave and I drove to the office of the District Coordinator in the town of Essex Junction to deliver, in person, the letter crafted by Joe Bivins. Geoffrey Green seemed to have arranged a neutral expression on his face, neutrality in his voice tones, determined, we supposed, to be an absolutely neutral arbiter in this quasi-judicial process.

He said that lawyers from CMC had told him that the company had indeed already received a Discharge Permit from the Waste Water management Division to drain the water out of the quarry and into the lake. We were shocked. How could that happen? Did not the fact that my family owned part of the quarry pond prevent such a permit? Mr. Green did not seem to have an answer.

He also told us that it seemed that part of the quarry property was a Federally Mapped Wetland. We didn't know what that meant. He drew out a large black and white map of Isle La Motte marked with strange combinations of letters. PSSA, PEMC. We had no idea, at that time, of their significance.

We had heard that the opposition lawyers were laughing about the case, certain that the summer people would be going back to New Jersey for the winter and then it would be all over. Geoffrey Green warned us that most people opposing projects through Act 250 lost their case.

"Well we are planning to be in the remaining one percent," I said, my confident air underlain by terror.

Having delivered the letter we departed, but not before gathering up all the literature—brochures, pamphlets, booklets, a Directory of Vermont State Government, titled "About Act 250"--anything that might conceivably be of use.

News travels fast on our small island. I stopped in at the village store, a small white frame building next to the small white frame post office, to pick up eggs and milk. Richard Middleton, Harvard Ph.D in the field of microbiology and now storekeeper at the Isle La Motte Country Store, picks up all the gossip.

"I understand that the quarry company already has a discharge permit to drain the water out of the Fisk Quarry," he said casually.

I was learning to assume a poker face which, I hoped, hid the storm of emotions evoked in recent weeks, by the most innocent of comments. "Is that so?" I said.

"That's what they say. Some of the guys working in the Goodsell Quarry stopped in here earlier today."

I reported the news to Merrill. He looked incredulous. "How can they possibly drain the pond? Didn't you once tell me that the boundary line of your property goes right across the quarry pond. There must be something about riparian rights here. What is a 'riparian right' anyway?"

I called a surveyor, Dave Peatman from Johnson, Vermont, who had surveyed the land that I had bought from the Halls just the year before.

"Would you come and just double check the boundaries here?"

When Nelson Fisk sold his quarry and shipping dock to the Vermont Marble Company in 1919 he drew a diagonal boundary line beginning at the lake shore near his old dock, stretching across the dirt road, across the quarry on the other side of the road, and back into the fields. By doing this he definitively separated a 20 acre parcel including the quarry and some of the surrounding fields and woodlands from his own homestead.

Sure enough, Dave Peatman confirmed the diagonal boundary line running from the shoreline, across the road, and right through part of the big pond in the quarry. Indeed, my family now owned part of the quarry pond. Surely this would help our case!

Finally, on October 27, a letter arrived from the District Coordinator's Office. It was a copy of the Advisory Opinion to CMC. I tore it open and read aloud to Merrill and Mary Jane.

"Ok!" I said. "He finds that the changes proposed by CMC do constitute a development and require an Act 250 permit. He says that the quarry was abandoned before 1971 and was not operating on that date and therefore does not qualify for an exemption as a pre-existing development. He says the only activity in the quarry has been for waste stone, rip-rap and rubble. Since the quarry doesn't qualify as a pre-existing development, it's not necessary to deal with the issue of substantial change. Hmm, it says they have thirty days to appeal this opinion."

It was good news.

October 28, 1995

I continued to communicate with Joe. "The long distance phone calls have to come to an end," he said early on. "Do you have a computer? Do you email?"

"Yes and no," I said. I had a computer but had not mastered that new fangled invention of email which had just begun to be popular in the early 90s. He patiently tried to teach me the process. "You need an email address."

I decided to use my initials: lvf@aol.com. But I had a heck of a time sending my first email to Joe. My message bounced back every time, informing me, rather rudely I thought, that there was no such address. One of my early attempts was entitled "Trying Again."

"Dear Joe, Disconcerting it is to send long epistles that (seemingly) end up floating around in outer space rather than reaching their intended destinations. I hope this communication simply goes quietly to Thetford rather than ending up circulating around the globe, which is where I envision my other messages to be. Linda"

Finally he figured it out. I had been spelling his name wrong. "Bevens" I had written. His email address turned out to be joe.bivins@valley.net. "You see," he wrote back, "how everything is better when you spell my name the same way that I do." I responded:

"I think that computers, like horses, can smell fear. I think they know when their riders are secure and when they can be dominated. I however, feeling no fear (at the moment) am quite confident that this message will get through. I'm not even going to try to make it short. I am determined that from here on in, this computer will understand who's in charge."

Looking back, it is impossible to imagine how, without the technology of email communication, we could ever have managed during the next three years.

Autumn winds had blown most of the leaves off of the trees, island docks had been pulled up, wood piles had been stacked up and covered, and last minute painting completed in preparation for the long Vermont winter. Joe had agreed to come to Isle La Motte to look over the entire situation for himself.

Shasta barked at the sound of heavy footsteps on the porch steps and a loud pounding on the old, wooden front door.

How do you describe Joe? A short, heavyset man, age 50 say, with balding head, spectacles, a little beard, plaid shirt, red suspenders, blue jeans, brown work boots, wool socks. A little hat set on top of his shining head. A twinkle in his soul.

He had been described to me as one of the state's foremost authorities on Act 250 land-use laws. One of his friends said "He has one of the three or four sharpest minds I have ever known. If I had to describe a perfect legal mind, it would be his." Other stories had Joe arguing cases in the Vermont Supreme Court, giving him the right to represent cases even though he wasn't a lawyer.

Today Joe passed up the offer of a cup of coffee, impatient to get out to see the quarry. He had his camera and made Merrill and me bring ours. I felt that a stout and brilliant plaid shirted angel had descended into our lives.

Joe made us take pictures. He had ideas and angles and perspectives in mind which I had never thought of. A shot of soils and plant materials scraped up from the quarry floor pushed into berms along the edge of the quarry. Photos of the expanse of scraped quarry floor making it look more like a parking lot than the magical meadow of mosses and wildflowers which had entranced us for so many years. He clambered up the eastern rim of the quarry and suggested shots which showed the proximity of the quarry to Lake Champlain. The photos revealed the delicate blues of the quarry ponds, of Lake Champlain just beyond, soft greys of rock walls etched with white fossil forms, the quiet rose of low shrubs growing around the ponds. We tramped through the woods and field which were also part of quarry property. I think back, marveling at how little I knew then about this land and how much I was to learn.

Over homemade vegetable soup at Fisk Farm, Joe conducted a seminar on Act 250 for me, Mary Jane, Merrill, Elva and Neil. "Act 250 is great in a lot of ways. Since it was passed in 1970 it has given citizens the opportunity to have some influence on development in Vermont. However, the fact of life is that developers have the advantage of money to hire lawyers and professional witnesses to win their cases. Citizens or even citizen groups don't often have that kind of money. It helps a lot if you can do a lot of the work yourself."

Joe explained that Act 250 sets out ten criteria which need to be considered by commercial developers in Vermont.

"I suggest that you learn them, memorize them even and decide which ones might apply to this project. The criteria have to do with air pollution (including noise), surface and ground water, storm water runoff, the storage of oils, fuels, chemicals etc., use of water for manufacturing or other processes, wetlands, impact on water supplies including nearby wells, control of dust, soil erosion, traffic and road conditions and general impact on local municipal services."

We were already confused. Joe buttered a piece of bread and continued. "The project should not have an undue adverse effect on the scenic or natural beauty of the area, aesthetics, historic sites, or rare or irreplaceable natural areas."

"That's us," we said. "We are scenic and naturally beautiful, the quarry is a historic site and it's a rare and irreplaceable natural area."

Joe continued. "It shouldn't significantly reduce agricultural potential of primary agricultural soils. If the project involves extraction of earth resources that it would not unduly harm the environment or neighboring land uses, and that the project would not endanger any adjacent public investment."

"You're kidding, right? You don't really expect that we're going to learn all this," I said. Elva just shook her head.

As he was saying goodbye Joe said, in an offhand manner, "I would be happy to represent you. I'd have to get paid something of course. And I should tell you that I've never been paid for this kind of work before. But I'd be cheaper than a lawyer."

He put on his little hat and walked out the door across the lawn to his rusty car of anonymous vintage.

And that was our first visit from the "ordinary citizen from hell."

Joe Bivins

6. From Swampland to Wetland

"When I first visited California, it was my good fortune to see the "big trees," the Sequoias, and then to travel down into the Yosemite, with John Muir...He met me with a couple of packers and two mules to carry our tent, bedding, and food for a three days' trip. The first night was clear, and we lay down in the darkening aisles of the great Sequoia grove. The majestic trunks, beautiful in color and in symmetry, rose round us like the pillars of a mightier cathedral than ever was conceived even by the fervor of the Middle Ages. Hermit thrushes sang beautifully in the evening, and again, with a burst of wonderful music, at dawn."
Theodore Roosevelt[13]

IF GEORGE PERKINS MARSH WROTE FROM HIS SCIENTIFIC UNDERSTANDING of the environment, John Muir, 1838 to 1914, was the poet of environmentalism, whose eloquent voice and passion for the wilderness would shape the thinking of many, including the future President Theodore Roosevelt. John Muir was born in Scotland in 1838, some 16 years before Roosevelt's birth. From boyhood on Muir had a passionate love of the out of doors. Of his childhood he wrote:

"Wildness was ever sounding in our ears...Oh, the blessed enchantment of those Saturday runaways in the prime of the spring! How our young wondering eyes reveled in the sunny, breezy glory of the hills and the sky, every particle of us thrilling and tingling with the bees and glad birds and glad streams! Kings may be blessed; we were glorious, we were free."[14]

When he was still a boy, his Scottish family emigrated to the New World where wild Wisconsin seemed like a paradise and "everything about us was so novel and wonderful that we could hardly believe our senses." As an adult, Muir explored the great landscapes of the West, becoming a naturalist, author, and an apostle preaching on behalf of the wilderness. He advocated the permanent protection of wilderness areas, co-founding the Sierra Club in 1892 with the mission of protecting Yosemite and other spectacular natural areas in the Sierra Nevada Mountains.

In 1903 he took President Theodore Roosevelt on a camping trip in Yosemite--seeking to inspire the president to protect the land. For Muir the wilderness was a place of refuge, of solace, of inspiration. Protection of the land was a spiritual imperative. "He was a great factor," Roosevelt wrote later, "in influencing the thought of California and the thought of the entire country so as to secure the preservation of those great natural phenomena--wonderful canyons, giant trees, slopes of flower-spangled hillsides--which make California a veritable Garden of the Lord."[15]

With Nelson and Elizabeth at the helm, the Fisk family estate took on a new luster. Elizabeth was known as a superb hostess and the couple entertained in style. In 1890, flush from the sale of ice from Lake Champlain to New York City, they remodeled the big stone house, refinishing seventeen rooms in oak.[16]

In 1882 Young Nelson became involved with politics, elected first to serve in the Vermont State legislature and then to the Vermont Senate. It was the same year that Teddy Roosevelt, just a year out of Harvard, entered the political arena, the New York Assembly. Later, Nelson Fisk was twice elected by his district as a delegate to the National Conventions of the Republican party, first in 1888 and then in 1892. In 1896 he was elected Lieutenant Governor of Vermont and served one term, 1897 to 1899. He started a store and postoffice with its own cancellation stamp in a frame building very close to the stone house to serve the quarry workers as well as farmers and others who lived on the south end of the island.

He also became president of the Fish and Game League. In 1899 and again in 1901 Nelson and Elizabeth hosted several annual meetings of the League. Which was how Vice President Theodore Roosevelt came to Fisk Farm.

From the moment we purchased the remnants of the old Fisk property, my family was acutely aware of the story. My father, whose field was public administration and had, for a time, served as City Administrator of New York, had always been interested in the progressive Teddy Roosevelt and his work in the area of government reform. My own interest in Roosevelt grew as I learned of his contribution to the conservation movement in this country.

Winding through the Champlain Islands and connecting them by causeways and bridges is Route Two, also known as the Teddy Roosevelt Highway. Of course in 1901 the best way to travel from Burlington in the south to the northern island of Isle La Motte was by boat--the means by which Vice President Roosevelt traveled to Isle La Motte--rather than by the arduous overland route on the then primitive roads and the occasional connecting ferry.

Route Two today is marked by grand vistas of the lake, rolling fields, several villages, and the shapes of the Green Mountains taking on the hazy blue shades of lake. It carries you south to 89 where you are whisked to Burlington or Montpelier or the quaint little town of Waterbury where some state offices were housed, particularly those managing the environmental health of Vermont.

Here was the Agency of Natural Resources, an umbrella for the departments of Environmental Conservation, Vermont Fish and Wildlife, Forests, Parks, and Recreation. The Wastewater Management Division was part of the Department of Environmental Conservation. Its mission: "to preserve, enhance, restore and conserve Vermont's natural resources and protect human health for the benefit of this and future generations."[17] Definitely a change from government efforts to preserve natural resources before the presidency of TR.

On November 1, 1995, Ross Firth and I made a trip to Waterbury to express our concern that a Discharge Permit for the Fisk Quarry may have been incorrectly issued to the company. In a large room with office cubicles and a forest of filing cabinets, a young man listened politely if unenthusiastically. He reluctantly took us to one of the cabinets lining the room and opened a drawer. Sure enough. After some digging, we found files labeled Isle La Motte Quarry. And sure enough, here were letters between the quarry's new owner and a Wastewater Division officer documenting--not so many months ago--the issuance of a wastewater discharge permit.

My heart sank. How could this have happened?

"Is there no appeal process?" I asked. "No possibility for public comment? I mean this allows the company to drain water out of the pond, part of which is on our family property." The young man looked blank. He did not register any sort of outrage or surprise. His whole attitude could have been summed up as a shrug.

"Well, there is a 30 day period for public comment, but that's come and gone," he said. The two men continued to sift through papers. I picked up another paper.

"But look! Wait a minute. This permit describes the quarry as being...this isn't the Fisk Quarry! This is a permit for the Goodsell Quarry." A map on the next page showed the site marked with an orange x on the east side of the island, not the west side.

Ross picked up the paper. "She's right. It says 'Isle La Motte Quarry' but it's the Goodsell Quarry not the Fisk Quarry! Why didn't someone catch this?"

What a relief! So, despite island rumor, there was no discharge permit for the Fisk Quarry. Not yet. What would have happened if we hadn't gone through all these papers ourselves?

Our next stop was to be the Wetlands Office, seemingly an important part of this puzzle according to the Wetlands Map which Geoffrey Green had shown us. It was part of the Department of Environmental Conservation. We didn't really understand what a wetland was. The concept seemed intimidating somehow. Surely there were technical definitions that you had to be an expert to understand.

The hall in which the wetland offices were housed was decked with posters of forests and fields, maps.

We were told to go to the office of Carl Pagel, State Wetlands Coordinator. Mr. Pagel turned out to be a large and friendly man. I showed him some of the pictures that we had taken. There were photographs of the woodlands behind the excavated quarry, an overgrowth of saplings and an undergrowth of sensitive fern.

"Beautiful!" he said.

He told us that wetlands are mapped in the US on something called the Federal Wetland Inventory Maps, put out by the US Dept of the Interior: Fish and Wildlife.

He gave us a large map of the southern half of Isle La Motte. Shapes--circles, ovals and amoeba-like shapes were marked PSS1C, PFO1C, POWH; And there was the Fisk Quarry marked PEMC and PEM/OWF. Again I was puzzled. What were these letters? What was PEMC? Carl told us that someone from his staff would make a visit to the site within the next week or so. He gave us her name: Cathy O'Brien. "She may be in the next office if you want to talk with her now," he said.

Cathy O'Brien was young and blonde and determined.

"I recently got a call from the president of CMC," she said. "He was very pleasant over the phone and said something like, 'I don't know what all the fuss is about. It's just rock cliffs that go straight down. There are no wetlands involved.'"

"I just happen to have some pictures with me," I said, pulling out an envelope containing the pictures that Joe Bivins suggested Merrill and I take. There were long dramatic shots from the cliffs looking west across the quarry ponds with the vast stretch of Lake Champlain just beyond. Mysterious dark woodlands with autumn browned ferns, red branched bushes glowing in a blanket of early morning fog.

Cathy said that it was possible that the company would have to apply for a wetlands permit, but her visit to the site would determine that. "After the application is submitted there is a thirty day comment period by members of the public. The company will have to prove that their activities will not have a negative impact on the wetlands 'functions and values.' "

Wetlands 'functions and values.' That sounded like Act 250 Criteria. I left the office feeling somewhat more clear about how to prepare both for the site visit next Tuesday and beyond. Might it be possible that we could stop them on the Wetlands issue and not even have to go through Act 250?

What is a wetland? In the Wetlands Office I picked up paper...brochures, pamphlets, anything that would help to educate us. I started to read. For much of this country's history, I learned, wetlands were regarded as a menace; they were called swamps, undesirable places, breeding grounds for mosquitoes and disease, a hindrance to agriculture, useless land. Junk land. You couldn't build on it; couldn't farm it. The best thing to do with it was to drain it, then turn it into agricultural land. In a 1912 publication by the US Department of Agriculture I read, "The term 'Swamp' is used to designate all areas which in their natural conditions are too wet for the production of any crop."[18]

Over time, however, attitudes began to change. Gradually it was realized that drained swamps did not always make good agricultural land and that the draining of land has adverse impacts on water birds and animals such as mink and muskrats.[19] Over time it was also learned that "wetlands are among the most productive ecosystems in the world." Not only that, said the brochures, but wetlands "control floodwaters, recharge groundwater, and filter pollutants; they are a habitat for waterfowl and other wildlife; they are sanctuaries for rare and endangered species; they have educational, recreational, and aesthetic value."

And then there were the letters. These, I discovered, are a classification code describing more specifically different types of wetlands. I finally figured out that the "P" in the cluster of letters PEMC stands for Palustrine or shallow ponds, marshes, and swamps. "EM" refers to Emergent Vegetation or plants which grow above ground but whose roots are happy in wet soil. "C" means seasonally flooded. In PEMA the "A" stands for temporarily flooded. A PSSI wetland is a "scrub shrub emergent wetland which, if left undisturbed, will gradually be replaced over time by trees."[20]

As I read the Vermont Wetland Rules, I learned that as of 1995 they were designated in Vermont according to class. There were Class I, Class II, and

Class III wetlands. "All wetlands in Vermont shown on the Significant Wetland Inventory maps are Class I or Class II wetlands unless determined otherwise by the Secretary or Panel," I read in the Rules. What was a Class III Wetland? "Class III wetlands are those wetlands that do not provide significant function and value according to the Vermont Wetland Rules."

What were these functions and how did they apply to the Fisk Quarry? After reading the Vermont Wetland Rules, I made a list of the functions that I thought might apply to the quarry property.

Function 5.3 Fisheries Habitat. Function 5.4a Wildlife and migratory bird habitat. Function 5.4b Mammals. Function 5 4.c amphibians Function 5.4d Reptiles. Function 5.4 E. Other. 5.7 Education and Research in Natural Sciences 5.8 Recreational Value and Economic Benefit. Function 5.9 Open Space and Aesthetics. This list seemed to be relevant to our situation. Perhaps I could use my pictures in an attempt to document the presence of these functions before Cathy O'Brien came.

I spent almost the whole night before Cathy's visit, sorting, pasting, and typing, creating a booklet which cited what I thought were the relevant wetland functions and laying out photographs as illustrations. As I look back, years later, I remember my passion and my desperation as I tried to piece things together. I am struck by the beauty of the pictures we had taken. About how much I was learning...how much I felt forced to learn...so very quickly.

I titled my booklet "THE FISK QUARRY" subtitled "Wetlands Area and Natural Habitat." I began with a quote by Teddy Roosevelt. "The nation behaves well if it treats the natural resources as assets which it must turn over to the next generation increased, and not impaired, in value."

"The Fisk Quarry" I wrote, "is located on the southwestern shore of Isle La Motte, the northernmost island of Lake Champlain. Extensively quarried in the nineteenth century by the Fisk Family, the quarry has been quiet for many years--except for the occasional removal of loose stone. Its dramatic beauty, the birds and animals and plant life which inhabit the quarry and its rare fossils make it a precious resource for the neighborhood and for the citizens of Vermont and visitors from all over the US and abroad to visit this beautiful area. All the photographs were taken in the quarry or on land adjoining the quarry in September, October, and November of 1995."

I interspersed letters with pages of color xeroxed photographs captioned by the wetland functions I believed they might exemplify, photo documentation, and quotes from neighbors.

"Listed on the National Inventory of Wetlands, the quarry consists of several acres of pond, emergent marsh, shrub swamp and forested areas," I wrote with a growing sense of authority.

By 9:00 am, the morning of Cathy O'Brien's site visit, I had finished my cutting and pasting job. My picture/text album was ready. To say that I was nervous is an understatement. I watched for cars, very few along our road in November. Eventually came the slam of a car door parked next to the barn. Cathy O'Brien walked across the lawn in a heavy jacket and waterproof boots. Standard working apparel for folks from the state Wetlands Office I was to learn. My real education about wetlands was about to begin.

We walked together down the gravel road and into the pathway that led to the main entrance of the quarry. "Look there," Cathy said, waving at the forest of red stemmed shrubbery near the big pond. "Red-osier dogwood."

What's that? I asked.

"It's a wetland indicator. There's a lot of it here."

I gave her a tour. "So this pond? We call it "Big Pond." And over here is "Turtle Pond." We find a lot of turtles sunning themselves on logs. Ok, and here's where the quarry company worked for three days in August." I showed her where CMC had dug a pit in the rock by the pond, scraping soils and vegetation and pushing them into a big berm by the water's edge.

Cathy headed toward the narrow fringe of vegetation along the northern wall of the quarry cliffs where a shallow stream connects Big Pond with Boulder Pond. "Look here," she said. "Beaver dams!" There were many tree stumps--sapling stumps really--whose tops came to a sharp point. "Beaver chew," she said.

I had never noticed them before.

I showed her the two beaver lodges on the edge of Big Pond which we had watched with fascination for many years. She talked about the difference between beaver dams and lodges. She pointed out snags...old dead trees with cavities which were prime places for certain bird species. She noted that the areas around the ponds were marshy.

"Marshes can be shallow or deep," she said. "Some have soil that is always wet, while others are wet only periodically. Shallow or deep marshes support a variety of amphibious plants, called 'emergents' that grow partly in and partly out of the water. Plants of shallow marshes include various grasses, sedges--especially bulrushes and cattails. A third kind of marsh is the wet meadow which may either flood during certain seasons of the year or just be basically wet all year long. You'll find things like sedges, green ash, maybe red osher dogwood in these areas. Places like low-lying farmland for instance."

Cathy explained that Vermont Wetland Rules state that a development cannot proceed if it negatively impacts one or more of the wetland functions of any given area.

"How," I asked, "can digging out this entire area, and draining the water from the ponds and marshes not negatively impact the wetland functions of this site?"

She shrugged. "I don't know," she said.

It was a comfortable and interesting walk. I was learning more about this place. After about an hour we parted; it was time for her to meet with the owner to hear about his plans for the area. I went back home, wondering what the outcome of this visit would be. Unbeknownst to me at the time, all of this information was going to be critical to our case. How could I know that much of conflict in the next three years was destined to be about water?

We knew there was bitterness among some of the islanders about our opposition to the quarry opening. Merrill worked with some of them on a job in the village: the creation of an apartment above the Isle La Motte Country Store. They would tease him.

"Hey Bud, just saw Linda comin out of the swamp with a six point buck on her shoulder and a bag a frogs."

But there was also anger. Merrill said he heard someone say in a local restaurant, "Some stupid bastards are trying to keep the quarry from going in." I was a stupid bastard, I realized in amazement. Frankly, what was being said behind my back terrified me. I felt vulnerable, a woman out of place in this world of guys in their pickups. Their guns.

"Hello," I said hesitantly to one of them in the vestibule of the Town Hall one morning.

"I'm not talking to your kind, damn you!" he snarled.

It has been a terrible thing for me in the past to be disliked and so when I first became aware of the anger I was devastated. Then I decided that my spiritual challenge was not reconciliation (for me a lifetime area of interest and involvement) but to develop the warrior in myself. Feeling that there were men out there who were probably calling me "witch" and worse, I decided to embrace the idea of witch and took it on as part of a new email address. I became islewitch. It had, I thought, many layers of meaning. There is a negative, strong quality about it, helpful because I needed a kind of oppositional strength at this time. But there is also a quality about the word that invokes magic, power; witches have also been thought of as female shamans. (Try asking me to dowse for water. I can find anybody's septic tank!)

Hunting season was on. Merrill's brother Jack came from their hometown of Bethel, Vermont to help him out on one of his construction jobs. On the second day of hunting season Jack shot a buck, heaved it in the back of his pickup and drove it to Merrill's house in the village. He was shining with the joy of it, the pride of it. He strung it up from a tree in the front yard. I duly admired and took pictures.

Actually I felt safer being connected with Merrill and Jack. Though Jack was naturally on the "other side," angry with flatlanders coming in and telling born and bred Vermonters what to do with their land, because I was Merrill's friend he loyally came over to my side. He adopted me into his tribe.

"You let me know what you want. If they bring their equipment in and start drilling you just let me know. I'll come up and hey, they could find their equipment doesn't start. A little sugar in the gas tank. Who will know?"

"Thanks Jack, but that probably won't be necessary." I was touched by his loyalty and glad that he wasn't on the other side.

Bitter days came, cold laced with sunshine, frost spicing the geranium leaves, icing the upturned soil in the cleaned out garden, sparkling on the tall brown spikes of goldenrod, milkweed, burdock and brambleberry in the fields. My dog Shasta and I went out into the mowed field, she racing around joyous to be free in large spaces, I bundled in winter jacket and wool cap. Apprehensive. I was due to leave for my winter home on November 7. I took lots of pictures before I left. November pictures--the quarry all silver and blue and white; water, sky and cliffs; a beaver swimming through the silver pond, mounded stick constructions of the beaver lodges. Red osier branches shining against the blue water of the quarry pond; dead tree stump leaning out of the marsh with holes of many sizes...condos for a great variety of quarry dwellers I was later to learn.

On one of my last days I wrote, "Here I am in this place of quiet, the vacation quality gone, beauty changing with the seasons, new and wonder filled forms emerging...silhouette trees against grey or blue or gold or purple skies and it becomes high crime not to have a film filled camera always at the ready. I go around taking pictures as an expression of my passion for this place, taking pictures to ward off the dread of losing the beauty. Another loss threatens my life. No, another learning opportunity, another teacher, another...I go around taking pictures..."

Lake Champlain

7. Reconsideration

"We have become great because of the lavish use of our resources. But the time has come to inquire seriously what will happen when our forests are gone, when the coal, the iron, the oil, and the gas are exhausted, when the soils have still further impoverished and washed into the streams, polluting the rivers, denuding the fields and obstructing navigation."
Theodore Roosevelt

IN THE SECOND HALF OF THE 19TH CENTURY the entire country had lost much of its forest cover. Wanton waste of the country's natural resources at the hands of the timber, railroad, mining, and other great industries of the time began to spark concern, and in response, conservation efforts had begun to form all over the country. Sportsmen, understanding that the destruction of habitat meant the destruction of hunting and fishing, started to form organizations with a commitment to a conservation ethic. The magazine "Forest and Stream" founded in 1873 contributed to this ethic and led, eventually, to the founding of the Audubon Society in 1905.[21] In 1887 Theodore Roosevelt a great lover of hunting, started--with his friend George Bird Grinnell--The Boone and Crockett Club which today declares itself the oldest wildlife conservation organization in North America. In 1892 John Muir cofounded the Sierra Club "to do something for wildness and make the mountains glad."

Environmental destruction in Vermont had resulted in the loss of the entire deer population; fishing was decimated by erosion and the resulting silting up of streams and rivers. Vermont's Fish and Game League was formed to respond to the bleakness of the situation and the resulting loss of wildlife habitat. Over the years the League restored the deer herd and lobbied to enact legislation with regard to hunting and fishing.

It also became a prestigious political organization; two of its annual meetings were attended by presidents--one by President McKinley in 1897 and the other in 1901 by Vice President Theodore Roosevelt. Both gatherings took place at the Fisk home on Isle La Motte. Both were hosted by Nelson and Elizabeth Fisk.

November, 1995
I returned to Princeton filled with a sense of dread. What would be the next step? The next shoe to drop. What would be CMC's response to Geoff Green's Advisory Opinion? My parents had made the move from Princeton to a retirement community in nearby Hightstown. They had a small apartment, the possibility of making new friends, and a health center in the same building in which they lived. I didn't want to share the events of the past few months with my mother who continued to be deeply concerned about my father. I felt alone with a heavy burden.

On November 22 a letter arrived. It was a copy of a letter from the lawyer of CMC asking the District Commissioner to reconsider his opinion that their operation would need an Act 250 Permit. In effect they said that active quarrying had been going on from long before 1970 and up to the present time. As proof they sent two affidavits. One was from the president of the company which owned the quarry, and the other one was from an employee.

The president said he had sold about 20 tons of stone from the Fisk Quarry to a contractor in Burlington, about 5 tons of stone to a contractor for stone mason work and about 30 tons of stone for erosion control. He also stated, "A customer recently requested that I sell him dimensional stone on an as needed basis." He then described what the operation would look like.

> "The dimensional stone will be taken using hydraulic cement and a portable electric diamond wire wet saw. The saw is quiet and produces no dust. No significant changes will be made to the quarry site itself. On average I anticipate supplying about one truck load per weekday of dimensional stone although fewer trips will be made when stone is not in demand, and during the off-season. I will only supply stone with the Selectboard's permission to use the local roads, considering the prevailing road conditions."

The employee had submitted a document saying that he had lived in Isle La Motte for his whole life, and that he had worked at the Fisk Quarry and Goodsell Quarry since he was 18. He wrote "Myself and other local residents believe that the Fisk quarry was active in 1950 and earlier, because in 1950 a local youth was known to have run the quarry's tractor all over the quarry." He quoted documents that indicated or seemed to indicate that substantial amounts of stone were taken out of the quarry by the Town of Isle La Motte for fill in 1959, 60, 62, 68, and the 1970s. "It is unclear how much stone was taken from the Fisk Quarry from 1980 to 1989 although it is quite possible that some stone was taken for miscellaneous local projects during that time."

Along with the two affidavits was a petition which stated:

> "We the undersigned year-round residents of the Town of Isle La Motte strongly disagree with the group calling themselves the South Shore Associates. There has

been some concern about the quarry located at the South end of the Island operating. We feel that a halt to the operation would hurt the Island economy as we have only a few small businesses that offer jobs to our local residents. Our island has suffered by the drop in the Canadian exchange and lack of tourist trade in the past several years, and we feel that the quarry, as a historic and tourist site could provide jobs, tourism, and attract business to our stores, motels and provide much needed economy to our small community."

It was signed by sixty-seven people. I had known many of them for years, and counted them as friends. It was cast as a testament that hard working local people would suffer if we prevented the quarry from being reactivated. I had always thought of myself on the side of the underdog, on the side of the economically disadvantaged. Having spent my adult life working for social causes, for the improvement of race relations, it was painful to think that I was now assigned by some to the ranks of the socially unjust and morally insensitive.

The moment was a defining one; for me this battle was going to be partly about learning to carry on with something that was unpopular. I would be seen in a negative, unflattering light. No longer could I play the role of reconciler. Of negotiator. The woman who brings people together. Now I was "Flatlander." Isle La Motte had always felt like an ultimate kind of home, a place where my husband's family had lived since 1803, a place of retreat, of solace, a place that you could go to heal. I felt redefined. Outsider.

After several days of extreme distress, I realized that a decision had to be made. I had three options. I could give up trying to "save" the quarry and hence the family home where, I felt, it would be impossible to live in the midst of noise and dust and destruction. I could try to carry on with the struggle feeling stressed and inviting—or so I believed—a recurrence of cancer. Or I could completely change my attitude and continue on, but in a spirit of serenity. Option number three seemed like a desirable but impossible option.

True the stress was due to the fear of losing our beloved home on the island. But it was also due to my sense of carrying a heavy load all by myself. It was the "it's all up to me" syndrome. I had been there before and understood the potential consequences to my health and well being. I must have help.

Geoffrey Green had indicated that this was the time to hire a lawyer.

And indeed, I didn't see how we of South Shore Associates could proceed by ourselves. What about Joe Bivins? What about Stephanie Kaplan, the crack environmental lawyer who was good friends with Randy and Joe. Could we hire one of them? If so, which one? And how much would it cost. How could I afford it? I had very little money and after the cancer in 1994 I wasn't working. I emailed Randy with my new found email capability, begging him for wisdom.

December 2
From Linda to Randy:
I guess it's time to start to crawl out of my mental morass and start thinking constructively about this quarry situation. The immediate issue is to figure out what to do. With this letter asking the District Commissioner to reconsider his decision, the active question in my mind is whether it's now time to hire a lawyer and if so to go with Stephanie or Joe? Facts:

1. We have 30 days (from last Wednesday) to respond to the latest communication from CMC. I suppose Geoff Green would extend it if necessary since there is no legal deadline involved.

2. Geoffrey Green said to me over the phone that now would be a good time to hire a lawyer and to file a legal response to their request for reconsideration, He wrote an opinion that the company must apply for an Act 250 Permit based on certain facts we submitted. They then submitted new facts and asked him to reconsider his opinion. They included an affidavit signed by someone who has been the caretaker of the quarry for years. It's probably not all that important, but it does need to be responded to by us within 30 days.

3. It's critical to keep costs down. There's no money, really.

4. Stephanie indicated that she could be quite flexible in terms of how we would use her. Said her rates are low because her overhead is low.

Wonderings just between you and me:

5. I get the feeling that Joe would like to work on this—though probably would start feeling exploited at a certain point if he didn't make any money. He once let slip the possibility that he could represent us at an Act 250 hearing. "I'd have to get paid of course" and "I've never done this before," and then quick change of subject.

6. I wouldn't want to lose Joe's help and input on this by hiring Stephanie.

7. I wonder if there might be some judicious way to combine Joe's legal mind and brilliance and the fact that he has all the background on this with Stephanie's brilliance and vast experience and legal status. And finding a way to pay Joe something and to pay Stephanie her fee. Though we can't really afford this.

8. Do you have any thoughts or reactions to the above.
Thanks endlessly. Linda

December 3
From Randy to Linda

I think quite a lot of Joe and Stephanie as expert advisors. Both are at separate cusps of life where money is a major issue so whatever you do, for all your sakes please don't gloss it over. Joe LOVES this work and would be extremely easy to exploit. Stephanie has provided freebie work for others and was heard to make disgruntled mumblings on the subject. I'm not sure I can be unbiased about either of these two. The closest I can get is feeling that the other possible "anti development" lawyers I've known would require extensive getting up to speed. You pay them to learn how to defend you! Stephanie wrote the book, so to speak.

Joe Bivins once said that going through the Act 250 process is like playing monopoly. If you can get it to the level of monopoly or chess then it can be fun.

Fun!

But what to do! Stephanie was indeed a "real" lawyer. And Randy said, in effect, "Stephanie wrote the book" on land use laws in Vermont. But then I knew Joe. I had been in contact with him. He knew the case. Should I use both of them? Randy had said that whatever decision I made would be a good one. It was up to me.

I emailed Joe and put the question to him. I signed it SWFH. He responded that he would like to do it and that his fee would be 25 dollars an hour. I knew that was an incredible bargain. I also knew I couldn't afford it but I said yes. Would South Shore Associates help out? I didn't know. Joe's first action was to write me a comforting letter.

December 3, 1995, 2:05 p.m.
Joe to Linda
Re: From Princeton with Despair

Dear Linda,
Don't despair -- you'll get there. You did have it VERY easy the first time around; the other side is simply beginning to wake up. Nearly all of the "new" information is from one source and it doesn't tend to change the earlier picture of the quarry very much--nothing indicates a regular pattern of daily activity and nothing indicates any great volume. Many of the other arguments you raised also continue to hold.

As to the petition, its impact is psychological rather than legal. It shows your group has some community work to do outside of Act 250. If you wanted to do a petition and worded it carefully you could almost certainly get several dozen signatures too. So it is still a little early to abandon Vermont, but coming back would probably help.
Take care,
Joe

ps I never did figure out what the "SW" represented in SWFH
Social Worker from Hell
Super Woman from Hell
Sharp Wily Fox from Hell
Satanic Wife from Hell
Sacred Wonder from Hell
Seventh Wonder From Hell
Somehow I suspect that none of these is what you had in mind."

What I had in mind was "Scared Woman From Hell"

December 3, 1995
from Randy to Linda

Linda. My erstwhile political allies around this town used to talk a lot about zen detachment and then leave me in the lurch. In your case, a little detachment might help a lot. You will be needing to psych out a variety of people over the coming months which will mean finding a way to rise up out of your love of the farm to actively get on your neighbors' and your opponents' wave lengths. Knowing that you can always fall to pieces among your comrades. If it's a question of your health, there's nothing for it: we will have to organize an armed milita and clear the bastards out immediately. Please advise.

I no longer felt alone. My distress lifted immediately. At least for now.

8. Affidavits

"Do what you can, with what you have, where you are."
— *Theodore Roosevelt*

THEODORE ROOSEVELT'S LOVE OF NATURE began early in life. A sickly child, he learned to love the out-of-doors, collected plants and animals, carried frogs in his hat, determined to become a naturalist when he grew up. His concern for conservation may have begun as early as 1883 when he took a vacation from his work in the New York legislature to visit the Badlands in North Dakota for a two week vacation. Here he fell in love with the beauty of the landscape. At the age of 25 he actually bought a ranch and a herd of cattle.

A year later at the age of 26, tragedy left young Roosevelt's life in ruins. His mother died in the Roosevelts' New York City home. Hours later, just after the birth of their first child, his beloved wife Alice died upstairs in the same house. "The light has gone out of my life," wrote Roosevelt in his diary.[22]

Five months later he left the East and went back to his ranch, taking a break from his work in the legislature and returning to the West looking to lose himself in hard physical activity. His cattle had done well so he increased his herd, and took up serious ranching for several years. The beauty and serenity of the land, the relentless physical activity and downright hard work proved to be healing in the wake of his terrible loss. "Nothing could be more lonely and nothing more beautiful than the view at nightfall across the prairies to these huge hill masses, when the lengthening shadows had at last merged into one and the faint afterglow of the red sunset filled the West," he wrote.[23]

It also gave rise to a passion for conservation which proved to be a central theme of his life, his presidency, writing, "I have always said I would not have been President had it not been for my experience in North Dakota."

Both my parents came from the northwest corner of Nebraska, from ranch country, not far from the Badlands of South Dakota. Though my parents emigrated to New York City early in their marriage, my childhood included trips to the West where my brother and I and numerous cousins rode horses on our grandfather's ranch, gloried in the great skies, sunrise over the prairies, the leaping grace of white tailed deer, the pheasants rising up in a flutter of concern at our quiet approach. It was here that I first learned a deep love for the land.

In their request for reconsideration, CMC or their lawyers were describing a reality completely at odds with what we had known, with what my family and all of our neighbors had experienced during the years we had lived next to the Fisk Quarry. How could we express our views. How would we tell our stories?

"Affidavits," Joe said on the phone. "Can you get affidavits from your neighbors describing their experiences with the quarry? We have thirty days to respond to what they've said, but we've already used up a number of them. It's December 4 now. And even though we have until December 27, we'd better get our stuff in before Christmas. Say by December 23."

Well...here I was in Princeton, New Jersey. Of the west shore neighbors on Isle La Motte, a dozen or more traveled year round between Isle La Motte and Canada. Mary Jane and Dave Tiedgen lived in Michigan; Joe and the whole Bajorski/Masalek clan was in Connecticut. Ross Firth, our president, said he would be away and couldn't participate. It was now December 4. How could we possibly get signed, notarized affidavits from everyone before Christmas?

Joe and I talked some more and finally worked out a mode of operation. I would call each neighbor and interview him or her by phone about his or her experience of the Fisk Quarry over the years, whatever it was. Since I can type almost as fast as people can talk, I would record what was being said. With the help of Joe I would put it into an affidavit format and send it by way of email to Joe. Joe might have a few questions which would necessitate another phone call. Finally, I would fax the affidavit to the specified neighbor who would review it. If what I had typed was accurate and complete, the neighbor would take the fax to be notarized, then send it to Joe in Thetford, Vermont by way of priority or overnight mail. Joe needed all the affidavits in hand in time to write a brief. The brief and all affidavits had to be completed and sent to the District Commissioner by December 22.

When you have something specific, something positive to do, I found that fear recedes. So while Princeton in the holiday season was decked with twinkling white lights, graceful boughs of greens, red velvet bows, and choirs singing in the town square, I was sitting at my desk. Phoning. Listening. Typing. Emailing. Faxing.

It was a marathon. I started by calling my Vermont neighbors just to tell them what we had in mind. "So if you would think about this, I'll be calling you later today or tomorrow to interview you."

This December Operation was the beginning of getting to know our neighbors; the beginning of developing a team. As I listened on the phone and typed, neighbors' statements were sweeter than Christmas carols. They expressed a love of place, a love of the land that mirrored my own.

All the affidavits began the same way. "NOW COMES NEIL HANNA WHO STATES AS FOLLOWS UNDER OATH: My name is Neil Hanna. I am over 21 years old and legally competent to sign this affidavit." And then each continued, each telling his or her story.

"The quarry has always been an interesting spot in the neighborhood," Neil Hanna told me over the telephone. "In the winter we'd go in and the kids would play hockey on the ice. Sometimes we'd have skating parties and then go back to the house for baked beans. There was a hill at the back and the kids would go and ski and toboggan there on the hill on the eastern edge of the quarry. In the summers the kids were always going in there collecting pollywogs and frogs. It was a great place for minnows. There was one place in there called Billy Goat Hill; people would throw their minnow nets out and collect their minnows.

"Another thing that comes to mind, there were a number of apple trees on the border of the quarry. Mr. Grant would pick them and once he grafted a branch from one of them onto a tree in back of his house. Throughout the 1960s to the present, there was always all kinds of beaver activity, including lodges, freshly gnawed trees, etc. Once a giant beaver made a mistake and a tree that he was chewing came down on him and killed him. There was other wildlife including herons and foxes. The quarry has been a very quiet and interesting spot in the neighborhood. A nice thing to have in the neighborhood.

"From time to time people would come to take out loose rock or riprap but there was never any quarrying per se. Loose stone was removed occasionally maybe once every few years. I remember someone taking loose stone out once in the 70s. Being so close to the quarry we would have known what was going on. Of course this past summer (1995) we could hear the company people over in the quarry. It was pretty disturbing. You could see the fresh cuts that they made. They also tore up a lot of the vegetation. It was not the sort of thing that you would want to put up with."

"Oh my," Elva Grant said. "The quarry. It was one of those spots you were drawn to. Some areas were marshy. There was a lot of low undergrowth, wildflowers, and lots and lots of cattails. And there was always a heron. And ducks. You would get families of ducks that would find a spot in there. We would look for interesting wild flowers and then we would go back in the fall to see if there were interesting dried flowers. From the time he first came here, my father would go into the quarry frequently. In about 1960 he started taking my children over to the quarry when they were too young to go by themselves (they would have been five or six when he started). He liked showing things of interest to the children such as the geologic formations, the fossils and the wildlife that lived there. Later in the 1960s and in the early 1970s the kids would go frogging and looking for turtles in the quarry. It was a favorite haunt of theirs."

"We built our house next to Fisk Quarry in 1958," Mary Jane Tiedgen recalled. "From 1958 for the next eight years I spent entire summers there with my mother and brother from June to the end of August. During those years I virtually lived in the quarry. It was my place of retreat and solitude and always has been. I was literally there every single day. There was no quarrying activity in Fisk Quarry. It was just a beautiful place for birds and animals and fish and plant life."

Mary Jane's brother, Jeffrey Williams also had memories. "I spent a lot of time in the quarry. I ran a minnow business and sold minnows to unsuspecting fisherpersons. I remember Stuart and Robert Sculley active in the quarry trapping minnows also. Stuart and I had competing bait businesses. We had a bit of a go around once but ended up being friends. I was also there during the hunting season. I hunted for ducks and foxes in the quarry; I would hunt for partridge, woodcock and rabbits in the woods east of the quarry—which is quarry property. And in the winter we would return to ice fish in the lake."

Their father, Carl Williams added, "I would say I visited the quarry almost every day. It was one of my favorite spots. I enjoyed the beavers. The red foxes had their homes in amongst the loose rocks at the back and I would go and watch the baby foxes grow up. It was so pretty seeing them running around in the wintertime on the snow. It was a beautiful sight. I also had minnow traps there for many years. When my son Jeffrey was at Michigan State there was a sort of new minnow in our trap that we had never seen before. He took several of them back to Michigan State to have them identified. They turned out to be stickelbacks, a minnow whose primary diet is mosquito larvae. So they are quite a plus in keeping the mosquitoes down. It was very good to fish with because it was a tough little minnow with a fin on the back."

My older son, Lyle Andrews emailed his affidavit. "Part of the specialness of growing up on Isle La Motte was Fisk Quarry. I was very young, maybe 6 or 7 when I started going over to the quarry by myself. That would have been in 1974 or 1975 and it continued into the late 1980s. The quarry is very close to the house, and part of it is basically our yard—my family owns about 40 or 50 feet into part of the quarry. I would go into the quarry maybe two or three times a week. All the kids in the neighborhood would go there: Mark and

Kevin Peacock, Elizabeth Shelley, Ann Orick, Daniel Sauve and his sister Mary Clair, Lars and Grady Turner, Granger and Sara Dale, and Judy Hanna.

"One of the most interesting things happened when I was 12. My friend, Mark Peacock and I made a raft and floated around the quarry pond. We plumbed the depths of the pond and made a map, giving names to the different rocks and islands. Some places were over 30 feet deep. Floating around on the raft gave us a new perspective on the water filled parts of the quarry because then we could get close to the beaver lodge and try to find the entrance. Of course there are fossils over there which it was educational to explore."

Bruce, my younger son also typed his affidavit and sent it to me by way of email. "My grandparents, the Fitches, bought the Fisk property on Isle La Motte in 1970 where I have spent my summers since I was born in 1971 until 1990 when I went to college. From the age of seven (1978 to 1990) I spent lots of time in the Fisk Quarry which is directly adjacent to my grandparents' property. As kids, my brother and my friends would go in the quarry several times a week—once a week at a bare minimum. Our favorite thing to do was to go out scaling the walls, and practice rock climbing. It was basically our giant jungle gym.

"There was a lot of animal life including beavers. Once my friend, Kevin Peacock (a neighbor whose family had a cottage just north of us on Fisk Point) and I were in there making a map of the quarry and we saw evidence of deer. The plant life most interesting to us was what was growing in the quarry pond. There were also bullfrogs, tadpoles, turtles and lots of leaches. And of course there are all sorts of interesting fossils. My brother, Lyle Andrews and Kevin's brother Mark did a whole exploration of the quarry by raft, poling it around, taking measurements of the depths and making a map."

The Scully family lived just north of our property. John Scully said, "Throughout the 1950s and into the 1960s my older brothers Stuart and Robert (nine and twelve years older than I) would go into the Fisk Quarry in the spring, summer and fall to catch turtles, frogs and tadpoles with their homemade traps. From an early age (say 1956 on) I would go with them. The quarry always had a special interest for all of us in the neighborhood because of the wildlife, the fossils and the things we could do there. In the winter we would skate in the quarry. Unlike the ice in the lake which would often be rough because of the wind, the quarry was always glass. You could skate all over the place. I don't remember the beavers in the 1950s but from the 1960s they have always been there. Now I bring my own boys who are ages 3, 7 and 9 and I go down to the quarry with them and watch the wildlife, especially the beavers which are a star attraction. The quarry is a special place to them as well."

Perhaps the most poignant statement came from John's father, Vincent Scully who wrote: "I am 83 years old and live in Montreal. Myself and family have had our Isle La Motte property since 1953. We use it year round. It forms part of Fisk Point on Lake Champlain and is near the old Fisk Quarry.

"I can say that had there been quarrying at the time I bought it, or even had it been cited as a possibility I would have had to continue my search for a place in the sun due to a health problem. The quarry is a place we walk to with our guests and tell about its history. We show off its beaver and sanctuary details. Also its our best local tobogganing spot.

"My three boys grew up free to roam and explore the neighborhood. The quarry was an important part of their lives. I believe that the reopening of the quarry will now will put my son's three boys (ages 3,7,9) at risk.

"I can only say, please leave the old abandoned lakeside quarry alone. I'm sure my humble reasons for asking this of you can be surpassed by others who equally feel this impending loss."

So each affidavit was like another. Though many of us didn't know one another, though we were different, though we came from different places, we shared a love for the wild life, the plants, the peace and quiet. We were also interested in the fossils though we didn't know, at that time, exactly what they were or what they represented.

To Joe's delight we ended up with eleven affidavits. As I typed phone interviews I faxed them to neighbors in Vermont, Connecticut, Michigan and Canada who in turn had their signatures notarized, then faxed them back. I sent them to Joe who began weaving them into a brief. I was very curious to see this document, having no idea what it would be like. Having no experience with such a thing as a "brief."

"How are you coming?" I would email Joe several times a day.

"It's coming along but where's the affidavit from Elva Grant?" he would email back. "And ask Neil Hanna about that beaver the tree fell on. I'm not clear about when that happened."

Finally, on December 22, he said that he was sending his brief as an attached file.

Part of this process was learning how to deal with computer processes. Such things as email and attached files were relatively new in 1995. I'll never forget the moment when it arrived. I printed it out. There it was, 18 pages all in 12 point Geneva font, looking—to my novice eyes—utterly formidable. I started reading.

"The legal issues to be discussed are simple and straightforward so far as they apply to this case. In general, commercial or industrial development require a land use permit under 10 VSA 6081. An exception to the permit requirement is made for activity already going on at the time Act 250 became effective (June 1970); this is the issue of pre-existing development.

Such activity remains exempt from the permit requirement so long as two further conditions are met: (i) there is continuity of operation and (ii) there is no significant change in the character or scale of activity from the immediately preceding period. The former condition addresses abandonment of operation; the latter refers to substantial change.

In dealing with the jurisdictional question of whether Act 250 applies to the Fisk Quarry, then, four questions need to be answered:

Question 1: Is the proposed quarrying activity a "development" within the meaning of 10 VSA 6081 and Environmental Board Rule 2?

Question 2: Was the quarry active in 1970 when Act 250 became effective-i.e.did the quarry qualify as an active ongoing pre-existing development?

Question 3: Has the quarry been continuously active from 1970 to the present i.e., does the quarry meet the continuity of operation test?

Question 4: Is the proposed activity identical in character, scale, and technological basis to such pre-1970 activity as has continued to the present--i.e., does proposed activity represent a substantial change from previously permitted or exempted activity?"

Joe proceeded to organize his presentation around these four questions. The heartfelt statements of neighbors in their affidavits became the basis for his arguments. In one of his final paragraphs he wrote,

"As in the pre-1970 period, the only workers present on the site on a regular daily basis were the beaver -- and their activity was centered on wood rather than on stone. The main 'products' turned out on the site were, first, children with an interest in natural processes and a love for wildlife; and second, adults with an appreciation for the beauty and the serenity of the setting. For some especially fortunate adults, there was also the joy of sharing some of their own childhood pleasures with their children or grandchildren. These are not the 'products' which CMC proposes to remove from the site."

To me this long document was like poetry. I read it again and again. I read it in the bathtub. I took it to bed with me. On December 23 I sent a cover letter, Joe's brief, and eleven signed and notarized affidavits to the Act 250 Commissioner of District 6. I also sent a letter to the neighbors:

December 23, 1995
Dear Neighbors and members of SSA (South Shore Associates),

Yesterday I sent documents pertaining to our recent marathon effort to respond to the quarry company's request to Geoffrey Green to reconsider his decision that the company needs to apply for an Act 250 Permit.

The process, while arduous, turned out to be deeply rewarding for me personally. The affidavits tell of our personal experiences in the quarry, and the love which we all share, both for the neighborhood and for the quarry itself. Carl's tale of red foxes dancing in the snow, Mary Jane's taking her daughter into the quarry at the age of two to share a love of nature developed in the quarry during her own childhood, Scully and Williams kids running bait businesses out of the quarry, Vincent—the neighborhood patriarch first settling in the neighborhood in 1953, Elva and Elaine gathering wild flowers in the quarry, Neil and his family skating on the frozen quarry pond and going home for baked beans, my kids rock climbing and poling a raft around the pond, taking soundings and making maps. I feel closer to you all as a result.

Also, I cannot say enough about Joe Bivins who is truly an unsung hero and warrior on behalf of the environment of Vermont. Via email and phone, he worked for two solid weeks with me on this process, guiding me in getting information from you and putting together a document which is truly impressive. His brilliance and knowledge as well as humor, patience, humility, tact and indefatigable hard work made the process both satisfying and, much of the time, downright fun.

Best to all,
Linda

Shortly thereafter the District Commissioner found, once again, that CMC needed to file for an Act 250 Permit. Then I received another letter. It was, I found after slicing it open, from one of the lawyers engaged by CMC.

January 4, 1996

"Dear Linda and Members:
Based upon the affidavits that your members have submitted, your members, and their children, have been using the Fisk Quarry for recreational purposes. Quarries are not recreation areas. They are working areas that may pose some risks to visitors. Until further notice, I am recommending that my client post 'No Trespassing' signs around the property's perimeter, and that the Quarry's access areas be restricted. This action will help protect unauthorized visitors from injury, and it will help protect the owners from having to defend a lawsuit if someone gets hurt.
This letter serves as formal notice to you, your members, and their children, that trespass upon the Fisk Quarry is prohibited. Please pass this information along to your members."

9. Dry Rock Beavers

"To waste, to destroy our natural resources, to skin and exhaust the land instead of using it so as to increase its usefulness, will result in undermining in the days of our children the very prosperity which we ought by right to hand down to them amplified and developed."
— *Theodore Roosevelt*

AT THE REPUBLICAN NATIONAL CONVENTION IN JUNE of 1900, President William McKinley was slated to be re-nominated as president. Who would be nominated as Vice President? Young Theodore Roosevelt, returned from his ranching in 1886, had both remarried and plunged back into politics. In the next few years he held a number of positions, having made a name for himself as a progressive reformer in the New York Assembly. In 1889 he was appointed by President Benjamin Harrison to head up the US Civil Service Commission. From there he became president of the New York City Police Board, then he became Assistant Secretary of the Navy under William McKinley, and finally, in 1898 at the age of forty, he was elected governor of New York. But this upstart, trust busting young reformer had many enemies who wanted him out of the way. Kicked upstairs. Nominate him for the vice presidency! Anything to get him out of New York politics where he and his trustbusting, reformist activities were a big pain for the wealthy capitalist crowd and the conservative Republican machine.

Roosevelt had no desire to be vice president. "The Vice Presidency," he stated, "is not an office in which I could do anything and not an office in which a man who is still vigorous and not past middle life has much chance of doing anything."24 However, overwhelmed by a tremendous wave of popular support at the convention (with only one abstention--his own) he reluctantly agreed, the Republicans won the general election, and McKinley and Roosevelt were inaugurated on March 4 of 1901.25

Just six months later, on September 6, 1901, Roosevelt found himself sailing north on Lake Champlain to Isle La Motte. He was a guest on the yacht Elfrida, owned by the wealthy Webb family of Shelburne, Vermont. He would be guest speaker at the annual Fish and Game League of which Nelson Fisk had previously served as president. After that he was looking forward to a vacation with his family in the Adirondacks.

The day was glorious according to subsequent newspaper accounts. The Elfrida arrived at the dock of the Fisk Quarry, a few yards south of the Fisk estate. I imagine Nelson Fisk meeting Roosevelt on the dock and escorting the vice president with his party over to the big stone house and the spacious lawn shaded by black locust trees. Here a huge tent had been erected and a thousand guests from all over Vermont, many of them brought to the Fisk dock by the steam vessel Chateauguay, awaited his arrival. A luncheon of chicken and biscuits prepared by the Methodist women of Isle La Motte, was served in the vast white tent.

There were speeches by the political luminaries of Vermont. As guest speaker, Roosevelt spoke of his interest in the work of the Fish and Game League.

> "Gentlemen, I believe in what you are doing. I believe heartily in the gospel of work, but a man will work better for a little play. Every man who works also needs to play. I am interested in all furred, finned and feathered inhabitants of the woods and waters. I am interested in the wilderness itself. These things prevent the tameness and monotony which sometimes comes into life. I do not need to impress upon you the democratic character of well executed laws for the preservation of the fish and game and forests. If you do not preserve them soon the only places where they may be found will be the great private preserves."[26]

Nelson Fisk was an educated man. He was a businessman and ultimately became President of The Fish and Game League, the closest thing in Vermont at that time to an environmental organization. Understanding that game animals and fish needed habitat and hunting needed strict controls, the League pushed for legislation, attempted to educate public opinion and indeed did what it could to heal the environmental devastation of Vermont in the nineteenth century.

On the day that Vice President Roosevelt stood on these beautiful grounds and spoke to a great crowd, Nelson Fisk would, most likely, have been bewildered to know that his busy quarry, not 200 feet away, was to become--a century later--the source of a bitter environmental dispute.

February 1996

My father was now often in a wheelchair. When I first returned to Princeton from Isle La Motte in the fall, every day I drove out to nearby Hightstown to visit my parents in their new retirement home--Meadow Lakes. I would take my father for walks through the halls, pushing an empty wheelchair, just in case. During one walk, however, my father lost his equilibrium and lurched forward to the point of almost falling. I was just able to get him into the wheelchair once I found the brakes. After that I found I could exercise by jogging while pushing my father in the wheelchair through the halls. It was a pace that he enjoyed. Frequently, when we returned to my parents' apartment, we found my mother practicing the piano. A Chopin Nocturne. A Brahms Rhapsody.

Each day as I returned to my house in Princeton, I would check my mailbox hoping, that among the bills, the bank statements, and the occasional postcard, there would be nothing from Vermont. But on one frigid day in February, I found in my mailbox a large official looking envelope with a Vermont return address. I opened it up at the kitchen table and found a notice stating "Petitioner believes that the Coordinator's jurisdictional finding was in error."

I called Joe in Vermont. "What the heck is this?"

"CMC is now asking the Vermont Environmental Board for a declaratory ruling," he said.

"And what, pray tell, is that?"

"The Vermont Environmental Board is sort of a higher court of appeals for the Act 250 system in Vermont," said Joe on the phone. "That means that the company is appealing Geoffrey Green's decision that Act 250 has jurisdiction over the Fisk Quarry. I'm kind of surprised. I expected that they would be filing an Act 250 application. I never thought they would appeal the decision."

However, Joe was taken aback and we neophytes were stunned by what happened next. A week later a notice arrived from the lawyers of CMC informing us that the company had filed an Act 250 application with the District #6 Environmental Commission. For Joe the whole process was a battle of wits in which he prided himself on being able to stay several steps ahead of the opposition. But he hadn't imagined that the lawyers for CMC would file to appeal the District Coordinator's decision at the same time they submitted an Act 250 application.

"What are they doing?" I asked.

In an unusual weary sounding voice Joe said to me over the phone, "It seems they're doing two things at the same time. They are applying for an Act 250 Permit and appealing the decision that they need an Act 250 Permit, both at the same time. And according to the rules, it seems to be legal."

What did this mean?

"It means," Joe said, "that we have to prepare, number one, for an Act 250 hearing and, number two, for a second hearing based on a challenge to the original decision that an Act 250 is needed at all. It means twice as much work for us."

"Can we do it?" I asked. Worried of course.

"Well the first thing, is to get hold of the actual 250 application that CMC has written. Then we should all--you and Merrill and me--meet up here. In Vermont."

March 1, 1996
Linda to Randy

It's now 4:30 am, dark and cold in Princeton, with no crackling wood stove to curl up in front of with superb coffee such as you are enjoying up in your frozen world. Anyway, I'm into my 'thinking about nothing except quarry' mode which I don't really like at all. Our kitten (teenage cat) is in heat and is yowling for sex with a black leather jacketed tomcat which motorcycled up on four paws several hours ago and prowls around the back door. I'm really unhappy about the quarry...feelings of being trapped by some large amorphous thing which I have to fight but don't know how and don't want to fight anyway. I keep telling myself that all my growth in life has come from just going ahead--through my feelings of discomfort--just keep going ahead.

March 2
Randy to Linda

Nobody could have said it better than you did speaking of that grueling strain between the peace you wanted up here in Vermont and the battle you got. War and peace, at least in my universe, are such huge basic categories. But consider. Catullus wrote a jewel of a poem about how peace, which he thought he needed, turns out to be "bad" for him.
Rad

Vermont was blanketed in several feet of snow. Joe, Merrill and I made plans to get together at Brooksies, a local joint in Sharon, Vermont and a compromise meeting point between Isle La Motte in the far northwestern corner of Vermont and Joe's home in Thetford near the New Hampshire border. Warm, smelling of maple syrup, bacon, hamburgers and hot turkey sandwiches, Brooksie's was a comforting place in the frigid, snow-covered landscape. Merrill and I sat waiting for Joe who finally walked in wearing a heavy, plaid woolen jacket and his standard hat. It was lunch time. I remember that he ordered a big ham dinner. I can't remember what Merrill and I ordered. Tuna fish sandwiches maybe. We began the process of going over the Act 250 application.

It opened with a summary. The applicant would quarry no more than 2,000 cubic yards, no crushers would be installed, no new blasting, a water-cooled diamond saw would be used to cut the marble, the saw to be powered by an "efficient" diesel generator. Both would be very quiet; sound at the property boundaries would be "negligible." On average 1 flatbed truck per day would haul the cut blocks away for processing; operations would take place within the existing quarry which "may expand over time." Any overburden or topsoil would be used in the process of reclamation. The duration requested for the permit was fifty years.

I was shrinking in my seat. I felt defeated already. But Joe was rubbing his hands together. He probably didn't actually say "boy oh boy...let's get at this," but that's the way he looked.

"Now let's get into the meat of this," he said in essence. "I want all of us to write down all the problems we see with this application."

We began with Act 250 Criterion One. Air pollution. "If the project involves manufacturing or industrial processes, describe any process air emissions, odors, or sources of noise and measures proposed to control them." CMC had written n/a. Not applicable.

Joe was already scribbling. "Emission Sources: Diesel generator or generators, 20 ton tractor trailer trucks."

"They don't say anything about trucks carrying away rubblestone," I said.

"That's right, they don't," said Joe. He looked at Merrill. "I suppose you have a fair amount of experience with work sites."

"You might say that. I grew up on a farm and was around farm equipment ever since I was born. I worked on a road construction crew when they were putting in Interstate 89 in the late 1960s. And I've been building things ever since I could lift a hammer." He said he was familiar with a large variety of tools and equipment including tile saws, brick saws, stone saws, stone drills, blasting equipment, loaders, jack hammers, air compressors, diesel generators, back hoes, bull dozers, cranes and water pumps.

Joe was impressed. "Ok, so what else are they going to need on this construction site?"

"Well, along with the tractor trailers and dump trucks, they'll need heavy machinery such as excavators, maybe diesel excavators to remove overburden and rubble stone. Diesel bucket loader to remove and load large blocks of marble, diesel generators to power equipment. Bobcat jackhammer, loader, scraper."

"How about compressors to run the drills?" said Joe. "And what about all the hydraulic fluid, oil and grease that they'll need to run this equipment. They'll need storage and disposal facilities for all of these things."

Merrill went on. "Lengths of metal track and rigging for drills and cutting machines."

"Air hoses, electric power cables, water hoses. Don't tell me that there aren't going to be emissions," said Joe.

"What about sound? I mean, it's only 150 feet away from our house. Less than that from Bajorski's house." It was the only thing I could think of.

"Oh it will all be very quiet," said Joe. "They say that right here on page one of their application. And look here at Criterion 1g. 'Indicate how storm water runoff will be disposed of without causing undue water pollution from litter, oil, salt, pesticides, and the like.' And look at the answer. "The project involves quarrying dimensional marble from a quarry that presently produces fill and rubble stone. A portion of the existing quarry fills with ground and surface water each year."

For the first time I interrupted. "A portion of the quarry fills with water each year? It sounds as though part of the year the quarry is dry. The quarry pond is never dry. Not only is it never dry, but some of it is thirty feet deep."

"You know that because your son measured it from his raft," Joe said, remembering the affidavits.

"Yes."

"How old was he?"

"Twelve."

"Well he was probably right but we might want to check that out again," Joe said making a note.

We continued to read. "The applicant will apply for, concurrently with this Act 250 permit application, a discharge permit to dewater the area and retrieve quarried stone that lies underneath the water."

"We keep talking about Linda's family owning part of that pond," said Merrill. "How can they de-water their part of the pond without her permission?" he asked Joe.

"Maybe they plan to build a barrier," mused Joe.

"What? De-water the pond? Kill the fish. Destroy the beaver habitat? What about the bullfrogs? Where will the ducks nest?" This was me.

"Well, I guess they think there's a special species of beaver that lives there," said Joe. "A kind of beaver that doesn't need water. A dry rock beaver. That's it, we've discovered a new and rare species, the Dry Rock Beaver. We'll contact the NonGame and Natural Heritage Program."

This especially appealed to what I think of as Merrill's "Vermont Sense of Humor." He laughed so hard that I was afraid that people would start looking at us. "The Dry Rock Beaver, I love it. Hey we've got an endangered species here."

Eventually we got back to reading. "As the quarry area is developed, a sump will be maintained to collect and detain ground and surface water that collects in the quarry. The water, some of which may be used to cool the cutting equipment and control dust, will settle into the sump area which will be dewatered periodically as permitted by the State. A discharge permit application will be filed within the next 10 days and a copy of that application will be filed with the District Commission."

"So they're going to have a sump collecting water filled with stone dust, oil, diesel fluid, grease and all the stuff from the machinery they use," Joe said. "Where are they going to discharge this stuff? In the lake?"

Our meeting continued on in this vein with Joe and Merrill taking the lead on most issues. Many things leapt out at us as huge problem areas to be challenged. On page 11 we were fascinated to read the following paragraph: "Cathy O'Brien from the VT Depart of Environmental Conservation Water Quality Division, Wetland Office, has informally indicated that the project will not have a material impact upon our water resources."

"What?" I said. "When did she say that? She didn't tell me that during our walk through the quarry."

"Check it out with the Wetland Office," said Joe. "And look here, the State Wildlife Biologist, John Austin, has signed off on their claim of no wildlife habitat. No wildlife in the quarry? How did that happen? Better check on that one!"

The application said that the project would have no impact upon neighboring wells. There would be no soil erosion involved. No adverse impact upon the lake. I was particularly interested to read that the adjoining property along the road to the north "is a summer camp, which lies vacant for most of the year."

"Hey that's our place," I said.

"Hmmm," said Joe " a summer camp which is a State Historic Site once visited by Teddy Roosevelt with eligibility status with the National Register of Historic Places, a summer camp with five buildings two of them made out of stone in the late eighteenth and early nineteenth centuries, a historic barn which is being used for art shows and music, and a B&B...this is a summer camp that lies vacant for most of the year? Pretty interesting." The application went on to say "a few more camps lie to the south, but the overall area is sparsely populated."

" So much for the Williams, Tiedgens, Bajorskis, Grants, Hannas, Firths and Scullys," I said.

March 8 8:05 p.m.
Linda to Joe
Dear Joe,

Thanks for the super meeting the other day in Brooksies. In the meantime (actually since last night when we talked) the following things have occurred. Merrill and I went to Waterbury today and met with:

1. Carl Pagel, Wetlands Chief. Carl, genial and friendly, wanted to know what was going on. It turns out that CMC has not filed for a CUD. We showed him the application where Cathy O'Brian is said to have informally commented. He snorted and said Cathy would be interested to see that. We showed him where they were planning to drain the quarry, use giant saws, diesel fueled generators, et al. We showed him the pictures again (he's got some in his files). We showed him John Austin's letter (who said there was no significant wildlife). He shook his head and said we should go talk to John and show him the pictures. I asked him if he would call John and tell him we were coming. He did, then made us two copies of a huge wetlands map showing the quarry as wetlands and said this map is what the Wetlands Office is going by.

2. We then went to Air Pollution Control Engineer, Doug Elliot, who wrote the letter. He was out, but his supervisor, Bryan Fitzgerald--very friendly and open-- sat down with us to review the situation. He gave us a lot of useful information which I will try to type up for you in the next day or so. We showed him where CMC had indicated in the application that they did not need an Air Control permit. He said that wasn't true. He said that they had simply supplied them with information. The company has not provided enough information for them to determine whether they need to be permitted. He said to be sure to bring that to the attention of the District Commission.

3. Carl Pagel had called ahead to John Austin who was at meetings in Essex Junction. Austin said he would be happy to meet with us at noon. So we drove north from Waterbury through the blizzards. Austin turned out to be an earnest young man. We reminded him of the letter he had written and started to show him the pictures. Joe, this was really fun. With the first picture his mouth dropped open. He said that CMC's lawyer had told him that the quarry was dry. With picture after picture his indignation grew. He was also embarrassed. He said that he had made his determination on three factors: a.The lawyer's telling him that the quarry was dry. b.Cathy O'Brien's comment as cited in the application. c.And finally, when he made the site visit, the area was all covered with snow and he had no idea that he was even standing on water. Frozen water. He was embarrassed but he also said he felt that he had been duped and wrote down a list of people that he wanted to call including the District Coordinator, Geoffrey Green, Carl Pagel, and several others. He said he would send a different kind of letter to the lawyer. I asked him to send us a copy.

4. Then we drove back down to Waterbury and saw the supervisor of the department of Nongame and Natural Heritage. He said that he would put a lot of weight on John Austin's opinion. We then went to see Todd Sternbach, our man in Wastewater. Todd said he had been watching, but no discharge permit application had come in from CMC. We thanked Carl Pagel for putting us in touch with John Austin. Then we drove back to the island. The End.
Linda

p.s. Will meet with South Shore Associates currently extant on the island tomorrow at 10:00.

pps. Is it possible that with this incorrect information as to the need to file for permits and the elimination of a whole section in Criteria 9, i.e., impact on existing use of surround lands and future development, that the application could be considered to be incomplete? I sure would like the month of April and some of May to work on this. Especially the wildlife habitat piece.

March 8, 1996
Joe Bivins to Linda

Regarding your question about an incomplete application. Alas, no: lies and inaccuracy are not the same thing as administrative incompleteness. However, we may be able to argue that no site plan has been filed (there weren't any oversized pieces of the application at the town clerk's office were there)?

March 8, 1996
Randy to Linda

As to the Dry Rock Beaver...I believe it may be a relation of the Eastern Desert Beaver. This little guy can readily be identified by his cute little double humped back.

10. The Qwarriors

"So any nation which in its youth lives only for the day, reaps without sowing, and consumes without husbanding, must expect the penalty of the prodigal whose labor could with difficulty find him the bare means of life."
-Theodore Roosevelt

1901

IN THE DAYS AND WEEKS AFTER ROOSEVELT'S VISIT TO FISK FARM on September 6, 1901, articles in many papers and magazines described the drama that unfolded on that fateful day.

"The summer outing of the Vermont Fish and Game League at Isle La Motte, in the northern end of Lake Champlain, came to a dramatic close with the announcement of the dastardly attack on President McKinley at Buffalo. The business had been transacted, the dinner eaten and the speeches made, and the thousand members and guests of the League were gathered in groups on the lawn of the Fisk mansion waiting for an opportunity to shake hands with Vice-President Roosevelt.

"The scene was idyllically beautiful. To the west the sun was sinking in a cherry-red wave of glory behind the Chateauguay Mountains[27], a penciled line of the faintest blue, while nearer other ranges came into darker prominence, till at the mouth of the Little Chazy the sentinel elms stood out almost in silhouette, casting black shadows on the lake glimmering with the sheen of iridescent silk, bluish-green shading into red with glints of azure and lapis lazuli, and, far off, a streak of the faintest, filmiest, ashen-gray.

"Vice-President Roosevelt, Senator Proctor of Vermont and other distinguished guests were inside the house, which is of stone, with a long stone wing surmounted by a belfry. The lake washes the lawn in front, while on one hand in the sward tennis court, and on the other, separated by a hedge of plum trees, the deer park, where the dining tent was erected.

"Suddenly all eyes turned toward the house as Senator Proctor, followed by President Titcomb of the League and ex-Lieutenant-Governor Fisk, appeared on the stone portico. There was a momentary hush of expectancy, pending the arrival of the Vice-President, but no apprehension of anything wrong until Senator Proctor raised his hand and, in a choked voice, said: 'Gentlemen, it is my sad duty to announce that word has just been received by telephone—I trust it may prove false—that—' Here a steamboat whistled, momentarily breaking the thread of the statement and giving the crowd, whose ears were strained to catch the words, time to realize that an event of more than ordinary moment had occurred. In a moment hats were doffed and the assemblage stood bareheaded, waiting anxiously for the name that each one was trying to fit to the fateful announcement.

'At 4 o'clock this afternoon our beloved President was shot twice by an anarchist in the Temple of Music at Buffalo, just as he had finished speaking and was shaking hands.'

"The Senator stood with bowed head, while a great sigh of horror went up from the listeners. Men's faces paled and then grew red with anger.

"Governor Fisk, with tears in his eyes, called out: 'I believe it is a lie; we will yet hear it contradicted.' His words had little effect, however, for the assemblage was inclined to accept the first statement as true. All were sickened by the conviction that another tragedy had come to stain the fair name of the nation, which, however innocently, had harbored a Booth and a Guiteau.

"Senator Proctor reentered the house, and a few moments later returned and announced that the report of the attack had been confirmed by an Associated Press dispatch, but that there were hopeful features and that the President was resting comfortably and was conscious. The crowd made their way to the steamboat dock, but before all had embarked a faint cheer went up from the house, and the word quickly passed from mouth to [28]mouth of a later dispatch containing the hopeful news that the President was likely to recover.

"Vice-President Roosevelt did not appear until after this last report, when he was rowed out to the Elfrida, Dr. Webb's steam yacht, which carried him at once to Burlington, from which place he proceeded shortly afterward by special train to Buffalo. During the speechmaking Mr. Roosevelt had frequently been mentioned as the next occupant of the White House. Little did the orators realize that even as they spoke the act of a crazy fanatic in a neighboring State had made the goal so perilously near!"[29]

When Roosevelt reached Albany, the doctors felt that McKinley was now out of danger and urged Roosevelt resume his plan to take his family on their vacation in the Adirondacks. However, while hiking Mt. Marcy, the highest Adirondack Peak, Roosevelt was met by a messenger, scrambling up the mountainside. A note told Roosevelt that McKinley was dying and that he should return to Buffalo immediately. A wild buckboard ride through a stormy night brought him to a train station at North Creek, New York at 5:22 in the morning. There he learned that President McKinley had died at 2:15 a.m. Vice President Roosevelt boarded a special waiting train which took him to Buffalo New York. On September 14, 1901, Theodore Roosevelt was sworn in as the youngest president of the United States.

A thousand members and guests of the Fish and Game League were gathered in groups on the lawn of the Fisk mansion waiting for an opportunity to shake hands with Vice-President Roosevelt. The opportunity never came.

March 1996

Shortly after my return to Princeton it snowed. White streamed out of a white sky, blowing through the spruce branches outside my study window. Patterns of white froth formed on storm windows. Car doors were frozen shut, windshield wipers immobile under their ice casings, streets silent, garbage cans waiting for pick up, wait in vain. Inside the quiet houses children looked through whitened windows, rejoiced, and went back to sleep. School buses dozed in silent parking lots. My very mind felt frozen. And there was so much to be done. The Act 250 Hearing based on CMC's application was scheduled to take place on April 15, 1996.

"There are a number of steps that need to be taken," said Joe talking by phone to me in Princeton from his home in Thetford, Vermont. "First we have to apply for your Party Status."

"What's that?" I said suspiciously.

"Well, it gives you the right to participate in Act 250 proceedings," said Joe. "It's not automatic. You have to request it, either orally or in writing. Basically you have to tell them--in detail--what your interest is and what the potential effect of the project is on the criteria on which you are requesting party status. Is that clear?"

"Well sort of. I'll have to think about it."

"If you are an adjoining landowner, you can get party status. So that's you and Mary Jane. Probably South Shore Associates should apply as a community group, which would enable all the neighbors to file testimony and would indicate to the Environmental Board that this was a problem for an entire neighborhood, not just several disgruntled landowners.

"Then there are other people who can get Party Status--for example--expert witnesses. These are people who can provide expert testimony in helping the District Commission to get a sense of the environmental impacts of the proposed development. Then there are Statutory Parties who have the right by law to participate; these include say, ANR (the wetland folks and John Austin for example are part of ANR). And the Town also has the statutory right to Party Status."

I sighed.

Joe wrote a Party Status application for South Shore Associates and Mary Jane Tiedgen and I applied as adjoining landowners. It was all done with Joe's guidance of course.

"My name is Linda Fitch. I am seeking party status to participate in the Declaratory Ruling hearing sought in the appeal from the District Coordinator's Advisory Opinion 6-089. My parents and I own the land which abuts the entire northern boundary of the Fisk Quarry parcel; I am representing my parents, who also own part of the old quarry itself and a portion of the federally designated wetlands therein..."

"My name is MaryJane Tiedgen. I am seeking party status to participate in the Declaratory Ruling hearing ....I am co-owner with my father, Carl Williams, of the south boundary of the Fisk Quarry on Isle La Motte, Vermont..."

"Do we have any expert witnesses?" Joe had asked as we began the process of preparing for the first Act 250 Hearing.

"What's that?"

"Well these would be professionals or witnesses with credibility who can testify on various of the Act 250 Criteria. We're going to be addressing the impacts of a mining operation on wildlife, wetlands, hydrology, roads, economics and aesthetics. So in addition to the neighbors, terrific as they are, we also need some expert witnesses? Usually they are paid," Joe added.

Where would we get the money?

As Dorothy in the "Wizard of Oz" discovered, solutions to problems frequently abound in one's own back yard. Asking clearly, I now believe, is essential to the process. I began a little ritual of "asking the universe. Tell it exactly what you need."

"Dear Universe," I would begin. "We need a wildlife biologist who can identify the presence of birds, mammals, wetland species including frogs, salamanders, fish, wetland birds, and it would be really great if he/she could delineate wetland boundaries." Wetland Delineation was a term that I had recently heard for the first time. It means the process of establishing the boundaries between "wetlands" and "uplands" (land which is not wetland).

Several weeks went by before the answer suddenly came to me. What about Dan Froelich who had spent Memorial Day weekend at Fisk Farm in the previous year? His parents lived in Princeton, not far from my parents' former home. My music teacher mother had once given recorder lessons to Dan when he was six years old. Dark brown hair, glasses, eager, loving the out-of-doors, Dan was fascinated with finding birds as though sighting each new bird species was like finding buried treasure or, more accurately, flying, feeding, courting, nesting, chirping treasure.

During his visit with us, Dan had crept and crawled and skulked, watched, listened, climbed through the brush, waded through mud, sat silently on rocks with field binoculars, notebooks. Could we afford him? I kept thinking. What if I offered him a VERY modest stipend plus room and board for several weeks in return for a report, for his role as an expert witness in our Act 250 Hearing. I finally called him.

Twenty-six-year-old Dan was between jobs. "Sure," he said happily.

"Hydrology is important," Joe said back in the beginning. "The first three criteria deal with water. We need a hydrologist."

"I don't even know what a hydrologist is," I had said to Joe.

"Well they're the ones who study water movement and quality. How water is distributed. It would be important," Joe explained patiently, "to understand what the impact would be of draining the pond, digging new pits behind your house (which would be filled with machinery) on such things as the groundwater, the surface water, the local wells, the wetlands and the lake."

Where on earth would you find a hydrologist? An hydrologist?

In late February as I finally got around to looking through my Christmas cards I came across a Christmas letter from a Quaker friend, Andy Mills, who was living in nearby Newtown, Pennsylvania. "I've decided to come out of retirement and go back to my old career of hydrology," Andy had written to his vast array of friends and relatives.

Andy is a hydrologist? I called him up and met him at a Middle Eastern restaurant--located conveniently between Newtown and Princeton--for lunch. I brought every scrap of material I had. Andy, tall, lean with greying hair, was a top flight hydrologist, with a passion for social justice. With a Ph.D. from the University of California, licenses from four states as an Engineer, Andy had been active in the civil rights movement in the 50s and 60s, lived in India for nine years as a missionary specializing in water supply, and worked in Egypt investigating water resources of the Sinai Peninsula. We had previously worked together on the teen pregnancy project in Trenton, New Jersey.

"Sure," he said over stuffed grape leaves and hummus. "I'll come up in early spring to spend a few days and do a study. Maybe you can send me some preliminary information. It would be helpful to get some maps. An aerial photo would be great."

"You might check in with my son, Lyle," I said. "He's very good with this stuff."

A day later Andy sent an email.

"I just got back from seeing Lyle. He helped me firm up the location of the ponds on the 1"=100' feet sketch map you gave me. I had had the aerial photo blown up to the scale of the sketch map and traced the results onto the sketch map. Lyle helped me a lot by helping me interpret some of the aerial photo as far as the edge of the excavation and the extent of the ponds. Then he scanned that part of the aerial photo into his computer and with my adjusting the contrasts, etc. we got improved resolution so we could "see" the pond and rock walls better. So that is done. What I would like to do when I go up is to take water levels both in the excavation a few places and in the well. I can do that with the steel tape I'll bring up. But we may need help from a local person in taking the cap off the well so that we can lower the tape in the well to measure the level. Then, I want to take elevation levels which will require a surveying level. It would be best if you could arrange to have your surveyor friend there when we are there. It wouldn't take a great deal of his time. I basically just need to have ground elevations shot at the location of the well and at three or four points along the quarry wall nearest your property. If you aren't able to arrange this, I can do it, as I'll bring my surveying level. I just thought it would be faster to have the surveyor do it, and possibly better."

Joe was thrilled. "How do you find these people?" he wrote in an email. "So anyway tell your hydrologist friend, that measurements (elevations) are important. I think he should probably do the lake levels at the same time." He should also study the aerial photos for major fracture lineaments. A surveyor would probably be more accurate but you or Andy would have to be present so there is a witness who can testify to it. Please ask Andy or Lyle to get us (that means ME) working copies of their computer generated map as soon as possible (that means yesterday--I'm a bit fanatical about maps). And by the

way," he added. "There's Criteria #5. That's roads. The project isn't supposed
to cause dangerous or congested conditions on roads or highway. Do we have
anyone up our sleeves for "Roads?"

Ok, roads. Who is an expert on roads? Now didn't Joe Bajorski say that
he was–what–some kind of expert on roads? Joe Bajorski was part of the
Masalak clan, a family whose summer cottage was just fifty feet south of the
quarry. Just opposite the cottage of Carl Williams and his daughter Mary Jane
Tiedgen. Last summer, Joe and his wife Leslie had been horrified by the prospect of a quarry operation within fifty feet of the vacation home of their extended family. "How can we help?" they asked then.

"What are his qualifications?" asked Joe Bivins now.

From his home in Connecticut, Joe Bajorski sent along his resume. "I'm
in the Connecticut Army National Guard as First Lieutenant where I held
dual positions as Unit Movement Officer and Maintenance Officer. I was responsible for the development of unit movement procedures, convoy procedures, and the development of unit movement plans. Then as maintenance
officer I was responsible for all motor pool (maintenance) activities. I had
oversight of 16 mechanics and 19 Tractor Trailers, 20 Five Ton Trucks, 15 Two
and One Half Ton Trucks, and numerous other wheeled vehicles. And then I
was External Auditor of Connecticut's Department of Transportation auditing
various highway and road construction projects. Determined both financial
compliance and performance according to contracts and bid specifications.
Audited Utilities, Rights of Way, and other construction activities."

"So I can do roads," he ended.

"He's on!" said Joe. "Now how about Criterion 8 where the project isn't
supposed to have an undue adverse effect on aesthetics, scenic beauty, historic
sites or natural areas? And then Criterion 9 which says the project conforms
with the Development plan of the town, the impact the project will have on
the growth of the town or region? Well there's no Development Plan, so we
have to say what effect, in our opinion, the project will have on the town."

Scott Newman and his wife Elizabeth lived in the center of the village of
Isle La Motte. As a historic preservationist Scott was deeply interested in the
history of the Fisk Farm/Fisk Quarry complex. He had applauded our efforts
to restore the old Horse and Carriage Barn on Fisk Farm and was now ready
to add volunteer efforts to the quarry project.

"I'll be happy to testify on the economic affects of the quarrying project,"
he said.

Scott had a Masters degree in Historic Preservation, and had begun a consulting business which specialized in studying and developing the links between cultural resource management and state and local economies.

"Oh, and I'm a member of the Governor's Task Force on Heritage Tourism which explores the economic implications of heritage tourism for the state of Vermont; I was a steering committee member of the Lake Champlain Bikeways Association which exists to support Travel and Tourism. And I am currently under contract with the Vermont Agency of Transportation to assess the impacts (including economic) of federally funded, licensed or permitted projects."

"Righto," said Joe. He was daily sounding more cheerful.

I returned to Vermont with boxes of papers, my scant Vermont wardrobe (consisting primarily of jeans, turtleneck shirts and sweaters, T shirts for warmer weather). Also my flute, my guitar, and my dog Shasta who was always happy to return to the wide open if chill spaces of Isle La Motte. It was still March; from the southern to the northern end of Lake Champlain the ice was slowly disappearing. Days were cold but early spring green had begun to show itself. On thorny branches were born the tiniest of green ovals outlined in the thinnest lines of red. With the guidance of Joe we had submitted our party status applications, gathered expert witnesses on hydrology, wildlife, historic sites, and road impact/road safety...so far almost all were volunteers which conformed nicely with our nonexistent budget.

It seemed as though we needed a War Room, a place in which we could all convene and work. I decided on the "Doctors' Office." This room retained its name from its former inhabitant, Dr. Charles Whitcomb, an osteopathic physician. He was the brother-in-law of Nelson Fisk, having married Nelson's younger sister, Nellie. Nelson Fisk had died in 1923 and his wife Elizabeth passed away in 1927. When, a scant two months later Dr. Whitcomb's wife Nellie died, the good doctor inherited the scant remains of the Fisk estate. Losing no time, he remarried one Harriet Stone the following February, some three months after the passing of Nellie.

When my family came in 1971, years after his death, momentoes of Charles Whitcomb were enshrined throughout the property. The big stone house had burned in 1923 four years before he assumed ownership. The fire had left blackened stone walls which, over the years, were taken down stone by stone for use in other building projects on the island. The wing of the stone house remained, so Charles Whitcomb had a new roof built over the walls. He then built a garage. He converted the old store and post office into a house, adding a front porch and an entire two story wing. A room on the first floor of the new wing became his office. Old timers who worked on the original repairs in the late 1920s and 30s remembered old Dr. Whitcomb fondly. He used to give them free osteopathic treatments after a day's work. As a final romantic touch, Dr. Whitcomb used old stone from the ruins to build a ten foot high rectangular edifice between the newly renovated Main House and the garage, a picturesque structure whose original purpose remains, to this day, unknown. In 1971 the office still housed several old leather osteopathic treatment couches; the glass door bookcases housed old osteopathic medical books; the original pine floor boards were covered with an oddly patterned and cracked linoleum. To the present day we call the room the Doctor's Office. When our family moved in, the Doctor's Office became my father's study. The old oak desk facing the lake held his typewriter. In 1995 when the Quarry War began, the typewriter was replaced by my computer (one of the early Macs but I have no idea which one it was).

Now the Doctor's Office became the War Room--the Situation Room. Emails, phone calls and letters flew back and forth among members of our team--scattered among the states of Vermont, New Jersey, Pennsylvania, Connecticut and Michigan--at a greater rate than ever before.

March, 1996
From Andy Mills to Linda
Hi Linda,

I don't know whether you have left for Vermont yet. For several reasons it would be better if I could go in about 2 weeks, preferably between Thursday and Sunday.

I want to take water samples when we are there. We need to get a dozen or so new quart mason jars in which to place the samples. I want to take two samples from your well (or from your inside faucet assuming you don't have a water softener on the line). And probably about three samples from the quarry pond. We will have a local lab analyze for the major mineral constituents, including pH, calcium, magnesium, sodium, potassium, chloride, sulfate, carbonate and bicarbonate. I suspect each sample shouldn't cost more than $80 to $100 to do. I hope you can afford it. Perhaps you can scout out chemical labs in the area and get quotes from them on analyzing for the above constituents. Let me know how all this sounds to you.
Peace, Andy

March, 1996
From Joe Bajorski to Linda, Joe, & Scott

I am going to focus our arguments against the quarry on a four mile stretch of West Shore Road. I feel that this stretch will provide us with the strongest arguments we can muster against heavy continuous truck traffic. I will argue that this four mile stretch is loaded with various limiting characteristics such as sharp curves, heavy residential pockets with children, poor drainage, weak foundation, rough surface, and excessive camber or superelevation. Additionally the construction of this four mile stretch would have to be characterized as a light duty road. The "dirt" portions are basically natural earth stabilized soil with what appears to be disintegrated stone, perhaps granite or marble. The paved portions are constructed of a bituminous surface treatment on natural earth, stabilized soil, or other select material such as light gravel. Again this road is not designed for heavy duty use and would suffer surface degradation as a result of the planned increase in truck traffic.

I must run now....if you have any comments or suggestions please write or call. ################### Sorry about that...pressed the wrong button."

With the early spring migrating birds, Dan arrived. Every morning he appeared in the kitchen briefly, then went out onto the land. With binoculars and notebook he would be gone for hours. Sometimes he would appear briefly and without a word head for his computer in the office. The scribblings from his notebook were keyed into the computer. Blue winged teal. A pair of mallards. Were they migrating? Nesting? Passing through?

On one rainy evening Mary Jane and I followed him into the quarry. Mary Jane later described it in testimony:

"It was a drizzly night and the quarry was alive with the sounds of the gray tree frogs as Dan identified them and the peepers. We had flashlights and you could see the floor of the quarry was covered with frogs. They were especially dense in the area between Turtle pond and Boulder pond to the east. The frogs were even sitting on the boulders. You could shine the flashlights and watch their throats puff up. It reminded me of a National Geographic special. I can't describe what it was like to stand there listening with the lights off except to say that it was one of the most magical moments that I have ever experienced."

Andy Mills drove up from Princeton. Andy, gentle, tall and angular, went out every day with his surveyor's level, taking water samples from our well, from the quarry pond water, filling mason jars, sending samples off to a laboratory.

Joe frequently drove back and forth across the entire state. Neighbors stopped in to see how we were doing. In the evenings people took turns cooking. We talked. After dinner we sang in the kitchen while washing dishes. Happily, while other people washed, I got to sit on a stool and play guitar.

One of the issues had to do with sound pollution. What would be the level of sound in a full fledged quarry operation? We actually bought a sound meter at Radio Shack in St. Albans and on April 6, Scott, Dan and Merrill went out to test it. They returned as I was preparing supper, slightly windblown but happy. They all talked at once, reading their notes.

"Ok, the ambient sound with a little wind off the lake is 53-54 decibels. And two diesel trucks revving at source? 96 decibels. One truck from a distance of 500 feet at Fitch property from road is 68 decibels. Two trucks from a distance of 500 feet? 71 decibels."

The next day, April 7, was clear if somewhat early spring chilly. The guys continued their investigations. They found out that at source the chain saw was 118 decibels.

"As I think about it" said Merrill later as they all crowded into the kitchen, sitting on the old wooden counters, the stool, the red chair, "they say in the application that the generator is 65 decibels at 20 feet—which is hard to believe since one engineer according to Scott said that the generator was louder than the Electric Saw. We need to test the chainsaw at 20 feet."

"Ok, here's what else," said Scott. "At the Fitch property line from the middle of the quarry 500 feet is 67 decibels. At the Fitch property from the far end of the quarry 900 feet one chainsaw is 61 decibels. At the Williams/Tiedgen property line from the far end of quarry is 75 decibels. It turns out that decibel levels of 61 and 67 are horrifyingly loud. We might think about replicating these tests at the site visit. Are there any more of those brownies?"

We made telephone calls trying to get specs on equipment listed in the Act 250 application. Conversations continued over dinners. On the night that Dan made a rice and broccoli dish with spicy peanut sauce, Merrill reported on his conversation with the Meyers Saw Company. "They make the Diamond Belt saw which CMC says they want to use. So basically the noise of the Diamond Belt saw is 85 decibels at source. It takes 125 to155 kilowatts to run it. All the motors are 75 hp. And here's something on water. The saw takes 50 gallons a minute of water. The guy I talked with said it's critical that the water be clean; otherwise it increases wear on the bar. Most quarries set up a series of settling pools; the water that is coming out of the saw goes back into one pool so the sediments settle in that pond; then the water overflows into a second and a third pool and you take the water out of the cleanest pool to flush the blade with. Once the sediment fills up the first pond you have to bale that out and start over. If you don't have a stream nearby then you have to bring in water to keep the pools filled. Most companies just get it out of a stream nearby."

"Hmm," said I. "And where, pray tell, are these settling pools going to be? And what were you guys doing with the bathroom scale outside? I noticed you took a piece of stone from my stone wall."

They explained that they were trying to figure out the weight of quarry stone.

"Say a cubic foot block of quarry stone weighs 150 pounds...that's a conservative estimate," said Merrill. "CMC says they want to take out 2,000 cubic yards per year on the average of 20 tons per day. One cubic foot weighs 150 pounds...conservative estimate. So 1 block per truck. If the block is 20 tons, it will contain 267 cubic feet of material. If such a 20 ton block contains 267 cubic feet, figure a dimension of 5'x6'x9'. With 20 ton blocks of that dimension there will be 202 blocks per year to make 2,000 cubic yards. If they work April through October that's about 30 weeks or 150 working days. That's more than one 20 ton block a day. It's 1 1/3 blocks per day. That's 30 percent higher than their projections for removal. What's for dessert?"

They had lost me before they began! "I think there's some apple pie left over from last night," I said.

Emails flying back and forth were more numerous than the flocks of geese flying northward over the lake. Joe Bivins was coaching everyone. There was an email to Joe from Scott who said:

"I really wouldn't want to get into a situation where their lawyer interrupts and says 'well this is all very interesting Mr. Newman, but what has this got to do with this Act 250 application?'
Signed........devil's advocate"

Joe replied.

"Dear Devil's Advocate, Your focus is on SubCriterion 9E(i): A permit will be granted for the extraction or processing of mineral and earth resources (i) when it is demonstrated by the applicant that . . . the extraction or processing operation and the disposal of waste WILL NOT HAVE AN UNDULY HARMFUL IM-PACT UPON the environment or SURROUNDING LAND USES AND DE-VELOPMENT. Surrounding land uses and development" means residential and vacation homes, and various aspects of tourism in the case of Isle La Motte. Your points on the economy are all relevant because they link to this Act 250 concern. So are the various letters and guidebook comments about why people should visit Isle LaMotte, the Fisk Farm area, etc. Also, Linda has a set of letters that might help you; you should also go through the affidavits for comments about why people chose to live here."

Members of the team got nicknames. Joe Bivins was "Mastermind." Merrill was "Master Scout." I was "North Witch," guarding the northern border of the quarry. Mary Jane, guarding the southern boundary, was "South Witch." Joe Bajorski's family cottage was across from South Witch's house; he became "Transportation Warlock." Andy Mills was, obviously, "Hydro Sage." Dan Froelich was "Godwit," a category of wading birds with long bills. The name "Godwit," we found, is Old English with god meaning good and wit coming from "wihte," or creature.

Then a letter arrived. This was from John Austin, the wildlife biologist who had thought there was no water in the quarry. It was addressed to the Assistant Land Use Attorney with copies to us and to the lawyers of CMC.

March 21, 1996
To: Jim Caffrey, Acting Land Use Attorney
From: John Austin, District Wildlife Biologist

"In regard to the above referenced permit application the Department has some concerns about the potential impacts from the proposed quarrying operation on wetland habitats. As indicated in the application, I submitted a letter to a Mr. Steven E. Schindler of Keyser, et. al. Attorneys at Law in Rutland, Vermont in response to a request to conduct a review of the site for issues associated with necessary wildlife habitats.

On February 16, 1996, I conducted a site inspection. My inspection of the site followed a telephone discussion with Mr. Schindler about the character of the site and the applicants' intentions for development of the site. My response indicated that no necessary wildlife habitats were observed on the property.

On March 8, 1996, I was asked to meet with a Ms. Linda Fitch and Mr. Merrill Hemond. Ms. Fitch is an adjoining property owner to the quarry site. Ms. Fitch provided me with information indicating the possibility that wetland habitats are located within the Fisk Quarry. This submittal included photographs that were taken during September, October, and November 1995 and indicate the presence of standing water, beavers, and wetland vegetation.

Based on the information submitted, it appears that I may have made an oversight during my original review of the site. Unfortunately the winter season in Vermont does not lend itself to the easy identification of wildlife values associated with wetland habitats.

Therefore, based on the information provided by Ms. Fitch, I hereby request additional time to review the Fisk Quarry site in greater detail to determine the presence or absence of necessary wildlife habitats. My primary concern regarding impacts to wildlife habitats on the Fisk property includes the proposed dewatering of the quarry pond and the destruction of wetland habitats via proposed quarrying operations. The de-watering activity was not disclosed to me during my discussion with the applicant.

Please contact me in the near future to discuss this matter in greater detail. Included in this submittal are copies of the information and affidavits provided to me by Ms. Fitch.

Yours truly,
John Austin
Cc: G. Green, Dist. Coord.
c. O'Brien Asst. Wetlands Coord."

Then another letter arrived. This time it was from Cathy O'Brien to the Assistant Land Use Attorney, again with copies to us and to the lawyers of CMC.

April 1, 1996
To: Jim Caffry, Acting Land Use Attorney
From Catherine O'Brien, Assistant State Wetlands Attorney

"On November 6, 1995, I called the president of CMC when I first heard about the above referenced project. I let him know that this quarry was mapped on the National Wetlands Inventory map and was therefore a Class Two wetland. I explained that a Conditional Use Determination would be required for this project under the Vermont Wetland Rules. On November 14, 1995, I met him on site and explained the regulations to him in detail. I have not heard back from him to this date. No Conditional Use Determination application has been received for this project.

In the Act 250 application that was submitted, I was represented to have said that the project will not have a material impact upon our water resources. I never made this statement. I clearly indicated to CMC's president that a Conditional Use Determination could only be approved upon the applicant showing that there would be no undue adverse impacts to any of the wetland functions or values. I was clear that the burden of proof is on the applicant for demonstrating that there will be no impacts. The Wetland Rules state that any impacts, other than minimal impacts, shall be presumed to be undue unless those impacts have been sufficiently mitigated.

From my brief observations of the site, I believe that the functions and values of this wetland include, at a minimum, wildlife and migratory bird habitat (function 5.4), recreational value (function 5. 8) and open space and aesthetics (function 5.9). Further fieldwork may show it to be significant for fisheries habitat (function 5.3) and water quality treatment (function 5.2)."

The letters from John Austin and Cathy O'Brien inspired me to write to a Vermont State Representative whom we thought would have an interest:

My neighbors and I are contesting an Act 250 Permit for the reactivation of the old Fisk Quarry adjoining my property for which an application has been filed. A District Commission Hearing is scheduled for April 15 on Isle la Motte.

This is proving to be a fascinating—if immensely time consuming and difficult process. After this I will be ready to testify anytime, anywhere about the experience of an ordinary citizen going through the Act 250 process. Specifically, I am writing to you now because I find that one of our tasks is to run around to various agencies correcting misinformation provided by CMC which affects agency comments and letters to the District Commission. I'm enclosing a letter which I have written to Cathy O'Brien of Wetlands as an example of this process.

This is not a complaint about the agencies or the people in them whom I have found to be dedicated, competent and caring. But it is an observation that a developer can influence the Act 250 process before the hearings ever begin by providing inaccurate or incomplete information.

As a caring legislator I thought that you might be interested. I would like to keep you updated if you don't mind.

Linda Fitch

South Witch came running over one morning full of excitement. I was in the kitchen doing the perennial dishes.

"We've got our geologist, we've got our geologist. Oh God, I'm so excited."

"What?"

"We were at a meeting of the Lake Champlain Committee, you remember I told you we were going. It turns out that the speaker was Charlotte Mehrtens. Dr. Charlotte Mehrtens. Dr. Charlotte Mehrtens who teaches geology at the University of Vermont. Anyway, when I told her about the quarry she had a fit. She said, 'they can't destroy my fossils. I haven't had a chance to study them yet.' So I told her about the hearing and she said she would come and testify. She'll be our expert witness on geology."

"O praise the Lord," said I, doing a little dance on the kitchen floor. "What shall we call her? Maybe 'Rock Angel'?"

11. Act 250--The Hearing

"There were all kinds of things I was afraid of at first, from grizzly bears to 'mean' horses and gun-fighters; but by acting as if I was not afraid I gradually ceased to be afraid."
-Theodore Roosevelt

1800s

BATTLES WERE RAGING BETWEEN the conservationists and the great railroad, timber and mining companies. Congress was, in no small part, dominated by representatives of the great syndicates which saw the land as a source of unending profit. Huge swaths of forest in the West were clearcut with no thought for the future.

Along with John Muir, a powerful influence in Theodore Roosevelt's thinking was Gifford Pinchot, son of a wealthy New York family. Gifford Pinchot's grandfather had made a fortune in the timber industry, clear cutting great expanses of North America. His father, James Pinchot, was, however, concerned about the rapidly disappearing forests and suggested to his son, young Gifford, that he might be interested in forestry. Gifford later wrote, "I had no more conception of what it meant to be a forester than the Man in the moon...But at least a forester worked in the woods and with the woods--and I loved the woods and everything about them."[30] There was no forestry program in the US so in 1889 Pinchot went to France to study. In France he began to learn about the scientific management of forests, what later came to be known as "sustainable forestry."

> "When I came home not a single acre of Government, state, or private timberland was under systematic forest management anywhere on the most richly timbered of all continents....When the Gay Nineties began, the common word for our forests was 'inexhaustible.' To waste timber was a virtue and not a crime. There would always be plenty of timber...The lumbermen...regarded forest devastation as normal and second growth as a delusion of fools."[31].

As a forester Pinchot became the advocate for long-term sustainability as opposed to short-term profit taking. In 1896 he was appointed by President Grover Cleveland to head up a newly formed United States Forest Service.

As the Act 250 date approached, I felt weighted by a terrible fear. Dizzied by it. My nights were drowned in dreams populated by big trucks rumbling down the narrow road. Dreams of water being sucked out of the quarry. Fish and frogs and turtles lying dead on the quarry floor. Beavers wandering around, desperately looking for their homes. Racket, banging, drilling, rock splitting ringing through the air. Excavators. Diesel fumes. Ugliness. Desolation. Loss of place. Loss of quiet. Loss of comfort. Cliffs destroyed. All of these things happening.

A friend of Joe Bivins—Don Avery—was working on a manual to help regular citizens negotiate the Act 250 process. One paragraph definitely described my state of mind.

"The weeks just before the first Act 250 hearing can be very stressful. You have probably never participated in a quasi-judicial hearing before. You don't know what to expect... You're probably obsessed with fear that the proposed development will ruin your life. You probably can't sleep. You're in an Act 250 no man's land and you need help!" [32]

It didn't help when, several days before the hearing, the roar of loud machinery filled the outside air and sound penetrated the house. We looked out the front living room window and saw a road scraper. Up and down the gravel road it went. Following that was a gravel truck, spreading gravel in thick levels to an extent never previously seen on the road. The process went on all morning long.

Mary Jane walked over from her house. "Would you believe? They've put gravel all over the place, along the sides of the road, in the ditches even. It almost looks as though they were trying to make the road look wider. For the Hearing!"

We were two days from the Hearing. Were we paranoid or could someone have been trying to change the look of our narrow, gravel lakeside road just before the Hearing?

On the night before the Hearing the Doctor's Office, previously the site of patients receiving osteopathic treatments from old Dr. Whitcomb, was crowded with Qwarriors working on their reports. Costco folding tables were lined up with Dan, Scott, Andy, Joe Bajorski and Joe Bivins typing at five different computers throughout the evening. Joe was reviewing reports, checking for errors, coherence, grammar and accuracy. Merrill walked around peering at each report. My friend Carol had come up from New Jersey to add moral support. By midnight we were still working. Carol and I were kneeling on the floor collating pages of reports of which we were making multiple copies. There, at midnight, was Andy—also on the floor—checking to see if all of his pages were in order. "Where's page three of this copy...?" We, scrambling to look for a stray page three.

"Just print it out again," Joe snapped. "People have got to get to bed. The site visit begins at 10 a.m."

Joe Bivins reviews reports.

Linda Fitch and Andy Mills collate pages of reports.

The morning of April 15 dawned--cold, grey and drizzling. Not the day to show off the beauty of the quarry or its setting by the lake. On this damp day birds, not to be seen, had taken shelter from the inclement weather. We were grabbing cereal...eggs... whatever would fuel us for the grueling day ahead.

Someone said, "I saw guys in the quarry looking at Big Pond. There was a truck with a Vermont sign on it. 'Agency of Natural Resources' or something."

I grabbed my blue winter jacket against the grey chill, jumped on my bicycle and pedaled down the road to the main quarry entrance. There, gazing at the stretch of water, cattails, and red oshier dogwood of Big Pond, were John Austin, wildlife biologist for the Vermont Fish and Wildlife Department and another person whom I later learned was Steve Parren from the Nongame and Natural Heritage Program of Vermont. I guessed that this was John's first visit to the quarry site since he had seen it covered with snow.

I greeted John but hesitated to say much of anything. It was such a bleak and dreary day. I worried that perhaps the pond wasn't as lovely or wasn't looking like the rich habitat that we had testified to. Maybe they thought those glowing affidavits were exaggerations or worse. But then I was worried about everything and bicycled back to the house, full of dread and foreboding.

By 10:00 it was time for everyone to gather for the actual site visit in the quarry. The District Commission members would be present along with the president and lawyers for CMC, neighbors, and the Qwarriors.

As we walked down the road to the main quarry entrance I distinctly remember walking behind Joe as though he would somehow protect me, short but wide as he was. Joe wore his red plaid flannel shirt, blue jeans, and red suspenders. His bald head was open to the elements, his Amish-type beard and sideburns making him look like a friendly and not particularly formidable character.

Cars belonging to the Act 250 District Commission members were lined up along the side of the narrow road. All the neighbors had gathered: Mary Jane and Dave were there, Mary Jane's father Carl Williams, tiny Elva Grant, Neil Hanna, Carl and Jeffrey Williams. John Austin and Steve Parren and, to our delight, there was Charlotte Mehrtens, Professor of Geology at the University of Vermont. She had made the hour drive from Burlington just in time for the site visit.

A photo shows commission members huddled in heavy coats and jackets by the shallow pit which CMC had dug in the three days of jackhammering back in August of the previous year. We walked to Big Pond, to Turtle Pond, to Boulder Pond; we looked at the beaver lodges, the beaver dams. We walked up along the quarry cliffs. Another photo shows the dark grey and silver water of Big Pond with a reflection of everyone standing on the cliff, looking as though we are all under water.

Charlotte Mehrtens was lecturing: "Vermont is famous around the world for these reefs. I've led a field trip of the International Geological Congress here. Geologists bring classes of students here from UVM and other universities around the country. I've brought the Governor's Institute High School students here. Fisk Quarry should not be quarried because there's always the chance that further quarrying will eliminate the rocks that you have now and you're not going to see what you see now. These things are not laterally continuous. If you remove a wall there's no guarantee that there's more of that stuff behind there. Taking the rock away eliminates the data source."

Finally, from the edge of the cliff that adjoins the back lawn of Fisk Farm we hiked back to the house, pointing out the proximity between the historic buildings and the proposed quarrying operation. From there everyone climbed into their cars and drove up to the Town Hall, where the hearing was to be held.

With winter jackets and coats removed, the contrast between the Qwarriors and the legal team of CMC was really obvious. The three lawyers were wearing grey suits and ties in subdued lawyerly colors. They carried brief cases. Joe, in his plaid shirt and red suspenders had transported his papers in cardboard wine boxes and plastic milk crates and now was rummaging around in a milk crate for a map.

During our weeks of preparation Joe kept repeating variations on a theme: "We need to be honest and clear and credible. Remember, the people on this panel are regular citizens. Except for Geoffrey Green, the District Supervisor, the panel members get hardly any money to attend Hearings. And of course they have to do a lot of work outside of hearings--looking at lots of paper, operation plans, applications, testimony."

We were all carrying our reports, stapled together in the wake of last night's marathon session. The panel members were seated in front of the room facing us, lined up in grey metal folding chairs before a long table. Before the start of the Hearing I walked up to the Chair and delivered another picture book, this time addressing Act 250 criteria rather than Wetland Rules.

John Austin from Fish and Wildlife and Steve Parren from Nongame and Natural Heritage were among the first to testify. "I want to state that I've changed my original recommendation concerning the site," said John Austin. "Based on our visit this morning," John Austin nodded at Steve, "it does indeed seem to contain habitat of some interest."

"Did you see anything of significance," he was asked by one of the opposition lawyers. My heart sank. It was such a gloomy morning. I had seen no birds or anything that seemed important. No bullfrogs, peepers, tree frogs on this early and cold spring day.

The two biologists looked at each other. "Well yes," John said. "Among other things we saw a loggerhead shrike."

It seemed that this was an unexpected coup. I later learned that due to loss of habitat the bird is listed as globally imperiled and as endangered in New York, Pennsylvania, Maryland, Virginia New Hampshire, Massachusetts and Vermont. So far so good!

Another item on the agenda was a request by CMC to play a video tape of another mining operation. Their point, it seemed, was to show off some of the latest equipment in the mining world--how sleek, efficient and quiet it was. It turned out to be very loud indeed--cheering us up quite a bit.

Throughout the morning there was testimony from those of us with "party status." Mary Jane was shaking as she spoke. "The company has assured the neighbors that the noise produced by the quarry operation would be indistinguishable from ambient background sound. The closest house is 250 feet from the work site. My boundary line is 75 feet away and there is no guarantee that they won't work right up to the boundary. It's hard for us to believe that giant wire saws, belt saws, diesel fueled generators, pneumatic drills, splitters, loaders, pumps, dump trucks, and 20 ton tractor trailer trucks which the company says they will use, will be indistinguishable from our usual background noise--the sounds of birds, frogs, wind and water."

Joe Bivins was sharp and brilliant throughout, cross examining both the lawyers and the president of CMC. Toward the end of the morning he pulled out a piece of paper. It was the map which Nelson Fisk in 1919 had made creating the boundary line between the Fisk Quarry and the rest of his property as he prepared to sell the quarry to the Vermont Marble Company. It showed, indisputably, that the property boundary started at the lakeshore, then crossed the road and the quarry pond and continued out to the fields in back of our house. Part of the quarry pond which CMC planned to de-water, had been retained by Nelson Fisk, passed on to his widow, Elizabeth Fisk, then passed on through several generations and was now owned by the Fitch family.

Joe presented it to the Chair of the District Commission and to the lawyers of CMC. It was like an exquisitely targeted bomb. The Chair gaveled the meeting to order and announced lunch. The Qwarriors departed silently, leaving a hubbub of lawyers and the owner of CMC standing in a little group pouring over the map.

We ate hoagies from Isle La Motte's Country Store, planning our afternoon's strategy. Much of our testimony had not yet been presented. But when we returned to the Town Hall there was a surprise announcement. The District Commission had decided to recess the Act 250 Hearing. CMC was ordered to submit a complete Operations Plan and to procure a Wetlands CUD (permit) and a Discharge Permit before any further Act 250 proceedings would continue.

If we had had hats we would have tossed them up in the air.

A photo shows what happened next. We are all sitting on the ground on a little peninsula of land next to the part of the quarry pond owned by my family. We had dragged chairs down from the front porch of the main house. Joe, Vincent Scully, Andy Mills, Joe Bajorski, Dan Froelich are sitting in chairs. Leslie Bajorski, Mary Jane and I are on the ground. Shasta, relieved that everyone is back from wherever they were, is sitting at Merrill's feet. Joe holds a bottle of champagne. The rest of us are holding little white plastic cups. There are definitely smiling faces. I recall that at one point the lawyers and owner of CMC drove by—presumably to take a last look at the pond. We waved.

"Don't get too happy, here," Joe said at the end of the afternoon. The setting sun was cooling off the day and the neighborhood Qwarriors had scattered to their various homes. "Remember that CMC has submitted an appeal to the Environmental Board contesting Geoffrey Green's advisory opinion that Act 250 has jurisdiction over mining in the Fisk Quarry. Now we have to get busy on that."

"O good grief. Now that our first Act 250 proceedings have been recessed we go back to the issue of whether Act 250 has jurisdiction here?"

"Righto!"

12. Action Al

*"This country has nothing to fear from the crooked man who fails. We put him in jail.
It is the crooked man who succeeds who is a threat to this country."*
Theodore Roosevelt *An Autobiography, 1913*

WITH HIS FRIEND ROOSEVELT now president of the United States, Gifford Pinchot rose to greater political prominence. Conservation was high on the agenda of the new president. In 1902 he established Crater Lake National Park. He signed the Newlands Reclamation Act authorizing funding for irrigation projects in arid western states.[33] In 1903 he established Pelican Island in Florida, the first federal Bird Reservation. But it was in his second term, begun in 1905, that he really got going on his conservation agenda.

Theodore Roosevelt won the 1904 election by a landslide, the largest popular and electoral vote in history up to that time. The nation was weary of corruption on the part of governments, politicians, big corporations and labor unions. He was seen as an honest, even handed politician with progressive, reformist views, fighting against what he saw as exploitation of the public, of the common man.

In 1905 he established the National Forest Service, appointing Gifford Pinchot as chief. During his time as President, the acreage of forest reserves rose from about 43 million to 194 million acres. In 1906 Roosevelt signed the National Antiquities Act, an important conservation tool enabling presidents to protect American wilderness and historical sites as national monuments. It authorized the president "to declare by public proclamation historic landmarks, historic and prehistoric structures, and other objects of historic or scientific interest" that existed on public lands in the United States.[34] In 1908 he established Muir Woods National Monument protecting the redwoods from threatened logging. In the same year he so designated the Grand Canyon. "Let this great wonder of nature remain as it now is. You cannot improve on it. But what you can do is keep it for your children, your children's children, and all who come after you, as the one great sight which every American should see."[35] During his tenure Theodore Roosevelt established eighteen national monuents.

Spring, 1995

Early morning. The spring sky is grey. Walk outside and feel warm air, see clear mountains, still lake. Ground soggy from inches and inches of rain in the past weeks so that cars could only park on one high spot on the lawn.

Shasta followed me out to my car and jumped into the back seat where she stood, paws on the back of the drivers seat, resting her chin on my shoulder. I drove to the store in the village, passed Allen Hall mowing his orchard with a brush hog behind his tractor, passed George Fleury's truck pulling out of Mabel Holcomb's old house, turn at the Four Corners, passed Phyllis the post mistress raising the American flag in front of the post office and drove into the gravel parking area of the Isle La Motte Country Store. The "guys" were sitting on the front steps with their cigarettes and coffee.

"How's it going?" I said.

They seemed friendly enough. No residual feelings about the recent Hearing were in evidence. "I'm perfect," one said. "Only problem is there hasn't been enough rain."

I respond. "Yes, yesterday I got worried because we had a whole two hours without rain." I bought a Styrofoam cup of coffee and a newspaper, spilling some of my coffee on the front of my jacket as I walked out the door.

"Like the way you're wearing your coffee," said one of the guys.

"Yeah? It's the latest thing," I said. Walked back to the car where Shasta was waiting impatiently. "I don't think I've had my breakfast yet," she complained.

I returned home where Carol was making more really good coffee.

"We've got this Environmental Board Pre-hearing Conference in Montpelier on the 29th," I said unnecessarily.

"So you're wearing your cloak of invisibility today."

"Yup." I went into the office. Set up the screen at the open door. That meant "I'm working. Enter at your own risk."

What's the Environmental Board?" I had asked Joe some weeks ago.

"It's sort of a higher court of appeals for the Act 250 system in Vermont," said Joe on the phone. "If a developer doesn't like an Act 250 decision on the District Commission level, it can appeal to the Environmental Board. It's like the District Commission. The Board consists of ordinary volunteer citizens but it does have a full time paid chairman." The Chair, at this time, was John Ewing.

On April 29 Chair John Ewing convened an Environmental Board Pre-hearing Conference in Montpelier. We all attended, sitting around a shining oval table.

"Mr. Chair," intoned the lawyer for CMC. "We are prepared to concede that quarrying for dimensional stone in the Fisk Quarry may well be subject to Act 250 jurisdiction. However, we believe that Advisory Opinion #6-089 was in error, and that based on the historical extraction of loose stone, that the Proposed Removal and Extraction Activities are grandfathered and therefore, exempt from Act 250."

Ok. So CMC was now saying that mining dimensional stone in the quarry needed an Act 250 Permit, but folks have been removing "rubblestone" and loose rock in the quarry all along, and so naturally Act 250 wouldn't apply to that operation.

CMC's lawyer continued. The company would be applying for an Act 250 Permit for dimensional stone cutting. So the only question for the Environmental Board to decide at this point was whether rubble stone removal needed an Act 250 permit. A new Hearing was scheduled for July.

It was now the end of April. It seemed as though we had hardly had a chance to breathe. Between now and July we had to prepare for a hearing in which CMC would argue that rubblestone had been taken from the quarry all along on a regular basis. I was exhausted.

May 8, 1996
From Linda to Joe Bivins, Mary Jane Tiedgen, Joe Bajorsky, Randy Koch

Gentle Readers,
I seem not to be able to lift a finger, so have taken to bed like a Victorian heroine and am reading novels with minimal amounts of socially redeeming value. I realize that I am a truly burned out being. However, events continue to unfold.

1. The Acting Director of the Lake Champlain Land Trust whose name is Karen Cady called yesterday and said that she had presented the Fisk Quarry purchase idea to the Project Committee and that they were very excited. She said that several of them would like to visit and suggested two weeks from now.

2. I called Charlotte Mehrtens (Paleontologist from UVM) this morning, and asked if she could come to Fisk Farm to talk long and eloquently about fossils in the quarry with several Lake Champlain Land Trust Board members. She was delighted to hear that there is some talk of buying the quarry and said she could be present at a visit on the 23rd of May.

Yours truly,
Victorian Lady going back to bed.

May 23, 1996
Linda to Joe

The Champlain Land Trust visit couldn't have gone better. Karen Cady, Acting Director to be replaced in June but who will continue on the Board, and Susan

Alden came. Charlotte Mehrtens arrived shortly thereafter. Dan was there as our charming and knowledgeable wildlife biologist.

We began elegantly in the absolutely perfect day with coffee and scones. On the front porch Charlotte held forth for about half an hour on the significance of the geology of the quarry, and indeed of the whole southern third of Isle La Motte. Fortunately Mary Jane taped it and I started to transcribe the tape yesterday.

Evidently one of the fascinating things about Isle La Motte geology is that if you start with the reefs at the south end of the island on Turners Point, go north to Fisk Quarry and further north to the LaBombard's property, the rocks go from older to younger but because of the tilt of the rocks they are laid out on a horizontal plane. So along with being the oldest reefs in the world they are distributed in a way that provides a great deal of information about successive geologic eras...When you put the three together it's as though you get a movie which tells an important story. Studied together they demonstrate some basic principles of biology including the principles of succession and evolution.

At the end Charlotte got quite passionate saying "If you have something that is unique for so many reasons and offers such a unique contribution, you don't just trash it. You go somewhere else and dig rock out. You go down to Middlebury or someplace where you are not destroying a resource of worldwide significance. The idea of quarrying these rocks is a stupid waste, a stupid way to use such a resource. If you have only one Grand Canyon you don't use the Grand Canyon for building stone. You go get your building stone somewhere else. The significance of these reefs is such that they should have designation as a US rare and historically significant spot. Every avenue of preservation should be looked into here all the way up to national Monument Status because they are of such significant merit."

The Lake Champlain Land Trust was to play an important role in our story.

We learned that our response to CMC's appeal to the Environmental Board, would be a more formal process than that of the District Commission Hearing. Though our crew of expert witnesses had constructed written reports for the April Hearing, those reports were not used as the Hearing was recessed. However, they represented a great deal of work which would be useful from here on in.

"So before the Hearing in July," said Joe, "everybody has to submit written testimony and send it in. It won't be so different from last December when we got affidavits from all the neighbors. But this time testimony has to be written out in the form of questions and answers. CMC prefiles first; we get to read their stuff, then we write out our testimony and file second. CMC reads our testimony, tries to rip it apart, and sends in the results in the form of rebuttal testimony. And then we read that and send in our rebuttals."

All the neighbors were able to expand on the stories they had told in their December affidavits. And several others would join in, adding new voices to the story. By this time I was a downright competent emailer.

June 17, 1996
Linda to the Qwarriors

Dear All,
Here is the little triumphant note which Mastermind was wishing for last night. All prefiled testimony is herewith sent, edited, sent back, edited, sent back, edited, (and almost thrown in the trash), then 24 copies made this morning, 12 of which were packed into a single giant box and sent to Montpelier via guaranteed overnight mail for a mere one million dollars and seventy eight cents, and other copies sent to a remaining 9 or 10 human beings for one thousand dollars and two cents with three to be delivered by hand for free. (That includes T. Warlock, the Scullys and Neil.)

By Thursday or Friday of this week we get CMC's prefiled testimony; then we turn into an army of scurrying ants getting rebuttal testimony ready by next Friday, June 28. In the meantime I will be digging out from under piles of paper et al. It's a nice feeling when one giant step is over with, even though it leads straight into the next giant step.

Mastermind has been, as always, masterful, competent and a wonderful team leader. It's nice to know that even if one screws up, he will always manage to sound happy about it.

Yours witchfully, Linda

June 22
From Linda to Ross and Neil,

Joe Bivins has been working all day on the matter of CMC's (he is now calling it Confused Marble Company's) testimony and our rebuttal testimony. He has developed a list of questions for Charlotte Mehrtens and for Ross both of whom he feels can offer testimony a bit different from the rest of us. However, he suggests that it will be useful for the rest of us to read the questions he has developed for Ross and think about our own questions and the answers.

Ross, when you finish the answers, if you would let me know I will type them up and send them back to Joe to be checked. I will then show you his edits if any, and will type up the final version. I'll do this for everyone.

This is one of those crunch times. If we can get first drafts from everyone this weekend it would be good. We have only until Wednesday to put the whole rebuttal package together. And then we have to make about 20 copies of everything and send it all out. (As you know, this is what he did last week for the prefiled testimony.)

Onward and hopefully not downward,
Linda

June 28, 96
Linda to the Qwarriors,

Thanks to the efforts of all, the requisite 12 copies of Rebuttal Testimony were hand delivered to the Environmental Board in Montpelier yesterday, others sent off in the mail and I will deliver copies to you all in the next day or so.

I was in New Jersey while we spent two weeks working night and day on the Prefiled Testimony which got sent out a week ago Monday for a Tuesday deadline at the Environmental Board. I then had two days to pack for the summer in Vermont and complete some family business, drove up here on Thursday and as I picked up my mail in the village found CMC's Prefiled Testimony. As I got to my house I fumbled in my purse for two things: my key and Joe Bivins' telephone number. Since then we have worked night and day to complete the Rebuttal Testimony, due yesterday.

Even Mastermind Bivins was staggering by 3:00 p.m. Wednesday afternoon, having done masterful edits, rewrites and coordination of some eleven (count-em) pieces of testimony and some dozen or so pieces of documentary evidence....maps, letters... He has worked doggedly for days on this and I have been trailing along in his footsteps typing away madly. Joe had another big presentation to make on Thursday, having just recovered from the marathon on our prefiled testimony, and that on the heels of another Act 250 case and that on the heels of something else...! Joe, if we win you will have a lifetime vacation spot. If not...well, we could all sit in lawn chairs with vodka and watch the blasting operations.

The emails continue to flow back and forth; a lot of correspondence from Mary Jane Tiedgen who worked furiously (and that is literal, just read it) on her testimony at long distance (praise the lord for email), neighbors coming over to dictate or deliver their testimony, wonderful photos popping up unexpectedly in my mailbox from Ross, (which we will use in the next District Commission Hearing) and various encouraging words from hither and yon. Elva, we missed you on Rebuttal Testimony since you were away this weekend, but we got you on the prefiled round.

As always the spirit has been wonderful. Special thanks to Joe Bajorski and wife Lesley who have been here for this round and have given ongoing help and support and expertise and lots of sneaky detective work. Late Wednesday afternoon, Lesley became Chief of the Proofreading Department, and if there are still mistakes it's only because Bivins and I were so tired that we let thousands of mistakes slip by, even as we were correcting thousands of others.
Joe and Lesley Bajorski came at 7:00 Thursday morning to accompany me to the printer's in St. Albans – a great help indeed!–So this is to say thanks to everyone. Everyone contributed wonderfully and I, for one, am very grateful!
Love to all, Linda

We may have had email in those days, but we didn't have such things as "attached files" and so great volumes of paper had to be sent by what we now call snail mail or delivered by hand. But we were way ahead of other folks; I don't believe the opposition lawyers, for example, had email. They would have been dependent on such horse and buggy technology as the telephone or the US mails.

During that same month of June I heard that there was to be an opening of a new state park in Alburgh...about fifteen minutes driving time from Isle La Motte. There was to be a ceremony and Vermont's Governor Howard Dean was to be present. I thought it might be a useful event to attend.

The Alburgh Dunes State Park is named for the sand dunes near the center and western end of the south-facing natural sand beach. The sand comes from glacial deposits remaining when the last glacier melted some 10,000 years ago. The preservation of this land and creation of a State Park was an enterprise in which we were very much interested, having become, so recently interested in preservation ourselves.

It was a warm sunny morning. At the park were a crowd of people, a tent, parked cars, and a speech by Governor Dean. At the end of his congratulatory remarks, the crowd headed down toward the refreshment tent. I suddenly noted that the governor was walking alone toward the tent. (Only in Vermont.) As I've told the story since then I've always added, "And Confucius say, 'Never let Governor walk alone.'"

So I walked quickly up to him, and said in essence, "Thanks very much for your letter in response to mine."

"What issue was this about?" he not unexpectedly asked.

"It's about the Fisk Quarry on Isle La Motte."

"Oh yes," he said. "In fact I was there this morning. Some people want to open a quarry there, but those neighbors are making quite a fuss."

Oh my gosh. CMC had gotten the governor to come to the quarry this very morning. And we hadn't even noticed. We were almost to the refreshment tent. I felt that I had 15 seconds to come up with a memorable sound bite.

"Are you aware that the quarry is the site of rare 480 million year old fossils, which are famous among scientists all over the world?"

He then said something in the way of, "I better not get into the middle of that." Though I was always and continue to be a strong supporter of Governor Dean, I did find that to be an awkward response. In retrospect he certainly didn't have much time to think it through. If he had had his wits about him, I suppose he might have said, "Well isn't that interesting," or something of the sort.

The gardens around our house in early July were blooming with hollyhocks, roses, and bee balm. The cone flowers were about to open. At Hall's Orchards a hundred sturdy trees and more were beginning to bear small green balls. Throughout each year Allen watches rain and sun saying, "I don't know, we could use some more rain/sun/warmth/cool/ to get a halfway decent crop this year."

We had received our licenses from the Department of Health as a Home Bakery and a small B&B. There was so much to do each day with cooking, cleaning, recycling, gardening, laundry, worrying about the well. Writing testimony, getting testimony from the neighbors, rebuttal testimony, typing, emailing. Carol testing out recipes for tea sandwiches, gourmet lemonade, fruit tarts, chocolate cake for our second summer of Tea Garden on Sunday afternoons. Sounds of hammering and the occasional buzz of a skill or circular saw were Merrill working in the barn. And then there was the cat who, having succumbed to the attentions of a wandering tomcat during the previous winter, suddenly gave birth to five kittens in an upstairs bedroom closet of the Main House.

On the first Sunday in July, leaving Carol to her cake artistry in the back kitchen, I went out in the early morning to set up the odd profusion of small tables which Carol had painted white the previous summer. I placed them carefully around the lawn, keeping in mind where the shade would be between 1:00 and 5:00, the time set for Sunday afternoon "Tea Garden."

I set the tea cups out on the old store counter in the tea room, brought out containers of lemonade and iced tea. I then went into the barn, opened the sliding door on its old iron hinges and stepped into the dark coolness. Wooden walls scarred by years of use by horses, the storage of hay and farm machinery, had been hung with color...paintings and photographs by my former sister-in-law, Betsy Andrews, and her daughter, Sue. And there would be music. In those early days of Sunday Tea Gardens, music was an impromptu family affair. We would sing...Carol, Jim, myself and whoever else was around and I would play the guitar. Or Carol would say, "Linda, go stand on the porch steps and play your flute." Wandering musicians often happened by. A cellist might set up on the lawn. We never dreamed that years later there would be two grand pianos in the barn, evening concerts with two pianos, string quartets, glorious singers, jazz.

July 10 arrived along with Joe Bivins. It was the day of the Environmental

Board Hearing and site visit. But unlike the grim and drizzling day of the April site visit when Act 250 District Commission Members and the rest of us wandered around in the dark and gloom of early spring, on this July day the sun shone brightly. Photos show us in informal warm weather clothing; Joe in a dark blue short sleeved shirt with red suspenders, Elva in a white sweat shirt, Jim in Bermuda shorts, Neil in bright red jersey. The District Commission members were somewhat more formal in suits, the CMC lawyers in grey jackets, ties, and natty dark pants. Clip boards. In one photo we seem to be gazing thoughtfully over Turtle Pond with its green summer cover of duckweed.

After the site visit we again convened in the Town Hall Meeting Room, sitting in grey metal folding chairs that, as in April, become harder by the hour. There were about thirty present; most of us constituting the opposition. The issue was whether there had been an ongoing rubblestone operation throughout the years. Each one of us who had presented prefiled testimony and rebuttal testimony was given the opportunity to speak.

Joe cross examined us first:

"In the period before July 1970 did you ever hear or see any drilling and blasting in the quarry?" "No," said each witness.

"In that same period did you ever see any extraction of rock by excavation or breaking rock loose from rock face using heavy equipment?" Each witness responded in the negative.

"In the period from July 1970 to the present did you ever hear or see any new stone excavation work at the quarry site?"

The consensus was that in the 1970s there was occasional and infrequent removal of loose stone left over from the quarry's operation in the beginning of this century--but that was picking up loose stone, not excavating new stone--and after 1980 or 81 even that came to an end.

The town had party status by statutory right so the Selectboard members were given the right to speak. One of them did speak up:

"I feel the availability of that rubble is a big asset to the town. Because of our erosion problems over here it helps us economically to have close access to rubble and 'riffraff.' "

"Riffraff." Was he referring to us? Or did he mean "rip-rap?"[36]

I talked about fossils and the generations of families who had enjoyed the quarry. But it was Mary Jane who really expressed the feelings of all of us: "The reopening of the quarry would affect our lives dramatically. My days on Isle La Motte are spent largely out of doors. That is what it is all about for me. I enjoy the lake, fishing from my point, sunrises over the garden, sunsets over the lake, the yard work, the gardening and just being out of doors to hear it all...birds, waves, wind, frogs...The air smells good and the sounds soothe the spirit. Our garden plot and future homesite for my daughter and her family is only 50 feet from the place where CMC proposes to begin quarrying."

She started to cry. "My husband and I plan to retire here year round. As much as this place is in our soul, how could we possible retire here if quarrying was taking place within ear and eye shot. The narrow dirt roads would no longer be safe for biking, walking, children and pets. We are used to seeing only an occasional car and often know who it is. The activity hours, whatever they turn out to be, would ruin outdoor breakfasts, lunches and dinners on the deck due to noise and traffic. I could go on and on. It would not be the same place. I would not want to be here."

The president of CMC said, "I intended to use high-tech equipment and did not plan to do any blasting. But if I am 'grandfathered' I might have to blast. I'm up here to work with the people. I'd like to provide some jobs; people here need jobs."

Now we would wait for the decision. It would take several months.

July 12, 1996
Joe to the Quarriors

Greetings to the Super Beavers and to all their friends and relations,
Dreaming might have resulted in a much more eventful trip, but I'm content. I did a lot of singing.

Arrived back to find all the rubble from writing the Findings of Fact, a large number of dirty dishes, and a mailbox completely full of paper including the lawyers' (I think we should call them Slimy and Moldy) final submission (as timely as it was worthwhile--and misaddressed on both levels). Also in the mailbox were the Corps of Engineers regulations (how about that for efficiency), a letter scheduling the Putney Paper hearing for August 27--so you can forget about seeing me the weekend before that one--but the one after looks good; a letter canceling the latest meeting of the committee on the groundwater rule (about which I had not heard in the first place) and various and sundry catalogs, advertising circulars and the like--a reminder that I still live in America. Most of those did not even make it into the house since my recycling facilities are on the front porch.

There is also an inch thick envelope for next Wednesday's hearing on the case Stephanie wanted me to take on. Well, there is always tomorrow. The telephone rang within fifteen seconds of bringing in the last box of documents from the car--one of the people involved in our local dump struggle giving me a lengthy update. (The long overdue ANR order has yet to arrive in my mail box.)

Sleep Well, Oh beaver queen, and dream of ever increasing ponds, marshes, and wetlands taking over the quarry. Thanks to all for making such a good dream-trip. I'm already missing you and your house full of your friends and relations, not to mention the rest of your brigade up and down the road.

Love to all, Joe

The Environmental Board site visit from left to right:
Arthur Gibb, John Ewing, Joe Bivins, Linda Fitch

My parents came in August. My father's short term memory was now greatly compromised. He spent his days sitting on the front porch watching the passing scene, the new kittens frolicking and tumbling over his feet. He was also able to appreciate Merrill's restoration of the old horse and carriage barn. "This is the most important thing that has happened here since the time of Nelson Fisk," he said enthusiastically.

Photographs show my parents sitting at one of the little white tables on the lawn on a Sunday afternoon, enjoying the ambience of tea and music on the lawn. I seem to remember during that afternoon, a neighboring cellist performing on the lawn.

Joe Bivins spent a good deal of time with us that month…feeling a compatibility with all of us as we did with him. Photos show my mother and Joe playing recorders together on our front porch Joe or one of me playing flute with Joe on recorder. The tradition of family music at Fisk Farm was alive and well.

Then it was early September, the roses faded, the last withered blooms of hollyhock clinging to their stalks, the final stretch of summer. There were grey and mellow days with gusts of wind from the southland, days hazed in grey rain, cool days so bright that lake and sky were almost unnaturally blue.

"I don't know," Allen Hall was saying about his apple crop. "The warm weather means they're not coloring up the way they should be. They're perfectly good but you can't get top dollar for them."

While we waited to hear the decision of the Environmental Board as to whether rubblestone had been an ongoing operation, discussion about the quarry was becoming public and even entered the political arena. Primary elections for State Representatives for the Grand Isle District (South Hero, Grand Isle, North Hero and Isle La Motte) were coming up. A Democratic candidate, Alex Feinman, was running for the office of State Representative. On September 3 he ran an ad in The *Islander*, the local paper. "Vote for Action Al" it said: there were two American flags and a picture of trim Action Al with mustache and a pleasant smile. The quarry was one of his targets.

"It's time that the people of the Islands support the Isle La Motte marble quarry. This marble is world renowned. It offers good paying jobs and apprentice programs will be starting. There are a few greedy people trying to stop it -- you know who you are."

We guessed he was referring to us and we thought we should respond. Merrill, being a born and bred Vermonter, was volunteered to put out a letter of response.

September 5
Merrill Hemond to *The Islander*

My name is Merrill Hemond. I am a voter and a tax payer in the town of Isle La Motte. I was born and grew up on a subsistence farm in Vermont. I have always made my living as a carpenter, builder, and general contractor. I'm very concerned by the candidate for Democratic State Representative, Alex Feinman.

I'm concerned about Mr. Feinman's political ad in which he comments that a few greedy people are trying to stop the Isle La Motte Marble Quarry by which I assume he means the Fisk Quarry. These "few greedy people" include over a hundred people who have owned family homes in the vicinity of the abandoned quarry for four generations, who, combined, pay over $32,000 dollars a year in taxes (the quarry pays 64 dollars a year), and who dread the noise, dust, and trucks of an active quarry operation right next to their homes. The "few greedy people" also include thousands of Vermonters who cycle and walk here on the quiet lakeshore roads. The "few greedy people" include tourists from all over the world who come here to enjoy the beauty and quiet of Isle La Motte and to spend money which bolsters our economy. The "few greedy people" also include geologists and students who come to study the world renowned fossils in the Fisk Quarry.

I am one of these "few greedy people," trying to protect my home and my business, which employs a number of local people during the summer. For the past three years I have lived on and worked to restore Fisk Farm to establish a place where people can come for lodging, the Tea Garden, the art shows, craft shows, concerts and other events. This is the kind of thing Alex Feinman says he wants on the islands. However, a quarry operation with diesel fueled generators, drills, splitters, saws, and trucks operating a few steps from our house would end any possibility of such a business or a family home for us and for our neighbors.

As a native Vermonter who has had to work hard to survive, I know the importance of jobs. Has Mr. Feinman really studied the impact of a noisy, dirty, industrial operation on the existing islands' industry of tourism and vacation homes? Does he know how many jobs and tax dollars are dependent on this industry? Maybe I'm a dreamer, but I'd like to find ways to preserve the open land, the clean water and air, hunting and fishing, the fields and farms, and our Vermont history as the basis for a stronger island economy. I'd also like to have a state representative who doesn't try to get elected by publicly calling me names, even if he disagrees with what I believe.

September 17
Alex Feinman to *The Islander*

I read Mr. Hemond's article in the Editorial section of the September 10 issue of *The Islander* regarding the Quarry. If he told the truth or the whole story in his long dialogue he might have a point. Mr. Hemond and his little clique are extremely greedy. I believe the citizens of the whole island should have a chance to understand what is really going on in Isle La Motte. If Mr. Hemond or any of his associates would like to hold an open debate on the quarry with real facts and figures I invite them to set the date and invite the public and have the "Islander" act as a mediator.

I do understand what life means and the value of the quality of life in Vermont. Mr. Hemond and his associates are only trying to build a bigger crying towel."

October 1
Islander ad by Alex Feinman

"Regarding the issue of the quarries - The quarries in Isle La Motte existed long before the Select Greedy Committee was. The little tea at noon and the little carpenters who work on the tea house only have their own goals in mind. These quarries are as important to Vermont as maple syrup is, both historically and economically. My question for the tea house crew is - Do you have a permit for your Bed and Breakfast and all proper state licensing?

I immediately sent off a polite little note to *The Islander* indicating that we had the requisite licenses.

A heavy, large envelope was delivered in early October of 1996. In it was the Environmental Board ruling. It was many pages long but in summary it said:

"The Board finds that under CMC's proposal, at least 100 truck loads would be exiting the quarry each year. This added volume of truck traffic in what has become a residential neighborhood could be expected to increase noise, dust, and traffic flow. The dirt road upon which these trucks would travel could be expected to require additional maintenance due to the size and weight of machinery brought in for removal activity, as well as carrying out the outgoing loads of stone. Within the Fisk Quarry, the vegetation and aquatic organisms could be expected to be impacted. The noise of the operation could affect neighboring residents, and a variety of impacts under the various other Act 250 criteria could be expected to occur. Accordingly, the Board concludes that the proposed operation would effect a cognizable change and that the potential impacts of such change would be significant

Accordingly, the Board has no basis upon which to afford CMC's Proposed Extraction Activities the status of a pre-existing development because, as explained above, blasting, active quarrying, and extraction from the rock face has been abandoned since the enactment of Act 250. The Board further finds that with respect to the removal of loose stone, CMC's Proposed Removal Activities would constitute a substantial change to the historical method and level of activity. Consequently, the Board declines to grant CMC an exemption from the requirement that its development be subject to Act 250 review."

Joe happened to be with us at the same time that we received this Declaratory Ruling. He was triumphant as were we all. "You know," he said, "I think they'll give up. I don't think they're going to go on with this."

In December, the following article appeared.

December 24
Burlington Free Press article reprinted in *The Islander*
Former Candidate Charged

Chef Alex Feinman who ran for the Grand Isle House seat in the September Democratic Primary has been ordered to appear January 23 in court on a charge of grand larceny.

The North Hero home of Feinman was raided last Tuesday night by Essex Police. Essex Detective Rick Garey said several pieces of antique furniture allegedly taken from an apartment ...in Essex in October 1995 were recovered during the raid off Blockhouse Point Road. Police used a rental truck to haul away the items including several antiques: a brass bed a dressing table and a mahogany sewing stand.

Feinman, 47, said he and his wife lived in the apartment but moved out after a dispute over the furniture and other issues with the landlady, Ruth Korzun. He said the dispute was thrown out of small claims court and he will contest the criminal charge in Vermont District Court. Feinman vowed to fight the charge. "She's going after me because I have a record," said Feinman. He said he remains on federal probation for an out-of-state mail fraud conviction. Feinman ran sucessfully for the Vermont House against James Senesac in the Democratic primary in September."

That was the last that we heard of Action Al.

13. Hard Times

"The nation behaves well if it treats the natural resources as assets
which it must turn over to the next generation increased; and not impaired in value."
Theodore Roosevelt

THERE WAS CONFLICT, not just between environmentalists and business interests, but among members of the environmental movement itself. John Muir was representative of those who wished to conserve the wilderness for itself. In 1892 he co-founded and became first President of the Sierra Club, whose mission was to "explore, enjoy, and protect the wild places of the earth." Gifford Pinchot, also a lover of nature and for years a close friend of Muir, began to advocate for what we might now call sustainability: "the planned use and renewal of natural resources," or nature for the responsible use of humankind. He advocated the scientific management of forests, opening forests to lumbering but stressing renewability and replanting. The two strands of thought have been called "conservation"--the preservation of natural resources for their sustainable use by humans--and "environmentalism"--the protection of natural areas and wildlife for their own inherent value. Teddy Roosevelt shared John Muir's almost mystical attitude toward non-human nature, but also believed--with Pinchot--in the sustainable use of natural resources.

Autumn, 1996
The early morning eastern sky was pale peach gold streaks and the mountains west were glowing with the deep reds and oranges of fall. Mother cat came in after her usual night out. After the birth of five kittens, and months of feeding them I would give her canned food as a treat for working so hard at mothering and being thoughtful and courageous. She adored canned cat food and always gave a little cat chirp of, no doubt, thanks.

My parents had been on the island during August, then returned to their new retirement community home near Princeton. After struggling with dementia for two years my father had become weaker and weaker.

In October my mother called and said that my father had become so disoriented that it was no longer safe for him to live in the small apartment in their retirement community and that he would have to go to the infirmary, to B Wing reserved for patients suffering from dementia. At that point we cried together over the telephone. It seemed as though it was the beginning of the end.

"I need you here," she said.

I went back to Princeton and spent October, November and December commuting out to the retirement community in Hightstown where my parents now lived. I took my guitar and spent the three months playing guitar not only to my father, but to all the residents in B wing. Music was the one thing that reached them all. It seems that when a brain is dying, music is the last to go. Friend Carol, also back from Vermont, joined me in singing duets, and reading poetry to the infirmary residents. My little dog Shasta played the role of therapy dog, delighting the residents with her charm, intelligence, and good manners. In early December I wrote in my journal:

I put Dad (very tired) in the wheelchair and we walked through the halls, saw the snow falling on the lovely trees, stopped at the cafe to get coffee, went to watch the geese on the pond except Dad slept instead of looking with the interest that he had three or four weeks ago. He leaves this life bit by bit, but we can reach him through music. After sleeping through the geese we went to the lounge and I played Christmas songs on the piano and he would smile and wave after each one and say, "It's something about rise up shepherd and follow." Or "Something like deck the halls." We came back to the nurse's station and sang Christmas carols, I playing the guitar which inspired Jeanie, an aide, to come and sing and work on decorating the tree in the patients' ward, and soon we were surrounded by patients and aides all decorating the tree and singing or moving their lips, wiggling their toes.

On Christmas Day Dad was too weak to leave his bed. Mother sat by his bedside while my sons, Lyle and Bruce, Bruce's future wife, Tobi, my cousin Jay and I gathered outside his door with guitar and Jay's double bass and sang all the old songs. It was Deck the Halls, Silent Night, and The Wreck of the John B. Dad lay with his eyes closed but one finger tapped along with the songs.

Dad died three days later, leaving us a pile of gifts. He left us his fighting spirit, he left his curiosity, his work ethic, his passion for the social well being of all, and a careful, mindful consideration for the world in which we live.

January 6, 1997, 9:22 a.m.
Linda to Randy
Dear Rad,
6:00 a.m. Coffee. Dark. Living room still in a chaos of chairs and poinsettias from the reception after the Memorial Service for my dad yesterday. Great celebrational event; folks coming from all over; incredible tributes and eulogies, music--recorder consorts, Schubert song, my cousin Jay playing Bach on the double bass for the service, folk songs at home later. Great obit in the New York Times last Tuesday (under the picture the caption, "The only NY public official who could rope, tie and brand a calf.")
All good but it's sad times.

Best,
Witch Woman

Joe had said that he didn't think CMC would continue the battle over the quarry. Most of the time Joe was right. But on February 26 a letter arrived in Princeton. It was from a wildlife biologist hired by CMC as an expert witness, announcing that that he had filed a CUD application with the Vermont State Wetlands Office on behalf of his client, CMC. The letter was dated February 14.

I called Mary Jane. She had also received a copy of the letter. We were shocked. We knew that once a complete application had been successfully filed with the Vermont State Wetlands Office, there was a fifteen day comment period. It was now, according to the date on the letter, twelve days after the filing of the application. Had we missed our chance to file comments and request a Hearing? In the confusion I sent a frantic email to Joe.

February 27, 12:51 p.m.
Linda to Joe

Dear Joe,
Just got this in the mail. It's dated February 14. It implies that the CUD was filed in the Town Clerk's Office before this date. If so, our fifteen days to respond has almost run out.
Linda

Joe got busy and drafted a letter to the Secretary of the Agency of Natural Resources.

February 27
Joe Bivins to Secretary, ANR Subject: in re Application of CMC Corp for a Wetlands Conditional Use Permit
REQUEST FOR STATEMENT OF CLARIFICATION REGARDING PUBLIC COMMENT PERIOD

A number of people entitled to notice and wishing to comment on a proposal to destroy very special wetlands for a proposed quarrying project are concerned that the time to comment may have virtually run out before they received notice of an "administratively complete" application....

The purported notice is dated Feb 14, 1997, but does not appear to have been mailed until considerably later. It is manifestly unreasonable to start the comment period on the date the applicant claims that a copy of an "administratively complete" application was filed with the Town Clerk when notice was not provided until substantially later...

Even worse than lack of timeliness is the failure of the letter to meet even minimal standards for notice seeking public comment. Nothing in the applicant's letter informs recipients that they can submit comments, much less provides information on the name and contact address of the ANR official designated to receive comments. The starting and ending dates of the comment period are not specified. Nothing is said about the procedure for seeking a public comment meeting. The notice and its timing is exactly the sort of letter one would send out if one's goal was to discourage public comment and try to make sure that there is as little of it as possible.

Under the circumstances I request that the Secretary issue a written statement that public comment will be accepted until some fixed date (say, March 31) that is reasonable in view of the untimely and inadequate notice and the significant threats to harm wetlands by the company. The statement should also indicate who will be receiving comment and how and where it is to be submitted.

Thank you for straightening out this situation.
Joe Bivins for South Shore Associates

It turned out that a final application from CMC was actually received by the Agency on February 21, 1997. Notice of the request was issued by the Agency on February 25 and a public comment period was extended to March 27. The mystery of the February 14 date on our notice letters was never solved. I received an email from my mother who, at 82, was a proficient emailer and who, despite the recent loss of my father, was closely following our situation.

"Dear Linda, I propose a marble statue of Joe Bivins and an ongoing invitation to Fisk Farm for the indefinite future. Love, Mother."

It was late March, grey, the temperatures in the twenties and thirties, the air raw, a scattering of tired snow on the lawn. With a reasonable time period now established for public comments, Joe, Merrill and I once again convened on Isle La Motte, settling down in the Doctor's Office/War Room.

There were two documents to analyze. One was the application for a CUD (Conditional Use Determination) from the Vermont Wetlands Office. This was written by CMC's newly hired wildlife biologist. What would he have to say? The other was a full fledged Operations Plan for the proposed quarry operation designed by an Engineering firm from the nearby town of St. Albans.

We started with the application. It was shocking. It seemed as though this newly engaged biologist had been given none of the background of the case.

"The purpose of the project is to extract marble...from the southern and southeastern portion of an existing quarry which presently produces fill and rubblestone," we read.

"Oh no, not this again. Tell me how he can say this," I said to Joe. The Environmental Board has declared that the quarry does not currently produce fill and rubblestone."

"And look here," said Merrill. He quotes John Austin's old letter saying there is no significant habitat in the quarry. He completely ignores John's follow-up letter and his testimony rescinding his position. And on this page here, he says that Cathy O'Brian said there would be no impact on wetlands. What! Did they forget to tell him this stuff? Did they think we wouldn't notice?"

Once again, guided by Joe, we got to work. This time it was a matter of writing out "Comments" as opposed to pre-filed testimony and rebuttals. The writers of Comments were to include Mary Jane Tiedgen, Mary Jane's brother Jeffrey Williams, Merrill, Joe, and myself.

The application was long on what were either deliberate lies or simply misinformation based on ignorance. It was very short on detail.

"I see that there is no mention of generators or saws or any equipment. Only that it's a quiet operation," said Joe.

The only way to really understand what CMC proposed to do was to read the Operations Plan, basically an engineering blueprint. That was a document written in a language of lines and angles and curves, a drawing of esoteric hieroglyphics unreadable to me not surprisingly, but it seemed to be legible to both Joe and Merrill.

"Hmmm," said Joe. "The plan calls for the work to be done in three phases. Let's see, in Phase One they'll start mining in the southeast corner of the old quarry excavation. They will begin at this point here, about 50 feet to the east of Turtle Pond. This is partly on the quarry property and partly on Carl Williams' land. I wonder if they know that. Ah ha, looking ahead they will be quarrying right through Beaver Dam Woods and Boulder Pond. Destroying Class II Wetlands as they go."

"Ok, see here," said Merrill. "The next part of Phase One is up on top of the cliffs overlooking Boulder Pond."

"What?" I said. "What about the trees, and ferns and..."

"Sure," said Joe. They'll cut down the woods, burn the brush, destump the land, and remove the soil. They don't mention, by the way, where they will store it. Let's figure this out." He spent a bit of time with his calculator. "How about 340,000 cubic feet of dirt. Ok. CMC plans to cut this forested area down, which is filled with deer trails and provides cover for all kinds of wildlife by the way. Brush will be burned, the land will be destumped, the overburden will be removed. CMC has not mentioned in its plan where it will store 340,000 cubic feet of dirt."

Joe warmed to his description. "Now that the wet woods are chopped down and the hydric soils are stripped off, CMC will quarry the marble down to an elevation of 102 feet. Obviously where there was an emergent marsh, a series of beaver dams, a wet woodland, and a frog pond with cattails, now is an ugly pit. Beauty is, of course, in the eye of the beholder. So perhaps it will be a lovely pit. They say that half of the site, twelve acres or so, will be cleared of trees and other vegetation, and then stripped of soil down to bare rock. That would be the meadow next to your land, Linda. So then they will create a 28 foot pit extending along the entire southern border of your fields. It will be full of machinery, trucks maybe. I'm sure it will look quite nice."

By this time, if I were a fainting woman I would have been lying flat on the floor.

"Now I'll talk about what happens in Phase Two. As we can see here, the area impacted in Phase Two is mostly an open wet meadow. It slopes gradually from east to west, dumping surface water into Big Pond, and slopes from south to north adding water to the wetlands on the northern boundary. Linda, is there any more of that coffee in the kitchen?"

"I think so, also some oatmeal raisin cookies if that would help to keep you going."

After Joe and Merrill had refueled, Joe continued. "The western boundary of Phase Two is presently a 24 foot high limestone cliff on the edge of Big Pond. The bottom of the cliff, as we know, is the wetland stream with pools of water and beaver dams. It's a great place for birds and beaver. At the top of this cliff approximately 50 to 60 feet wide is a thicket of apple trees, shrubs, vines, berry bushes and large trees."

Merrill chimed in. "One of these big trees has a deer stand in it which a lot of the local hunters use to watch from as it overlooks the quarry floor, the wet meadow and a very well defined deer trail, which is used by the deer frequently. The deer use the trail to get around the open meadow and fields without being seen."

"Trust you to know about the deer trail." Joe continued. "The dimensions of the Phase Two quarrying area are approximately 240 feet wide by 600 feet long, east to west. According to the operation plan they will be removing some 720,000 cubic feet of overburden which they will have to truck away or stockpile someplace."

Joe was on his calculator again. "If they do that the pile would represent approximately 2,000 truck loads, with 14 yards in each truck. Will they stockpile it on top of Phase Three? If they do how will they prevent it from blowing away in great dust storms or how will they prevent it eroding into the adjacent wetland and onto the fields owned by Linda. She won't mind that, will you Linda? You're an open minded type."

"In any case, it doesn't really seem likely that they will use hand tools for this. But the application doesn't mention any equipment at all. I don't think the person who prepared this application looked at, or much less understood, the Operation Plan. Interesting," mused Joe a moment later. "The application says they don't need a discharge permit."

Merrill was looking closely. "But look here. The Operational Plan has these surface drainage patterns for the proposed new pit area."

"I don't see what you're talking about."

"Look here on the plan at the 104 foot contour line. Look where it goes...right from Boulder Pond to Big Pond. This is a ditch on the 104 foot contour line. They are going to cut a trench into the stone, that drains from Boulder Pond to Big Pond. Boulder pond is going to be a sump pit for their whole operation."

I went off to the kitchen in despair. Later the side door slammed and through the dining room window I saw them headed over to the quarry.

Later Merrill said to me, "Joe could not see that trough. For some reason he just couldn't see that that would be a man made trench that they had drawn into the Operation Plan. He didn't get it until I took him down into the quarry. I said, 'Look at the contour elevations drawn on the plan. And look at the flat quarry floor. Where on the floor are these lines that go down a foot. There's no dip on the quarry floor. These lines on the map are a trough in the rock draining from Boulder Pond to Big Pond. Here's Big Pond. Here's Boulder Pond. This is just a trench to get the sludge and crap and stuff from here to here.' When Joe finally got it he said 'Wow this is great. They're trying to pollute Linda's pond.'"

They pored over it for days. Joe was good. For him, unlike most of us, the plan with its technical details and elevations wasn't a document of incomprehensible Sanskrit. But it turned out that Merrill with no engineering training could read it so clearly it seemed that he could, amidst contour lines and notations, see trees growing and birds singing.

"So how did you learn about this stuff?" I asked him. "Reading blueprints, I mean?"

"I think the first time I came into contact with blue prints was when I was working on the construction of I-89 as a college student. I was working for the state. At first that was mostly taking apart plywood forms that were used for concrete culverts. Then I got moved to work on a stretch of Main Street in Plainfield, Vermont. I got to know the guy who was the operator of the heavy equipment for that job. His job was to dig for all the storm drain culverts. I was working as a laborer with a shovel. The problem was that the foreman was not really doing his job and we kept running into the old lines...gas, sewer, water. I was just a laborer...the one that had to jump down in the hole and shovel every time we hit one of these lines--gas lines, sewer lines--that were running under the street.

"I got kind of tired of shoveling so then I started going into the construction site office every morning where the engineer, who was watching over the project for the state, stayed. He would be looking at the blueprints showing where all the pipes were located, their size, location, all the elevations that had to be shot with a transit. The blueprints had all these numbers and had to be followed carefully so he started showing me how to read blueprints. The numbers, the abbreviations, what the lines meant. So from then on the engineer and I started working with the guys on the machines so they stopped breaking lines. The job really picked up then and we got back on schedule. In the meantime the foreman was sitting in his truck drinking. I thought it was a lot of fun of course. I also became involved with blue prints when I was in the Navy and went to school to become a quartermaster, steering ships in and out of harbors. I wasn't in the Navy all that long. But later of course I also had to be involved with blueprints when I was building houses."

One day I came upon them laughing their heads off.

"Look here," said Merrill. He started laughing again. "They actually think they are going to make a buffer zone for wildlife on top of the cliff."

"What are you talking about?" I said coming in to the office with another cup of strong, therapeutic coffee.

"Ok, so imagine this. You know that the wetland rules require that there be a 50 foot buffer zone between the development activity and the wetland. Ok, so Beaver Dam Woods is mapped as a wetland on the inventory maps.

And of course the northern boundary of this strip of wetland is the cliff. So in the application they are proposing to leave the cliff and the top of the cliff for 50 feet—on the other side of which will be the quarry pit."

"I don't get it," I said.

"Ok, look," said Merrill as though he were talking to someone who had just (barely) graduated from kindergarten. "As CMC quarries through Phases I, II and III, the soil (they call it the overburden...as though the soil is somehow burdening the land) and bedrock will be removed down to an elevation of 99 feet as shown here on the operation plan. What will be left is this 25 foot high, 50 foot wide stone plateau jutting out between Big Pond and the new quarry pit. If you were to take a walk along this buffer zone, you would walk along the cliff until you reach the section which now overlooks Beaver Dam Woods. At this point, you would stop because there would be a new quarry pit in front of you and on either side of you."

"How the heck is this a buffer zone for wildlife?" I asked. We knew that the thicket on top of the cliff provides a corridor of cover for animals such as deer, fox, raccoon, skunk, rabbits, coyotes, to get around the edge of the field from the eastern woodland unseen. Deer frequently use the thicket to pass safely by the adjoining field. Ruffed grouse and deer feed on fallen apples in the thicket.

"Seriously, let's think about this," said Joe who didn't look all that serious. "How does a stone wall 25 feet tall and 50 feet wide surrounded by a pit which has been completely severed from its natural connection to the woodland in the east still maintain the wildlife functions that it did before quarrying started?"

"Easy," said Merrill. "The deer will boat across the quarry pit, scale the 25 foot cliff and get into the thicket left standing on this stone wall perched in the middle of nowhere. Same with the beaver that use this area as a source of trees. The woodpeckers will have a field day drumming on all the dead trees cut off from their natural source of groundwater flow. So the application is really saying that even though the buffer zone is not so useful as a wildlife passage, animals will be able to go through the woods to the south, come out on West Shore Road and wander up the road, dodging any cars or trucks that happen to pass, making a nice safe corridor around the project."

"So tell me again," I said. "How then does this particular buffer zone serve to protect wetland habitat functions?"

"Beats me," said Joe. "I think we should call it 'The Great Stone Buffer Zone.'"

So we got busy writing our comments. And on March 23 Mary Jane and I both wrote letters to Cathy O'Brien asking for a Hearing, as permitted by Vermont Wetland Rules.

But we continued to be outraged about how the incorrect information deliberately included in applications to the state lingered on. In my frustration I wrote to John Ewing, Chair of the Environmental Board.

3/20/97
Dear Mr. Ewing,
I am writing to express my shock and dismay at an action taken by a company regarding the proposed Fisk Quarry Project on Isle La Motte.

You will remember the Environmental Board Hearing which took place on Isle La Motte on July 10 in which CMC appealed a decision by District Coordinator Geoffrey Green that CMC needed an Act 250 Permit for a rubblestone operation in the quarry as well as for the quarrying of dimensional stone. It is my understanding that Environmental Board Declaratory Ruling #319 issued on October 2, 1996, found that CMC needs an Act 250 Permit for the removal of both rubblestone and dimensional stone.

In accordance with a ruling by the District Commission #6 CMC has applied for a CUD from the Vermont State Wetlands Office before resuming the Act 250 process. However, in spite of protests by the Assistant Wetlands' Coordinator and in spite of Environmental Board's Declaratory Ruling #319, CMC persists in describing the site in the CUD application as an existing quarry which presently produces fill and rubble stone.

This document says "I hereby certify that the information provided above or attached to this application is true and accurate to the best of my knowledge and is signed by the president and owner of CMC and the Fisk Quarry. As he very well must know, this statement is contrary to Declaratory Ruling #319 issued by the Environmental Board on October 2, 1996, after a comprehensive Hearing and Site Visit by the Environmental Board on Isle La Motte on July 10, 1996. And this may well be a way for CMC to avoid Army Corps of Engineers jurisdiction since the application later says, "Mike Adams, Project Manager, Army Corps of Engineers Regulatory Division has verbally indicated that if the project is in an active work area that it will not require a Corps of Engineers permit.

What good is it for the state to spend citizens' time and tax dollars on a process designed to protect the natural resources of the state when rulings are so casually and willfully disregarded, apparently with impunity.

Am I wrong to think that the process should at least be played by the rules? Can nothing to be done to ensure that it is? It seems to me that even a letter of warning by some state authority to an applicant when misinformation is provided would help. I cannot tell you the amount of time and care that we have spent in trying to provide honest and scientifically based information in this process, trying always to scrupulously abide by the rules. Can nothing be done to ensure that the "other side" do likewise? I appeal to your sense of justice and fairness.

Best wishes,
Linda Fitch

I sent copies to everyone in the state I could think of: Governor Dean, John Austin (Wildlife Biologist), Cathy O'Brien (Wetlands Coordinator), Barbara Ripley (Secretary of Vermont Agency of Natural Resources, John Freiden (Vermont legislator), David Deen (House Committee of Natural Resources).

There was another issue. After extensive wandering through the fields and the woods during the previous spring, Dan Froelich thought that the woods just east of the old quarry excavation might well be wetlands. Part of these woods were owned by CMC; land adjacent to the woods was owned by the Hall family. Dan wanted to follow up on this idea and back in December, with the help of Andy Mills, he had sent a letter to Cathy O'Brien suggesting that the quarry woods and adjacent woodlands to the east should be investigated as possibly being wetlands. Twenty-six year old Dan was nothing if not thorough.

"The Wetlands Inventory Map shows a scrub-shrub seasonal wetland (PSSIC) near the Fisk Quarry in addition to the mapped wetlands within the old excavation. I am inclined to think that the southeast corner of the Fisk Quarry property is part of this PSSIC wetland for the following reasons. ˘

By scaling the location of this PSSIC wetland and plotting it on the USGS topo map and on a map showing hydrologic features of the Fisk Quarry property, it appears that the mapped wetland is approximately 800 to 900 feet east of the eastern edge of the main quarry pond, and about 200 to 300 feet east of the eastern boundary of the quarry property. In the spring of 1996, we observed the presence of a relatively extensive marsh in woods, located in this same area, which extended westward into the quarry property. As described below, the hydric soil, Swanton fine sandy loam extends from the southeastern section of the quarry property to the mapped PSSIC wetland area indicated on the Wetlands Inventory map.

The PSSIC wetland area was plotted on the agricultural soils map and we found that the soil of the wetland and the marshy area extending from the quarry property consists of Swanton fine sandy loam(SdA). The Swanton soil is of course a hydric soil, considered prime if the soil is drained.

I enclose copies of photographs of this area taken in April 1996 showing the extent of standing water on the southeastern section of the Fisk Quarry property as well as a map showing hydrologic features of the property. I would be interested in your perspective on this matter."

In response to Dan's letter Cathy O'Brien promised to make another site visit. "I think we should have our own wetlands expert to study the area as well," said Joe. After some research we came across the name of one Jeff Parsons who said he would make a visit as soon as possible. "But I can't do it until May," he said.

April arrived, the world was a bit warmer, and green shoots began pushing up through the blanket of fall leaves covering the garden. The Wetland Hearing was scheduled for April 31. Throughout that month we worked continuously, preparing our testimony. Dan could not be with us so Merrill became our wildlife expert, spending many hours walking the land, taking notes and photographs of plant life, wildlife, and water after rainstorms.

"You know," he said at one point, "I think we're missing something. I really think the whole north meadow owned by the quarry company along with your adjacent land is a wetland. The soil is wet. The perc pipes that someone conveniently installed in the quarry field show water at the surface or just below the surface of the ground. We really need this Jeff wetlands person to come in and analyze the whole field. It would be really good if this could be done before the Hearing. By the way this morning, standing on the cliff I saw two mallards and two wood ducks in Big Pond."

According to the letter from one of CMC's lawyers we were not supposed to go into the quarry though "No Trespassing" signs had never been posted. And though part of the cliff side of the quarry belongs to us, part of it belonged to CMC and Merrill was not that eager to be seen during his scouting expeditions. One day he came in around lunch time. "I was up on the cliff which overlooks Big Pond and the quarry floor. I was standing in the trees and I saw one of the Goodsell Quarry guys and someone else, I'm not sure who it was. I saw them coming through the opening onto the quarry floor. I was in the trees and ducked down. They seemed to be looking for something or someone. So I was watching them. They went around Boulder Pond and started coming up on the cliff level. I ducked into the trees to see what they were up to. They came closer and at that point I couldn't make a run for it so I crawled over to the edge of the cliff and was hanging off the face of it in order to avoid detection. They still couldn't see me but I saw them. My eyes were just level with their feet. They just stood there just about 20 feet away and me dangling down the side of the cliff. Finally they started walking again; they went onto your land across your lawn (talk about trespassing)! on their way out. I waited until they got to the road and then sprinted back to your land."

We contemplated changing his Qwarrior name from Master Scout to Master Burglar.

Several days later Merrill had another report. "Hey, guess what! I just saw CMC's president, the new biologist they hired, Cathy O'Brien and someone else from the state. This must be the site visit to investigate the east woods that Dan wrote to her about. Anyway, I saw them at the end of the visit and went down to the gate and met them when they were coming out. I said hi ....very friendly and they were friendly too. Cathy looked really tired."

"No wonder," I said. "I hear she's pregnant. But I wonder what they decided about the east woods. Do they think it's a wetland?"

"I can't imagine them thinking anything else," said Merrill.

Several days later we got the news .

April 17, 1997
Linda to Qwarriors
Flash!!! Wetland Determination

Great News Folks!
Cathy O'Brien has just told us by phone that the Class II Wetlands DOES extend up to and into the east quarry boundary. For those who have an Operations Map, what the Operations Map shows as Class III Wetlands, have now been determined to be Class II Wetlands. This puts a major crimp in CMC's plans for the excavations in Phase I. Special kudoes to Godwit who raised this issue in the fall, to HydroSage who helped Dan write the letter to Cathy raising the issue, and to Master Scout (Merrill) who has scouted vigilantly for many hours getting supporting photographic evidence.
North Witch

Just in case we didn't have enough to think about, Joe had another bit of news to pass along. "It turns out," he said one day, "that there is a Marble Quarry Exemption Bill in the works. Act 250 exemptions are special interest legislation we don't need - - Act 250 is already getting to look like a moth-eaten sweater. And in this case one of the major persons behind it is the president of CMC who wants an exemption because he doesn't like the decisions he has already gotten from Act 250 on the Isle La Motte Quarry. Time for some more letter writing, Linda. Get cracking on your computer."

April 2, 1997
Linda to David Deen

Dear Mr. Deen, I understand that Bill # H266 will be presented to the House Committee of Natural Resources. This bill has been inspired by CMC which would like to reactivate the Fisk Quarry on Isle La Motte.

The Fisk Quarry Case is an excellent one to use, I think, when considering Bill H266. It affords legislators an opportunity to consider the kind of site that could be impacted without ANY OPPORTUNITY FOR STATE REVIEW if marble quarries were exempted from the Act 250 process. In the Fisk Quarry Case, almost all of the Act 250 Criteria are involved including: water quality (groundwater, Class II Wetlands, Lake Champlain); air quality (almost all quarries need Air Quality Permits), noise pollution (because of the use of diesel fueled generators, pneumatic drills, air compressors, giant saws, etc.), traffic safety, road damage, wildlife habitat, historic sites, aesthetics, property values, and damage to tourism. On top of all this it is an internationally famous geological site.

Furthermore the Fisk Quarry case is an excellent model to study for a better understanding of the critical importance of citizen participation as the only way to counter erroneous and incomplete information provided by some developers to leanly staffed state agencies which do not have the resources to thoroughly research each and every proposed development site.
Sincerely,

Linda Fitch

14. The Darkest Day
"When you're at the end of your rope, tie a knot and hold on"
Theodore Roosevelt

"Good morning everyone. I trust there's coffee?" Joe had just come down-stairs to the dining room of the Main House. He was dressed in his usual jeans and a blue plaid shirt. He walked into the kitchen, grabbing his favorite brown mug from the 1920s glassed-in kitchen cabinets, poured some very dark coffee from the coffee pot, and came back to the table. "Yes, I'll have some scrambled eggs thank you very much. I need my strength."

It was April 31. At 7:00 that evening we would be in the Town Hall to testify at the Wetlands Hearing. Joe had stayed overnight in what we called the "Green Room," a west room overlooking the lake, freshly painted by Carol several years previously with her handmade quilt and curtains to match.

"I hope you're feeling especially strong today," I said. "Do you need more toast?"

"I have a bit of headache but it will disappear shortly. Not to worry." Joe waved a piece of paper with rough blue lines drawn in incomprehensible pat-terns. "I'm going out to the quarry to check some of your new ideas about the wetlands in the quarry," he said to Merrill. "You're right about there being wetlands in addition to those mapped on the National Wetland Inventory."

"Yeah, there's water running right out of the Eastern woods across the quarry floor and into Boulder Pond," said Merrill. If they hadn't scraped off the vegetation there would be cattails on what's now rock, along with cattails in the pond. So you want to get drawings to present tonight?"

"Right. Why don't you take a last look at the engineering plans and then we can compare notes. Just in case we've missed something."

"How can you have missed anything? You've been weeks on those plans." I started clearing the table. Merrill and Joe had spent days and weeks analyz-ing the plans, going out into the field, coming back. Endless discussions. Now they both left the house, Merrill headed toward the field, Joe to the old excavation.

There were piles of dishes from everyone who had been through the kitchen that morning. It was a relief to simply work on cleaning up. Wipe down the stove. Put the just washed iron skillet on a flame to dry quickly, then hang it up in its place on the wall. Observe the greening grass and the first daffodils through the kitchen window.

After a while I heard Joe come in through the side dining room door and go to the Doctors' Office—the computer filled "War Room." I thought he might like coffee. I went in to ask.

Just outside the office I heard an odd sound. Then I saw him. He was lying on his back on the brown carpet in the office. He seemed to be choking. Then I saw that he had vomited...he still seemed to be choking...I ran to him...he seemed unconscious...having a hard time breathing...he was choking on his own fluids. I tried to turn him over so he could breathe but he was so heavy that I could only push him to his side and then hold him there in place, trying with all my strength to keep him from flopping back...then calling...calling for help...but no one was in the house. I tried to get to the phone (we had no cell phones in 1997) but it was not within reach and I felt that I had to hold Joe on his side, not to let him fall over on his back. In retrospect I'm not sure how it happened but somehow I finally reached the phone and dialed whatever numbers I could think of. Whatever I had in my memory. I remember now ....911 and Mary Jane Tiedgen. Neil Hanna maybe.

In a few minutes Merrill came in, shocked by what he saw.

"Help me help me!" I gasped. Thank goodness Merrill was able to help prop Joe onto his side with cushions. Put a pillow under his head. The rest was a blur. The Rescue Squad...oxygen...Joe being carried out on a stretcher. I jumped in the ambulance to ride with him. I think Merrill followed the ambulance in his car. Or my car. The ambulance raced over the country roads for a wild forty-five minute ride to the hospital in St. Albans. What had happened to Joe? The ambulance crew had called ahead and Emergency Room staff at the Northwestern Medical Center were waiting for us at the door. Joe was carried in, still unconscious. We waited tensely in the waiting room. Soon doctors emerged. Joe had suffered a major stroke we were told. He would be taken to Fletcher Allen Hospital in Burlington where they had better facilities...yet another forty minute ride.

Nowadays they say that there is medication which can alleviate some of the damage if given in time to a stroke patient. I don't know that there was such medication at that time. In any case it wasn't given to Joe at the Medical Center in St. Albans. Merrill and I followed the ambulance by car down Route 89 to Burlington. Joe's family? How could we notify Joe's family?

Where do they live? Isn't it somewhere in the South? Do we have phone numbers? We didn't. But we called Stephanie. We called Randy.

We were in the hospital. Stephanie and Randy came from their respective homes in Calais and Randolph. Mary Jane arrived, having broken speed limits driving from Isle La Motte. We found a pay phone and called the Wetlands Office. We reached someone named Stephen Syz who, we learned, would be in charge of the proceedings that evening.

"Can the Hearing for tonight be postponed?" I asked desperately. "We can't be there." I told him that Joe...basically our "lawyer," our chief expert witness, our mentor, our...had had a stroke and was in the hospital. There was no way that we were going to leave him.

Stephen Syz said he would get back to us. We must have called him back as we were in the hospital, not reachable by telephone in an era without cell phones. He said that he had called the lawyers for CMC who had told him that they would not postpone the Hearing.

"But we can't be there," we said.

"I know," he said. His tone of voice was grim.

So the Wetlands Hearing, for which we had prepared for months, would go on without us. It would be a totally one sided Hearing.

Late that night we drove back to Isle La Motte. The Hearing was over. The Town Hall was dark. We wondered what had happened.

Early in the morning we drove the fifty miles back to the hospital in Burlington and found Joe in a private room. We were able to speak to him. That is, we could speak. He could not. With a kind of sign language he tried to convey his questions. "What happened?" "You've had a stroke. You were brought to the hospital yesterday."

He was able to understand what we said. And then, in sign language, "What about the Hearing?" We told him that we hadn't been there. Typical of the old Joe, he kept trying to draw us out--in sign language--for more information. We told him all we could.

For several days we maintained a vigil in Joe's room. Stephanie, Randy, Mary Jane, Merrill. Many others came from around the state. I began to fantasize about Joe's life once he left the hospital. He lives alone in Thetford. When he is ready to leave the hospital perhaps we can take him back to Isle La Motte with us. He would live with us. We would help him to recuperate. Take care of him. Provide therapy. Perhaps he would be able to learn to speak again.

At a certain point he was transferred from the intensive care unit to a regular hospital room. We were uneasy about this but it didn't seem as though we had the power to do anything about it. Joe's daughter, Linda, arrived and joined the group keeping vigil.

During this time I received another emergency call. This one was from my son, Bruce in Connecticut. Tobi, who some months later became my daughter-in-law, was very ill and needed someone in the house while Bruce was at work.

Leaving Joe with a large flock of concerned friends, I drove down to Connecticut where Tobi really needed assistance. She was weak to the point of being bedridden for much of the time.

I stayed in touch with the Vermont situation by phone. A day or so later I got a call from Merrill. He was weeping.

"We lost Joe."

In a haze I heard him saying that Joe's parents had finally been found and his mother was coming up from Georgia. She hadn't yet arrived and didn't yet know that Joe had died.

Tobi urged me to go back to Vermont saying that her mother was coming soon and that she could manage. I remember driving north through the loveliness of the May afternoon, weeping. Joe. Our teacher. Our dear friend. Our brother.

By ten o'clock at night I arrived at the hospital. Merrill met me in the hospital corridors. He said that Joe's mother was in the cafeteria and that we should join her there. The room was dark and empty of people. She sat in a metal cafeteria chair. Stoic. Somehow I remember her as being very stoic. Intelligent. Warm. In shock.

Merrill told me that he had come in that morning to find Joe lying in bed in a darkened room with his daughter, Linda, sitting in the hospital chair looking, just looking at his monitors.

Merrill sat with her in silence for a little while, watching the wavy lines on the monitor screen and the occasional beep. "How's he doing?" he asked.

Linda looked at him." "What do you mean?"

"Well, did he have an ok night? How are his vital signs this morning?"

"I called you this morning and left a message," said Linda. I guess you didn't get it My father's dead."

In the next terrible moments, Merrill learned what had happened the day before. Joe had suffered some kind of problem--he wasn't sure what it was--resulting in irreversible brain damage. Brain death. The doctors told Linda that there was no hope of recovery. "I knew that my father wanted to be an organ donor so his body is now getting mechanical support to keep his organs viable until they can be used."

Merrill also told me that just before leaving Fisk Farm that morning to come to the hospital in Burlington, he had gotten a call from a friend of ours who worked as a staffer for the Vermont State House Natural Resources Committee. She told him that the owner of CMC was going to testify at 8:00 a.m. the next morning before the Natural Resources Committee, making a plea for the passage of legislation exempting marble quarries from Act 250. "You should be here to testify for the other side," she said.

It was now close to midnight. Joe's mother must have found a hotel. And we decided that we also had better get a hotel if we were to drive south to Montpelier the next morning to testify before a committee at 8:00 am.

We awoke at 6:00. Exhausted. Dirty. Still in shock. No change of clothes, though I must have had clothes in the car from my Connecticut excursion. We got in my car and drove the thirty-eight miles south to Montpelier, Vermont's state capital. We made our way through the State House, searching desperately for coffee, and eventually found ourselves in a small conference room.

Was CMC's president with his lawyer? I don't remember. I do remember his start of surprise when we walked in the conference room. How could we possibly have known about this meeting? Always civil, he said hello and, always civil, we responded. Again, I have trouble remembering how the gathering began. But close to the beginning I recall that we were called upon to mention our "lawyer," Joe Bivins.

"Joe died yesterday," one of us said.

CMC's president was genuinely shocked. "What? Really? Oh no! Why I just saw him a few days ago. I met him in the quarry."

That would have been the day of the Hearing. He and one of his colleagues had been wandering around looking at areas in the quarry just as Joe had been. Later that day, after we had frantically telephoned the news that Joe was in the hospital, Steven Syz of the Wetlands Office had called CNC's lawyers asking for a postponement of the Hearing because of Joe's condition. The lawyers refused. Had CNC's president been part of that decision? Had he not been told that Joe had had a stroke?

Some of the members of the Committee wanted to know who Joe Bivins was. The Committee Chair said, "If this is true, it's a tragedy for the state of Vermont. Joe Bivins has been one of the most eloquent and powerful defenders of the environment in the state. This is truly a sad day!"

I can only remember the gist of the rest of the meeting. Basically the president was making a plea for the exemption of all marble quarries from Act 250. The amusing part—insofar as we were capable of being amused on this terrible day—was the extent to which he needed to be reminded of certain details. He would look to us to help him out with one piece of information or another...."Let's see, when was that Act 250 application filed?"... "What permits were we supposed to get?"...and we were ready to remind him. It was, in some sense, a mirror of the relationship throughout the process. He was a nice guy. We were nice people. Despite the battle, we tried, always, to keep it that way. But the importance of our being there on that day lay in the opportunity to present our side. Our point of view. The impacts of quarrying on the animals, plants, the people living near the site and the proposed destruction of an ancient community of life forms engraved in stone and known by scientists throughout the world. The Committee listened to us all.

We drove back to Isle La Motte in the afternoon. Beyond weary.

May 9, 1997
Randy to Friends

Joe is gone.
Joe Bivins has died. On Wed night at 10 p.m. he underwent a brief period of extremely low blood pressure and irreparable severe damage was done to his brain despite valiant efforts by the medical staff. This morning he was conclusively determined to be brain dead. His body is still on the breathing machine while preparations are made for organ donation.
His mother and his daughter Linda will be moving down to Thetford and beginning to settle his affairs and plan a commemorative gathering. They want help and guidance from his friends.

I'm too sad to say much more.
Randy

May 10, 1997
Linda to Qwarriors

Dear Friends,
Some of you know already, others do not. Our very beloved Joe Bivins, mentor, environmental warrior, musician par excellence, philosopher and leader has died. Joe Bivins suffered a serious stroke at my house ten days ago. We believed that he was recovering in the hospital, but he suffered a serious setback on Wednesday night, having contracted some kind of infection which precipitated a disastrous drop in blood pressure and massive damage to the brain. He was kept alive on life support until his mother arrived from Georgia and until the final tests on his brain were done, then was pronounced dead on Friday morning, May 9.

Joe was an organ donor and by now someone is alive because he gave his very strong heart. He gave us all his heart and his courage and now he will live in our hearts forever. We must continue to work for the principles for which he gave his life.

Love to all,
Linda Fitch
ps There will be a service somewhere in Thetford next Sunday. I will have further
details in another day for any who are interested in attending.

The Thetford Congregational Church was packed with people from around
the state. Joe's love of music had included his participation in a choir of Shape
Note singers. On this day, the choir sang their hearts out. People talked.
People wept.

May 21, 1997
Article in *The Burlington Free Press*
Advocate's private side full of gusto
By Sam Hemingway

They said goodbye to Joe Bivins the other day. On a sunny Sunday afternoon,
Bivins' many friends crowded into the Thetford Congregational Church to pay
their respects and, maybe, have him back in their midst one last time.

Who could blame them? Bivins, 51, was one of a kind. He was a passionate environmental advocate who could have made a good living as an Act 250 land-use
consultant, but often took his pay in homemade meals and pieces of pie instead.

The story is well-known by now. How Bivins so pursued the fight to close a contaminated landfill in Thetford that an opponent called him "the ordinary citizen
from hell." How, clad in suspenders and a flannel shirt, he argued the case before
the Vermont Supreme Court despite being a non lawyer--and won.

What isn't so well known about him are all the other things Bivins was. An accomplished trumpet player. A volunteer teacher of African culture in the Thetford schools. A founder of the statewide Citizen Participation Network.

Another untold story about Bivins is the environmental fight he was waging in Isle
La Motte the day he was felled by a stroke that led to his death May 11. The case is
a classic. CMC recently had purchased the long inactive Fisk Quarry on the island's west side and had plans to reopen it. The trouble for the company president is the quarry is part of one of the oldest coral reefs in the world, containing
fossils more than 450 million years old.

"It records one stage, one snapshot of evolution, competition, adaptation, succession," wrote Charlotte Mehrtens, a University of Vermont geology professor, in a
report last year. "If that movie frame were gone, you would not be able to interpret or place what happens before or after in any context."

And then there's the wildlife in the quarry, particularly the birds. More than 100
bird species have been sighted on the 18-acre quarry. "Only the Missisquoi Na-

tional Wildlife Refuge in its vastness produced similarly impressive numbers," remarked California ornithologist Dan Froelich in a 1996 letter.

The president of CMC has disputed the site's natural uniqueness. "I'm not a geologist, but anybody can come up with anything if they're opposed to something," he said. He insisted his quarrying would "not bother the wildlife," and said he wanted to abide by the Act 250 process. He voiced support for the law, the state's landmark development control measure, but admitted he was behind a legislative bill to exempt marble quarries from permit review.

Bivins got involved here the same way he got involved with all the other cases that crossed his path: Someone called for help. Linda Fitch was the someone. Fitch lives next to the quarry in the old Fisk house, the house where Vice President Teddy Roosevelt learned President William McKinley had been shot.

Fitch had already begun investigating how to stop the company from mining the quarry when she hooked up with Bivins in the summer of 1995. Within three months, the Environmental Board had ruled an Act 250 permit was needed before extraction could begin.

"He was our mastermind," said Mary Jane Tiedgen, a leader with Fitch of the South Shore Associates group formed to fight the quarry. "Whatever the hearing was he knew what steps we had to take to prepare for it. He was smart, scary smart."

The day Bivins had his stroke he was doing what he loved to do: preparing for a hearing in the home of friends, in this case going over information at the Fitch home in advance of a scheduled permit hearing.

Tonight at 7 at the Isle La Motte town hall, the Fisk Quarry battle continues. Fitch and her group will be ready. But what happens when the next case comes up that Bivins would have fought? Who will take his place?

Relief interlaced with terror. Those were our emotions when we learned that the Vermont Wetlands Office would give us another chance. A second Hearing was scheduled for May 21. Without Joe there were five of us to testify: Mary Jane Tiedgen, Joe Bajorski, Scott Newman, Merrill Hemond, and myself. We figured that the Hearing would begin with presentations of the project by the engineering company, expert witnesses, and perhaps the CMC president. Then it would be our turn. Mary Jane would talk about habitat. I would talk about the fossils. Joe Bajorski would talk about the roads. Scott would talk about the economic impact. Merrill would try to explain the project as it had been mapped out by the engineering firm and then talk about the problems associated with the plan.

The team went without sleep for two weeks. We would wake up in the middle of the night thinking of all the angles. We went over the salient points again and again.

On the morning of May 19, two days before the Hearing, Jeff Parsons showed up. This was the wetland specialist whom we had called back in April asking him to take a look at the field. He was youngish--in his thirties we guessed--bearded, and enthusiastic. We learned that he had an M.S. from the University of Vermont in Natural Resources Planning, and work in the areas of wetland assessment and delineation, along with interests in field ecology and conservation biology.

We walked out to the field. "Well, it's early yet so you can't completely tell what's going on here plant-wise," he said. "But so far it looks like plenty of red-osier dogwood, green ash stems, sensitive fern. Look over here...some species of horsetail." I left him as he explored the site.

Later that day he returned to the house. "So I dug a soil pit. I'll write all of this down in an official letter, but what I found is silt loam soil with a low chroma matrix and mottles at 14 inches...ok ok I'll write it down. But basically it seems as though the field is probably all wetland or has wetland sections within it and should be looked at closer and delineated later in the season. Oh, and I went down to the ponds in the old quarry excavation. Kind of neat in there. Frogs, fish, a great blue heron. And a beaver over in that big pond. Yup...I'll write it all up today. Do you have a computer I can use?" We escorted him to the War Room.

Merrill quietly continued to work on his presentation. With colored crayons he made a large map on several sheets of newsprint. On the night before the hearing, we could hear hammering in the basement where he was building a homemade wooden easel on which he would display his flimsy newsprint crayon sketches.

The Town Hall was packed. Our trembling team of five sat on the left side of the hall. On the right hand side was CMC's Team. Among their presenters were several lawyers, several engineers, and their wildlife biologist. The room was full of Isle La Motte residents. A panel of men and women from the Vermont Wetland Office sat at a table at the front of the room. In the back of the room were four or five husky men in flannel shirts, standing with arms folded.

Before the meeting began, we were handed papers by lawyers from CMC. What was this? Good heavens! It was a change in the Operational Plan developed by Cross Engineers. The plan now showed a Detention Pond and Sump. Nowhere had it appeared in the original plan submitted to the Agency.

Indeed in their original application of February 21, it was stated that no discharge permit would be needed for the proposed quarry operation.

Evidently, since that time, the Discharge Permit Section of the Wastewater Management Division had informed CMC that a discharge permit would be needed along with a new Operational Plan showing how CMC would deal with water discharge from their proposed quarry operation. We discovered that on May 19, two days before this second Hearing, CMC submitted an altered Operational Plan to the Vermont Wetlands Office showing a Detention Pond and sump and an overflow ditch to discharge contaminated water from the quarry pit.

We had been given no advance knowledge of this. No opportunity to study it or prepare comments on it. The Chair of the Wetlands Office panel asked what we wanted to do? Did we want to postpone the meeting? We asked for an opportunity to talk about it and went into a group huddle. Merrill was studying it closely. Finally he looked up and said, "We can do this. Let's go ahead."

CMC began first. The engineers brought up a sleek aluminum display easel and set up their complex engineering plan. (No Power Point presentations in those days!) They talked for close to an hour, pointing to various aspects of their plans, explaining where the excavation would take place, where surface water would be drained.

Then the wildlife biologist for CMC stood up. He testified that no new buildings would be constructed, no crushers would be installed, there would be no new blasting, and a water cooled diamond wire saw and belt saw would be used to quarry the marble in the southeastern portion of the quarry. He explained that the quarry area is surrounded by natural vegetation on all sides which would act as a sound barrier and visual screen. "There are no wetlands, drainage ways, or riparian waterways except for the quarry hole itself which periodically fills with surface water. The area is and will remain a hole in the ground. The only water entering it at present is the precipitation incident to the surface of the ground within the pit." No great blue herons, green backed herons, deer, resident muskrats, fish or minnows on either occasion. No fresh sign of beaver.

Finally it was our turn.

Mary Jane Tiedgen stood up. "I find it alarming that a professional can find so little wildlife in the quarry. There are two beaver lodges, in Big Pond and several beaver dams in the wooded area connecting with Boulder Pond. They all connect to the big pond and are wetlands unto themselves, providing homes for frogs, birds and waterfowl that I have seen on my many trips to the quarry. Boulder Pond and the Big Pond are a favorite place for the big Blue

Herons and the mallards. Season after season the Mallards nest and raise their young in the quarry. It can be quite startling to be walking in the quiet of the walls and have a mallard flush out in front of you. The little killdeer also nest there and go into the noisy injured bird act when you approach the nest area. The East wall is also where the foxes used to have their den. The herons hunt frogs in the East pond by the boulders (Boulder Pond) since the pickings are plentiful and the water is more shallow than in the deep quarry. You can also observe small minnows or some small fish in Boulder Pond so the herons may eat them also."

Scott Newman, taller than all of us stood up, looking over the crowd. "This case is interesting and important in the context of a larger question, and that is the use of land and natural resources--not only in Isle La Motte--but in the entire Champlain Valley region. A critical industry in the Lake Champlain Region is tourism, as indeed it is an important, two billion dollar industry for the entire state of Vermont.

"Conserving the island's natural qualities is vital to maintain tourism, and maintaining tourism is vital to support town revenues and local employment. The first part--that maintaining the islands natural resources and aesthetic qualities is vital to tourism is intuitively obvious. Isle La Motte has no Disneyland, no theme parks, and no carnival rides. There are no McDonalds restaurants or Walmarts. The reasons visitors come to the island are found in almost everything ever written about the island. For example, here is a quote about Isle La Motte from a Yankee Magazine article, "...a bucolic setting with apple orchards, open fields and lake views...the roll of the land seems gentle, all apple orchards, and farmland and cottages clustered along the shale of the shorelines, every bit as beautiful as Cape Cod used to be..."

"As far as jobs are concerned--tourism is undeniably the largest local employer by far. Some of the comments of the opposition in the past have underestimated the economic activity on the Island as consisting of an apple orchard and a general store. In fact the island has several restaurants, lodges, campgrounds, a bed and breakfast, an art gallery, marinas, the country store and St. Anne's Shrine--all of which hire hardworking residents from Isle La Motte and neighboring communities to keep their businesses competitive and our tourism industry vital. In addition, they and the dozens of vacation property owners create local and regional jobs for snow removal, landscaping, painting, carpentry, plumbing and heating contractors, builders, house cleaning, electricians, oil suppliers and others. Whatever keeps the tourism industry vital in Isle La Motte keeps all these people employed in this community."

We applauded mentally.

When I began to talk about the fossils in the Fisk Quarry one opposing Isle La Motte resident said, "I can't stand this," and walked out of the room. I continued, tremulously, reciting what I had learned from Dr. Merhtens from the University of Vermont.

Finally it was Merrill's turn. Merrill would have to make the case by himself that Joe had planned to make—Joe—whose articulate, sharp, and eloquent speechmaking capacity had once persuaded the Vermont Supreme Court to make a decision in his favor.

Shy and completely unaccustomed to speaking in public, Merrill made his way to the front of the room and set up his homemade wooden stand next to the slick aluminum easel where the Engineering Plans were still in place. He tacked up his crayon drawings and began to speak.

"According to their Operations Map on file with the Wetlands Office, CMC plans to start mining in the southeast corner of the old quarry excavation. Beginning about 50 feet to the east of Turtle Pond which is partly on the quarry property and partly on Carl Williams' land, they will quarry a series of 14 steps starting at the 115' elevation."

He may have been scared, but he was talking with a kind of quiet, but confident authority. A hush fell over the room as he continued to speak.

"The next part of Phase I takes place up on top of the cliffs overlooking Boulder Pond. This area is forested with a variety of trees, ferns, and other plant life. It has standing water at various times and is wet throughout the year. This forested area is connected with a federally mapped wetland (PSSIC) which starts in the woods and goes east to the foot of the hill on Halls' land. CMC plans to cut this forested area down, an area which is filled with deer trails and provides cover for all kinds of wildlife. Brush will be burned, the land will be destumped, the overburden will be removed. CMC has not mentioned in its plan where it will store 340,000 cubic feet of dirt.

"Where fox, deer, partridge, coyote, beavers, muskrat, spring peepers, spotted salamanders, grey tree frogs, all lived will now be an ugly pit. All the water that flows on top of the ground from the eastern wetlands would be shut off. All the water that saturates the hydric soils and slowly permeates down into the bedrock and the fractures of the bedrock, would be shut off. The water that flows from an underground stream located in the southern face on Carl Williams' property and flows across the surface of the old quarry excavation would be shut off. The total loss of the recharge source for Big Pond would be devastating."

At this point the room was silent. The Wetland Panel members were craning their heads to hear every word.

"There are some design problems with the Operation Plan. For example, this filter Berm bed. On the Operation Plan a filter berm bed has been located between the parking lot, stone stock pile, loading area, truck turnaround, fuel storage and refueling area and the wetland here known as Big Pond. The berm is sitting on the quarry floor running from what is now Beaver Dam Woods 240 feet west to the pit excavated during the illegal operation of CMC in August, 1995. The pit, by the way, was carved out of the wetland and buffer zone of Big Pond in 1995. The ditch creates a spillway for water from the proposed quarry pit to the wetlands of Big Pond. According to the Operation Plan, filter fabric will be laid in this ditch and the crushed stone will be put on top. Dirt will be put on top of that. The function of the filter bed is to filter sediments out of water that runs through it.

"Water passing through the filter bed would come from several sources. It would come from the parking lot, truck turnaround, loading area, fuel storage and refueling area which are up gradient from the filter bed. Water entering the bed from these areas would be laden with mud and sludge from trucks and loaders involved in the quarry operation. Also, contaminants from the fuel storage and refueling area from spills, leaks, the breaking of hoses, etc. would flow with the water into the bed. Since the bed does not slope in any particular direction, the water with its pollution could go east into the proposed mining pit or west into the wetland of Big Pond, or pass through from one side of the bed to the other. How many years will the fabric survive? Certainly not for the life of this permit. How long would it be before a slimy coat of mud would make the filter fabric impervious to water penetration? At what point would the crushed stone bed fill with silt and no longer function?

"From my experience in building and working on muddy construction sites, a single rainstorm overnight can clog a crushed stone filter system. This mining operation is going to be a very muddy site at all times. Once the bed is clogged the muddy water will seek out the lowest point and flow into the wetland. An additional problem is the fact that water carrying gasoline, diesel fuel, hydraulic fluid from broken hoses, etc. will not be filtered by either the filter bed or the silt fence, but will pass directly into the wetland adversely affecting plants and animal life there." After an hour of this Merrill paused. "Do you have any questions?" he asked the panel.

After his presentation our team refrained from breaking into applause, but certainly there was a hubbub of conversation and many people in the room came to shake Merrill's hand. Indeed, one of the engineers crossed the room, shook his hand and said, "Nice work."

May 22, 1997
Linda to South Shore Associates and Qwarriors:

Dear All,

Merrill says to say that at our Hearing last night, we kicked their asses, even without Joe. We got surprise evidence at the last minute; opponents had changed their Operations Plan; we protested with a vigor worthy of Joe. After consulting among our selves we decided we would still go on with the Hearing (we decided that much of our arguments concerning impact were still valid) but we demanded that a copy of their new map and a written narrative of their change be provided and that we be given fifteen days to respond to this change. (We write more confidently than we speak.) We got a week to respond (the other side was vociferously protesting). However we know the site and the issues so well we can get a lot done in a week.

Presiding was Stephen Syz and John Willard. Up against us was one lawyer, three engineers, a hydrologist brought in at the last moment (we figured out later that they had whisked him down to the site fifteen minutes before the Hearing started) and a Wetland Ecologist. The other side spent an hour presenting the plan. Then it was our turn.

Merrill had made a magnificent map and a homemade stand to set it on. We had had a two hour rehearsal session before the hearing and had decided exactly who would speak, when, and in what order. Amazingly, it all went as planned. Everyone was terrific. Habitat, aesthetics, noise, groundwater, paleontology, economic impact...one after another without a hitch. Merrill had been suffering...anguishing...for weeks, knowing that Joe would not be there to back him up. But when it came to his turn he was simply superb! He sounded so honest, so credible, angry in a soft, quiet, way and had the technical details down so incredibly thoroughly...We were SO PROUD! Joe Bivins was sitting there invisibly with a wide grin on his face.

When the whole thing was done and as people were getting up to go, the Chief Engineer came over to us with a grin on his face, shook Merrill's hand and said he had done a great job and said to us all that he had never seen such a well organized group. Damn Right! That's because Joe was with us the whole time.

Love, North Witch

Joe would have wanted some of his ashes scattered at the quarry. That's what his two daughters, Roberta and Linda, told us. The Qwarriors gathered on the quarry cliff. Neil Hanna brought three large boulders on his front loader placing them under the apple tree which grew on the edge of the cliff. Joe loved the little yellow apples which he found on this tree the previous fall. They were tart, tiny, misshapen, beloved by deer and wonderful for making applesauce, apple pies, apple crisp.

We dug a small hole at the base of the middle boulder and in it we carefully shook some of the ashes. Other ashes were gently tossed over the side of the cliff and floated down into the water of Big Pond, below. We sang. Our poet neighbor, Patrick Bradley had written a poem and read it.

In the days ahead we continued to receive email from friends of Joe.

Dear Linda,
So much love to you and to all the others in the incredible support group surrounding our dear Joe. We send you our strongest hugs. Somehow in the tears and rain, I hope we never forget the Light that has just gone to shine somewhere else, not the light that has gone out.

Whatever the hereafter is, I guess we now have to remember Joe as the one up there who is working to change the environment of heaven to be a truly better place. If ever there was anyone who could make a place better, they just got the best advocate we had on this planet.

Craig and I thank you so very deeply for keeping us in complete touch - may we all now be able to carry on the load with a bit of that brilliance and care which was our dear Joe's.

Fondly, Elizabeth and Craig

I grieved as for the loss of another brother.

Music on the porch: Joe and Linda

15. Keeping On
"Courage is not having the strength to go on;
it is going on when you don't have the strength."
— *Theodore Roosevelt*

1908-1913
BATTLE LINES BETWEEN THE ENVIRONMENTALISTS AND
CONSERVATIONISTS were drawn over the battle ground of Hetch Hetchy.
Herein lay the great divide between John Muir and Gifford Pinchot. Hetch
Hetchy was a valley in the Sierras which John Muir saw as one of the most
magical natural wonders in the country.

> The Hetch Hetchy Valley, far from being a plain, common, rock-bound meadow, as
> many who have not seen it seem to suppose, is a grand landscape garden, one of
> Nature's rarest and most precious mountain temples.....Sad to say, this most pre-
> cious and sublime feature of the Yosemite National Park, one of the greatest of all
> our natural resources for the uplifting joy and peace and health of the people, is in
> danger of being dammed and made into a reservoir to help supply San Francisco
> with water and light, thus flooding it from wall to wall and burying its gardens and
> groves one or two hundred feet deep.[37]

Gifford Pinchot, on the other hand, supported the City of San Francisco's
desire to dam Hetch Hetchy as a source of water for the city. Water shortages
and the great San Francisco fire had alerted the city to the need for a reliable
supply of water. "The benefits to be derived from use as a reservoir far out-
weigh the valley as a place of beauty," Pinchot wrote.[38]

Muir argued that there were other water sources that could meet the
need. "Dam Hetch Hetchy!" he wrote. "As well dam for water tanks the people's cathedrals and churches, for no holier temple has been consecrated by
the heart of man."[39]

The battle raged from 1908 to 1913, with newspaper articles and citizens
all over the country taking sides and making passionate arguments. It was the
first time that the use of nature, of wilderness, became a focus for national
emotion. For Muir and many others all was lost when Woodrow Wilson

signed the act which permitted construction of the dam. But to this Hetch Hetchy is regarded as a pivotal moment in the history of environmen talism in this country, when the US citizenry rose up to do battle on behalf of a beautiful wilderness. To this day, the Hetch Hetchy argument continues, carried on by the very organization which Muir co-founded one hundred and twenty-five years ago: the Sierra Club.

Spring 1997
I longed to collapse. Or to run off to some desolate city where I wouldn't care if the streets were being jackhammered. The reality of my father's death and of Joe now gone, began to sink in. As a sidebar kind of tragedy, in April the cat had collapsed suddenly and mysteriously on the kitchen floor. We picked her up to rush her to the vet, but she died in my arms before we reached the car. It was a mysterious death and even the vet, after examining her body, was unable to explain it. Her remaining kitten--now a young adult--mewed piteously for days, searching for her mother in every closet, every corner, under every piece of furniture.

Short of running away, I thought it might make me feel a bit better to try to organize the basement. "Organize!" my father might say if we were at breakfast or lunch or dinner. "I wonder what the dictionary says about that word?" The upshot of it would be our pulling out the dictionary and going to the O's. "Organize. To form as or into a whole consisting of interdependent or coordinated parts; to give organic structure or character to; to put oneself into a mental competence to perform a task." Perhaps if I organized the basement I would put myself into a mental competence to perform the challenges ahead.

I went downstairs into the dark, old fashioned basement and approached the work bench with trepidation. My father's mind was down here--visible in labels and boxes and jars and a sign admonishing tool users to return their borrowings. Disarray in his once ordered realm had taken over in the past few years since his illness had begun, like weeds in an untended English garden.

There were: dirty tools, pipes, drains, electric air pump, cans of old epoxy, a paper bag with rusty screw eyes and hooks; there was a damp packet of sandpapers of different coarsenesses, a two speed angle drive for polishing, sanding and drilling, an electric engraver. I faced these things as though they were demons buried in the deepest recesses of soul--a holdout of disorder on Fisk Farm.

An ancient jar from before our time labeled "Rottenstone used for top of cherry table," lumber marking chalk, seamless bicycle tube. Household Goop, glue gun, glue sticks, replacement metric screws for cutter blade assembly,

cular saw, skill saw, soldering kit, electric sander. Chaos in-
tract order? So much to do!

; to file comments on the revised plan which CMC submitted
to the w.. ; Board just before the Hearing. To do this we wanted to talk
directly with someone from the Wastewater Management Division about the
new plan.

Merrill telephoned Randy Bean of the Wastewater Management Division
"You know that this plan provides for water from the quarry company's detention pond to be discharged onto Linda Fitch's property."

Mr. Bean explained that this aspect of the plan was a civil matter over
which his office had no jurisdiction. "You'll have to hire a lawyer for that."

A lawyer? On top of everything else we had to deal with? With what
funds?

There was another issue. This had to do with the Army Corps of Engineering (ACE). I knew nothing of the Army Corps but we had noted that in
the ACT 250 application as well as the application for a Wetlands Permit,
CMC had stated that an Army Corps of Engineers Permit would not be
needed for this project. Was this true? We knew now that we had to check
everything out for ourselves.

On May 28, Merrill and I drove an hour south to the town of Essex Junction, for a meeting with a Mike Adams and a David Killy of the Army Corps
of Engineers. In their application, CMC had declared that the operation did
not need an ACE permit. Was that indeed the case?

We were directed to a spacious room with a large table. Merrill spread
out the Engineering Plan and I pulled out the various applications, the original Act 250 application and the application to the Wetlands Office. Both by
this time were somewhat wrinkled with wear and decorated with the occasional coffee stain.

"As you can see in this Wetlands CUD application," I said, "it is stated
that no ACE permit is needed because the project is and I quote, 'an active
work site.' "

"And it's not?" one of them asked.

I shook my head. "Before this Wetlands application was ever written,
both the Act 250 District Commissioner and the Environmental Board ruled
that the Fisk Quarry is abandoned. No active work site."

"Interesting."

"Also, the application indicates that only .21 acres of wetlands will be impacted, but take a look at this Operation Plan," said Merrill spreading out the
oversize document on a table. "Here is a substantial pond about 2 acres in

extent. The pond itself is designated as a Class II Wetland on the Federal Wetlands Inventory Map. Over here to the east are Class II Wetlands. Lake Champlain is right across the road here, about 40 feet from the site. The pond seems to be connected with the lake through fractures in the rock. Here is the extent of the pit that will be excavated over time. Oh and over here? This is Fisk Farm, a state historic site. It's hard to imagine how all of this will not be affected. But we're not really sure what the Army Corps regulations say."

Mr. Adams peered at the map for several moments, then looked up. "Well the Army Corps has jurisdiction over activities involving discharge, dredging or filling in all waters of the United States, including not only navigable waters of the United States, but also inland rivers, lakes, streams and wetlands," he quoted as if by memory. "Also, you say there's a State Historic site next to the quarry property? That automatically makes it eligible for the National Register of Historic Sites. If they need an ACE Permit, that will trigger a review assessing the impact of the quarry operation on the historic Fisk Farm buildings."

"We'll send a letter of intent to the company president," said David Killy, after scrutinizing the plan and glancing at the applications.

Again, there seemed to be no penalty on either permit applicants or those contesting permits for deliberate misrepresentations of fact in the permitting process—or for that matter—violations of those permits once they are received.

Joe had taught us much. Work hard. Let nothing slip by. Always tell the truth. Don't exaggerate. Document everything. We had learned a lot. But we still needed help. Who could replace Joe?

When I was first trying to decide who to call on for help in the early days of the Quarry War, it was a choice between Joe Bivins and Stephanie Kaplan.

"Either one could do it," Randy had written to me. "Joe is really smart. But Stephanie wrote the book." I had finally chosen Joe because I knew him and he knew the case. Since then I had gotten to know Stephanie, a very well known lawyer with a long history of environmental work in Vermont. A close friend of Joe Bivins, she was among the first who arrived at Joe's bedside after his stroke. She sat for hours in vigil with the many friends during the several days that Joe struggled for his life. Would she help us now? Harassed as she was by an overwhelmingly busy schedule, she said yes. A great relief!

And then, another Joe arrived.

Joseph Kennedy from Pittsburgh, PA was a childhood friend of my son, Lyle. His mother, Jean, and I became close friends when our sons were toddlers. It was the late sixties. The shooting of Martin Luther King gave rise to race riots all over the nation including Pittsburgh. Jean invited me to join an organization called the Panel of American Women. This was a national organization that began in Kansas City, Missouri in the 1950s, designed to combat prejudice by enabling people to learn about different races, religions, and cultures. A given panel might consist of a white Protestant, a Catholic, Jew, and African American. In our panel I was the WASP and Jean was black. It was a set format. Each panelist would speak for three minutes about her personal experiences with prejudice in front of various organizations--church groups, Rotary Clubs, and others--then encourage questions from the audience. (As the WASP I always felt like the 'heavy.') Jean and I had many conversations in our respective living rooms, exploring the nature of prejudice. Our toddlers played freely in the other room while their mothers were busily discussing our plans to transform the world. I'm not going to describe the moment when our young sons, trying to figure out how to make chocolate pudding, carried a box of pudding mix all over the house leaving an odd brown powdery trail in their wake.

Beginning in the 1970s young Joseph had started to visit us regularly in Vermont during the summers, coming to feel it as his second home. I regarded him as my third son. Upon graduation from college, Joseph went to Cornell Law School where he became the first African American editor of the Cornell Law Review and after the Bar Exams he joined a prestigious law firm in his home town of Pittsburgh. This year Joe's annual visit took place over the Memorial Day weekend.

Joe had been closely following our battles from afar in Pittsburgh. When Joe Bivins died, though they had never met, Joe Kennedy mourned with us. When he arrived in Vermont he walked out to the quarry cliffs and stared at the rock which had been placed under the apple tree in memory of Joe. It rested between two other boulders which had been transported by Neil Hanna's front end loader. After sitting quietly for awhile he announced, "This is where I want to be buried."

Joe had been under a great deal of pressure at work that year. "I was thinking," he said over dinner. "If I can wangle some time off could I stay here for the summer?"

We thought it was a great idea.

By the end of May with lilacs blooming in clouds of purple and white, with apple trees in transcendent blossom in Halls' orchards, we submitted our objections to the Wetlands Office regarding the change in the Operations Plan which tried to answer a fundamental question: how and where would waste water from the quarrying operation be discharged?

On June 10 yet another site visit by staff from the Wetlands Office took place. The entire office came out, trekking through the quarry and the surrounding fields and woods. Making sure, we supposed, that they all understood the entire situation before making a final decision on whether to issue a permit to CMC.

Throughout June, Carol was busy in the kitchen testing out recipes for chocolate cake, fruit tarts, and tea sandwiches. She refreshed the motley array of little tables that would be set out on the lawn each Sunday afternoon with bright white paint. She swept out the first floor of the "ruins" of the old Fisk mansion where tea and lemonade, cakes and scones would be served between 1:00 and 5:00 on Sunday afternoons.

I was scanning this year's crop of heritage hollyhocks, which appear every year from generations of seed planted by Elizabeth Fisk. They bloom in a rainbow of color from deep red to pale yellows, apricots and pinks during the first week of July. It looked as though we would have a profusion of bloom this year, but the old fashioned roses which formed a screen behind them were beginning to insist on some of the hollyhock space. A ruthless use of sharp clippers was called for.

But however lovely the season, however interesting the summer activities—art shows, music, gatherings of friends and family members promised to be—apprehension hung over us, clouded our days with concern as we waited for the decision of the Wetlands Office. If a wetlands CUD (permit) was awarded to the quarry company, the fight, we believed, would be over. Our arguments, our testimony, our photographs, all pertaining to such issues as habitat, aesthetics, water pollution, if not accepted by the Wetlands Office, would be gravely weakened in our Act 250 fight.

Joe Kennedy returned at the beginning of July. Having long been interested in cooking as an antidote to the rigorous life of the mind in corporate law, he had begun a tradition on high holidays at Fisk Farm of brining and smoking a turkey. The Fourth of July was approaching. This year we invited Stephanie and her boyfriend, Randy and Randy's wife, and many of the Qwarriors to join us for the holiday. On July 2 Joe and I planned a food shopping trip. "I want to stop at the post office to pick up the morning mail. Maybe there will be something from the State," I said as we drove north toward the village.

Post Mistress Phyllis in the tiny white frame Post Office handed me a large pile. Amidst the usual junk—unsolicited advertisements and brightly colored circulars—was an envelope which caught my attention. The return address printed in the left hand corner was the Agency of Natural Resources. Department of Conservation, the Water Quality Division.

"This is it," I said, handing it to Joe who was waiting in the car.
"Give it here," said Joe. "I'll read. You drive. Carefully please."
The letter was addressed to the president of CMC with copies to all of us on the Service List.

"This is to forward the Department's decision to your application for a CUD to extract marble through a portion of a Class Two wetland and buffer zone on West Shore Road in Isle La Motte, Vermont.

I regret to inform you that we are unable to issue a CUD for the proposed activity due to the projected impacts of your proposal on the wetlands and the functions protected by the Vermont Wetland Rules.

You should be aware that this decision may be appealed to the Water Resources Board, should you wish to do so.

Sincerely,
Wallace M. McLean,
Director Water Quality Division

"Oh gosh!" I said.
"Way to go!!" said young Joe.

July 2, 1997
Linda to Qwarriors
We Won! CUD Denied!!!!

Dear Qwarriors All,

Great news! The letter came today. The CUD was denied. In thirteen pages Stephan Syz wrote Findings of Fact and Conclusions of Law which, by and large, were a delight to read. Joe Kennedy and I were on our way to Burlington to shop for Fourth of July food, first stopping by the Isle La Motte Post Office to pick up the mail. He read the thirteen pages to me which lasted until we hit the Winooski exit. Oh Happy Day!!

Joe Kennedy says: "It is indeed a Happy Day. Linda has asked me to summarize and/or excerpt a few highlights from the 13-page long decision.

First, the Water Quality Devision adopted all of our terminology; the wetland areas are referred to as Big Pond, Turtle Pond, Beaver Dam Woods, etc. through-out the decision—just as we have always referred to them.

Second, the Division agreed entirely with our arguments about the seepage of ground water into the quarry through the walls on the north sides of Boulder Pond and Big Pond; it was even noted that these seeps were observed by members of the Division during their last site visit, "even though it was during a dry pe-riod."

Third, there were numerous pointed references to the failure of "The Applicant" to prove any of its assertions regarding the minimal adverse impact that the resumption of quarrying activity would pose.

Fourth, the Division [as Joe Bivins predicted] concluded that the protected functions of the wetlands that would be adversely impacted by the proposed quarrying include at least the following: surface and groundwater protection; fisheries habitat; wildlife and migratory bird habitat; recreational value and economic benefits; and open space and aesthetics.

Finally, the Division announced that it will be launching its own investigation into the illegal scraping that occurred in 1995. Merrill and I are in complete agreement that this decision constitutes an absolute "slam dunk" in our favor and that it is unlikely that "The Applicant" will even bother to appeal it. We will be celebrating our victory this evening with a champagne toast at the monument we have erected to Joe Bivins; the monument overlooks the Quarry that he fought so hard to protect, and we can think of no better tribute to all his efforts and his memory than to share this moment with him."

Thanks for saying it so eloquently, Joe! (Linda speaking.)
Love to all!

July, 1997
The first Sunday Tea garden. Paintings by Vermont artist Valerie Ugro were hanging in the barn. Joe was recruited to help with the hanging. "So how did you ever get involved with Fisk Farm?" Joe asked her

"Thanks for helping with this," said Valerie--a lean outdoorsy type in jeans. Ski instructor in the winter. "I have been artistically, emotionally really...connected to the Fisk Farm and quarry since oh...I think it was 1980, when I first visited Isle La Motte. I was on my bike as per usual. I came across this place by accident. It seemed amazing ...the old stone ruins covered with ivy, the stone cottage, the abandoned overgrown quarry. I wanted to come back. I came back...I think it was 1985 and that second visit inspired me to come back and paint this magical site, the ruins, the old buildings, the quarry. So then in 1995 I heard that there was a new B&B and tea garden and art shows at the Fisk site. I immediately came and asked permission to photograph and sketch scenes around the property. Linda gave me permission to wander around and suggested maybe I would be interested in doing an art show in the horse and carriage barn they were restoring, from the paintings and sketches that I was doing. Last year I finally had compiled enough art work for a show at Fisk Farm which turned out to be an incredible success. So now I'm the official art director of Fisk Farm. I'm using my connections with artists all over Vermont to bring them and their work to the Fisk Farm Horse and Carriage Barn for shows."

"Very cool," said Joe. "You seem to be hooked."

It's not hard," said Valerie. "And you?"

"Since the age of ten," said Joe.

In the middle of the first shining Sunday afternoon, as visitors sat on the lawn overlooking the lake, with their iced teas, their cucumber dill sandwiches, their slices of diabolical chocolate cake, lemon poppyseed cake or fruit tart, Merrill came up to me. "Someone's mowing the quarry field."

My immediate thought. "Oh my gosh. They've read the report from Jeff Parsons talking about the wetland plants and they're trying to destroy the evidence." Jeff Parson was the wetland specialist that we had engaged in April.

"I think I'll just go out there with my camera," Merrill said. When he returned he reported that indeed someone had been mowing the quarry field, which hadn't been mowed for several years. An employee of CMC was present.

Was this an attempt to conceal the evidence of wetlands in the fields adjacent to the quarry property which CMC had proposed to excavate? Maybe they were, indeed, planning to appeal the Wetland Office's verdict.

"I got plenty of pictures," Merrill said.

Originally the entire area had been owned by the Fisks. Many of the old-timers knew the fields behind our house as "Fisk Flats." The Vermont Marble Company had bought a piece of it back in 1919 from Nelson Fisk. The rest was purchased by the Hall family from Elizabeth Fisk's estate in 1935. And then, in 1994, I bought ten acres from Allen Hall and his mother, Mina, along with the old barn. Though "Fisk Flats" was not delineated on Federal Inventory Maps it seemed to us increasingly clear that most, or perhaps all, of what had once been Fisk Flats was a wetland. Jeff Parsons thought the Fisk Quarry field along with my land exhibited signs of being a wetland. In his report of May 19, two days before the Wetland Hearing, he had written "I visited the site in mid-May and the vegetation was not mature so only some initial observations could be made. The field consists of an unidentified monocot, a species of bedstraw, red-osier dogwood, green ash stems, sensitive ferns, a species of horsetail, and an unidentified goldenrod." Andy Mills' hydrology report supported this observation.

In the days following we continued to explore. Throughout July, when we weren't baking, mowing, planting, weeding, hanging art and hanging laundry, we roamed the entire extent of Fisk Flats. We regularly peered into the perc pipes, white plastic pipes sticking some eight inches out of the ground. You could see the water shining in the pipe, always very near the surface. I generally went barefoot to feel the damp or dryness of the soils underfoot. We made observations of the plant life. Much of my 10 acre section of the Fisk Flats field was truly wet. One area on my property was thick with cattails.

"You can see the ditch where the field was drained for farming," Merrill said. "Block up the ditch and there would be cattails all over the place." One question followed us around. What would CMC's next step be? Would they appeal the Wetlands Office decision?

It was a hot summer. Grass that barely fringed over island bedrock was brown. Orange day lilies were on their last lap and the cone flowers on the south side of the ruins looked peaked as did the daisies, fresh last week perhaps but now wishing for rain.

Toward the end of July a group of people stopped by to see the art show in the barn. As usual we provided a tour of the property and then walked across the lawn to show off our spectacular cliff side view of the quarry. One of our visitors identified himself as a staff member of the Water Resources Board and indicated that he was aware of our conflict with CMC. Little did we know that in the days ahead his visit would turn into a problem.

An official looking letter in the mail answered the question that had haunted our days and nights. Would CMC appeal the decision handed down from the Wetlands Office. The letter was from Randy Bean of the Wastewater Division. Back in May we had asked Randy Bean to keep us apprised of any communications from CMC with regard to our case. Now Mr. Bean wrote,

"On May 19,1997 CMC submitted an operations plan which included a Detention Pond and a Sump. Since then I have been informed by CMC not to proceed with their original application as they have decided that given certain problems with their first operations plan, they need to develop an alternative operations plan to deal with water discharge."

So now we knew that CMC would appeal. They would appeal the denial of the CUD by the Wetlands Office to the Water Resources Board, an appeals Board comparable to the Environmental Board for Act 250. Not only would they appeal, but they were thinking about changing their plan. Again!

Joe Kennedy was cutting up an onion for a marinara sauce for supper. He didn't hold back. "Look! They shouldn't be able to get away with this. Clearly an appeal to the Water Resources Board should be based on the plans received and then denied by the State Wetlands Office, not on plans which are in the process of being revised when the appeal is made for heavens sake! We should suggest that this appeal be denied as not ripe for jurisdiction...or something."

"Not ripe for jurisdiction." We thought that had a nice ring to it, but we weren't sure how to proceed. Stephanie was as yet not available. We discussed the issue for days.

"Look," Joe would say, "First they tell John Austin there's no water in the quarry. Then they submit an Act 250 Application saying the quarry fills with water several times a year and they'll have to pump that out in the process pumping part of your pond dry. Then they submit a Wetlands application saying they won't be 'de-watering' the quarry and so no discharge permit is needed for the quarry operation. Then, just before your Hearing on May 22 Wastewater Management says that they need a discharge permit and a plan showing how CMC will deal with water discharge. Ok, so they do that and you guys get hit at the Hearing with an altered Operational Plan. Which shows a Detention Pond and Sump, and an overflow ditch which CMC calls a filter berm bed."

He continued. "Ok and so then you guys get ten whole days for Comment...without Joe Bivins' help I might add. And you say 'Hey we have problems because this will contaminate the protected wetlands in the quarry, will affect Linda's family's part of the pond, and will discharge contaminated water on Linda's field.' OK, so now they are thinking of changing their changed plan? Their Operation Plan is turning into a moving target. If they are going to appeal the decision Wetlands made, on what plan are they planning to appeal. You really should make a motion to dismiss."

I wrote to Mr. Bartlett of the Water Resources Board citing some of the above. I finished my letter by saying: "On these grounds we are considering filing a formal motion to dismiss this Appeal pursuant to Rule 21 of the Water Resources Board Rules of Procedure, but wanted first to informally express our concerns to you."

A pre-conference hearing was scheduled to take place on September 9. Toward the end of August, Stephanie joined the team and talked with us about strategy. "Better get the neighbors lined up again," she said.

September 6, 1997
Linda to the Neighbors

As you know, CMC has appealed the State Wetlands Office's decision to deny the company a Conditional Use Determination (Wetlands Permit). A Hearing will be held by the Water Resources Board on Thursday, September 11, at 10:30 a.m., in the Isle La Motte Town Hall.

It will be helpful if as many neighbors as possible attend that meeting. Even more important, will be a large neighborhood turnout at the official Hearing - which is yet to be scheduled.

Stephanie Kaplan (former Environmental Board lawyer) is assuming Joe Bivins' role as our guide, mentor, and legal counsel. She has suggested that we follow the strategy that Joe established which worked well for us in the Act 250 Hearings; according to that plan Mary Jane Tiedgen and I will file for separate party status as adjoining landowners and Stephanie will file for party status for the neighbors as South Shore Associates. This will give any neighbor who can and wants to do so, an opportunity to testify. The more neighbors who are prepared to testify, the stronger our case will be!!!!

I have also sent a memorandum to the Water Resources Board suggesting that a motion to dismiss the appeal might be in order since we have reason to believe that the original Operational Plan filed with the Wetlands Office is going to be changed somewhat. It remains to be seen whether this will fly, but the Water Resources Board Counsel, Kristina Bielenberg, telephoned the other day to say that the Water Resources Board is now duly notified of this issue and it will be something to be discussed on September 11 at the pre-hearing conference.

Please call if you need further information (or even if you don't). Working together is what has worked for us in the past and is what will help us now!

On September 9, we received a copy of a letter from Kristina Bielenberg, Legal Counsel to the Water Resources Board, to CMC.

"The Chair of the Water Resources Board has asked me to send to you a copy of a filing the Board received on August 22, 1997. This is a party status petition from Linda Fitch. Since the Chair will discuss the procedural status of this appeal at the pre-hearing conference, it would be helpful if you were prepared to respond to Ms. Fitch's allegation that you are pursuing a new Operational Plan before the Agency of Natural Resources and that therefore this appeal should not go forward."

Things were never easy. Ever. On the same day another copy of a letter arrived.

William Bartlett, Executive Officer, Water Resources Board to Kristina Bielenberg, Legal Counsel Water Resources Board

I am writing to disclose the fact that I paid a casual visit to the Fisk Farm Bed and Breakfast on July 27, 1997. On that occasion I met and talked with Linda Fitch and a number of her friends and patrons. This visit came about when myself and two friends, after an afternoon of boating on Lake Champlain using a nearby public access area on the west shore of Isle La Motte, stopped at the Fisk Farm to visit their Art Gallery. At the time of my visit I was aware that CMC was considering appealing the denial of their Conditional Use Determination, but the appeal had not yet been filed.

During the course of this visit my companions and I, as well as other visitors, were given a quick, informal tour of the buildings and grounds of Fisk Farm, including a brief visit to a vantage point overlooking a portion of the quarry owned by CMC.

During this visit, which lasted less than one hour, there was a general discussion of the history of the buildings and site. When the discussion first touched on the fact that there were plans to reactivate a nearby quarry I mentioned my association with the Vermont Water Resources Board and requested that there be no discussion in my presence of CMC'S plans for reactivation of the quarry or of any issues related to those plans or the likely appeal of the company's denial of a Conditional Use Determination. This request was respected throughout my visit.

I do not believe that my casual visit to the Fisk Farm on July 27, or the general discussions that occurred during the course of that visit are in any way improper or compromise my possible participation in this proceeding as staff to the Water Resources Board. However, I would ask that you disclose this information to all prospective parties at the September 11, 1997 pre-hearing conference."

What effect would this have, we wondered.

On September 11 we convened again at the Isle La Motte Town Hall for a pre-hearing conference regarding CMU's appeal of the Wetlands Office denial of the CUD permit. Present were Stephanie representing South Shore Associates, Mary Jane, and myself. Because this case was an appeal of the decision by the Wetland Office of the Agency of Natural Resources (ANR), they were now parties defending their decision. They would add their evidence supporting this decision to ours. On this day they were represented by their attorney, Jon Groveman.

The cast of characters from CMC was, of course, present. This was not the crowded venue that we faced in May. And yet it was fraught with tension. Would we be able to make progress on our hope of having this appeal dismissed?

But other issues arose. Chair Davies brought up the letter with information that Mr. Bartlett had visited Fisk Farm in late July and asked the Board's Legal Counsel to read into the record the disclosure statement made by William Bartlett, Executive Officer of the Board.

"Are there any objections to Mr. Bartlett serving as staff to this case?" asked Chair Davies.

No objections were raised.

"In that case we shall proceed. There will be an opportunity in the future for filings of any written objections."

Chair Davies then noted that Party Status was granted to Linda Fitch and her mother, Violet Fitch, to Mary Jane Tiedgen (as adjoining landowners) and to SSA to be represented by Stephanie Kaplan. The Agency of Natural Resources was granted party status by right.

"Mr. Chairman," said the lawyer for CMC. "I object to the granting of status to the South Shore Associates on the basis that SSA has failed to demonstrate that its interest cannot be adequately represented by existing parties, that is the Fitches, Mary Jane Tiedgen, and the Agency of Natural Resources."

"Objection overruled," said the Chair, "on the basis that the members of this organization, some of whom are adjoining property owners, have interests which may be distinct from those of other parties (i.e.: potential effects of proposed activity on their water supplies and on specific, wetland values benefiting their properties). I also note that, unlike the Fitches and Ms. Tiedgen the SSA is represented by counsel. However, I advise the above mentioned parties to coordinate the presentation of their case as much as possible."

"Mr. Chair," said the lawyer for CMC. "I have received a communication from Representatives Thomas Alberico and Fred Maslack requesting party status."

Good heavens! These were the lawmakers behind Bill # H266 to exempt marble quarries from Act 250. We had attended a hearing regarding that bill the morning after Joe's death.

However, Chair Davies declined to grant party status to the representatives. "Would the parties identify any other preliminary issues?" he asked.

I stood up. "As I mentioned in my party status application, because there has been some indication that CMC is considering a change in its Operation Plan, I question as to whether this appeal should go forward. We are thinking about filing a Motion to Dismiss."

Chair Davies looked at CMC's lawyer. "Are you prepared to respond to Ms. Fitch's statement?"

The lawyer stood up and cleared his throat. "I will discuss with my client whether he is prepared to proceed with the present appeal based on the plan submitted on May 19."

Andrew Rauvogel, Counsel for the Agency of Natural Resources, spoke up. "We feel that if the Appellant is planning to redesign the project, a remand to the ANR would be appropriate."

Chair Davies looked at CMC's lawyer. "Your client has until October 10 to decide whether to proceed with the appeal as originally written or to remand the proposal to ANR for jurisdiction. In the meantime," he continued to all of us, "if the appeal goes forward a site visit for the full Water Resources

Board will be scheduled for November 4. After that we will ask for pre-filed and rebuttal testimony from all the parties, and will issue a schedule for the same."

The hearing was over.

Fall was well on its way. In the morning the rising sun now shone over the quarry through the office window over my right shoulder as I sat at my computer. The garden was still yielding, with green and purple basil still lush, the ground covered with red and green tomatoes, and flowers still bright and luxuriant against the grey stone of the workshop and Dr. Whitcomb's monument. Joe Kennedy had returned to Pittsburgh. With summer folk gone the island was quiet, with only an occasional car passing by.

In September there was a day of high excitement when I received a postcard from my younger son, Bruce, and his girlfriend, Tobi. Unbeknownst to all their parents they had gone to the Bahamas. "We're having a wonderful vacation," they wrote. "We'll see you when we get back from our honeymoon." Honeymoon! My son had gotten married. There was a flurry of phone calls between parents and grandparents as we all tried to absorb this momentous news. Tobi's father said, "I always said that if she eloped I would pay for the ladder. Guess I won't even have a ladder bill." It was a happy moment.

All seemed quiet for the moment with regard to the Quarry War, but if you listened quietly there was an almost imperceptible sound, like carpenter ants gnawing at the foundations. Though I hesitate to make an analogy between carpenter ants and a representative of the Vermont legislature...

October 9, 1997
Linda to Quarriors

Dear Lawyers, witch, warlock, and others....
Recent development is that Rep. Alberico has been writing to Stephan Syz of Wetlands expressing his "deep concern about the cavalier attitude of people who break the law by trespassing on legally posted property, and a state system that accepts as legal evidence any information gathered in this illegal manner!!!!"

On September 30 he (Alberico) wrote to William Davies, the Water Resources Board Chair, complaining about a disclosure which William Bartlett (Executive Director of the Water Resources Board) made at the pre-conference hearing. The Hearing order stated "The Chair asked the Board's Legal Counsel to read into the record a disclosure statement made by William Bartlett, Executive Officer of the Board. In that statement, Mr. Bartlett disclosed the circumstances of a brief visit he had made to the Fisk Farm and Fisk quarry site in the company of Linda Fitch and others just prior to the filing of the present appeal." Alberico goes on in his letter to say, "I questioned the appellant (that would be CMC's president) as to the request to visit the site. He stated that he did not give permission to anyone to visit the site!"

Based on all of this, William Bartlett has recused himself in a memo to William Boyd, Chair of Water Resources which I also received today. It states in part, "It appears that Mr. Alberico is under the impression that I trespassed on quarry company property to observe its quarry operations in Isle la Motte. I can understand his confusion given the wording of the pre-hearing conference Report and Order at page 2. However, as is evident from the content of my Disclosure Statement, dated September 9, 1997, I made my observation of the quarry from a vantage point which I believed to have been on property owned by the Fitches. Indeed, I have no recollection of crossing a fence line, of passing a 'no trespassing' sign, or of observing any landmark which would suggest that I had left the Fitch property and entered upon land owned by CMC."

In return I wrote a letter to Representative Alberico saying in part,

I want to assure you that Mr. Bartlett did not visit the Fisk Quarry Site, but simply viewed it from a vantage point on my property which is very easy to do since the quarry site abuts my lawn and my entire southern boundary of some 500 feet. Indeed some of the quarry pond is on my family's property which the company did not realize when an Act 250 application was first filed; evidently the owner had not had a survey done at that time and was planning to drain a pond partially owned by my family.

The quarry site also abuts the entire northern boundary of my neighbors' property, Mary Jane Tiedgen and her father Carl Williams. In fact, according to several surveys, her boundary actually crosses the quarry floor on which, for a period of time, CMC had stored a pile of wooden pallets.

All the neighbors along the West Shore Road would be very pleased if you would pay us a visit. Perhaps when you saw how close the quarry site is to our homes you would better understand the depth of our concern about the proposed operation of CMC. The plan proposes to quarry not only the wetlands but also (according to the Operational Plan presented to the Agency of Natural Resources on May 19, 1997) to clear cut a woodland, strip off the top soil on some twelve acres of land and create an entirely new twelve acre pit filled with noisy machinery in the midst of a quiet residential neighborhood of retirement homes, on the shores of Lake Champlain. The project as outlined in that plan also proposes to discharge water from CMC's detention pond/sump directly onto my adjoining field.

I appreciate your concern on behalf of the company. We would appreciate the opportunity to share our perspectives with you as well."

I wasn't particularly surprised when the Representative did not write back. But at about the same time, the following letter did show up.

October 9, 1997
CMC Lawyer to Kristina L. Bielenberg, Esq. Legal Counsel, Water Resources
Board
Re: CMC
This letter will confirm that the Applicant is not going to redesign the project and
will pursue the Appeal on the present design.

At the time we didn't imagine the extent to which this letter would eventually
change our lives.

16. Site Visit
"Let us speak courteously, deal fairly, and keep ourselves armed and ready."
Theodore Roosevelt, San Francisco, CA, May 13, 1903

THEODORE ROOSEVELT MAY HAVE COME DOWN ON THE SIDE
of Gifford Pinchot on the issue of Hetch Hetchy—the pragmatic, utilitarian
side. But he also shared the poetic, spiritual perspective of John Muir. For
Roosevelt as for Muir, wilderness was a source of uplift and solace, of healing.
And in the end his presidency was a victory for both conservation and environmentalism. Inspired by the poet Muir, buttressed in the halls of policy
making by the forester Pinchot, and driven by his own love of nature, when all
was said and all was done, Roosevelt had created four National Game Preserves, five National Parks, eighteen National Monuments, twenty-four Reclamation Projects, and fifty-one Federal Bird Reservations, and one hundred
National Forests. By the end of his presidency two hundred and thirty-million
acres in all, were set aside for the people of the United States.

Now that William Bartlett was no longer in charge, the Chair of the Water
Resources Board, Bill Davies, was coordinating the appeal process. One of the
requirements of an appeal process to the Water Resources Board (not surprisingly) was a site visit which, we learned, would take place at the Fisk Quarry
on November 4, 1997. Chair Davies was not leaving anything to chance; he
would brook no time-wasting on this visit. CMC and the parties were required to agree among ourselves, well ahead of time, on an exact schedule for
the tour; we were to agree on sites to be visited, why, and the length of time
the visit at each site would require. Negotiations for our side fell to me.

In the midst of the autumn glory on Isle La Motte, I spent hours on the
phone, with a young woman lawyer, Katie Buchanan, from the office of
CMC's lawyers, discussing an itinerary for the site visit. After a great deal of
genteel argument, we finally established between ourselves a plan; it involved
the determination of nine so-called stations. We would spend ten minutes at
the edge of Big Pond observing "habitat, vegetative and hydrogeologic fea-

tures." Station two would be the proposed location for an office trailer, portable toilets and employee parking. Next, was the proposed site for quarried rubblestone and fuel storage. Next go to Boulder Pond, etc. etc. There were nine of these stations. This itinerary had to be completed by October 31 for a teleconference involving representatives of all the parties. CMC insisted on eliminating such points as "Beaver Lodge, duck nesting site, signs of habitat for American Woodcock, indications of karst, rock fractures, etc. from the site visit plan, arguing for language that was more neutral.

I emailed a lawyer for the Agency of Natural resources. "If this draft is acceptable to the Board and to ANR, Fitch, Tiedgen and SSA are prepared to accept it essentially as it is."

Nov 2, 1997

Rain poured out of the sky, shrouding everything in wet grey. It was all about water; rain pounded on the roof; pond sized puddles formed across the island; water gushed from culverts into the lake. It was a wet, wet world and it was two days before the site visit. Our Site Visit Agenda had been approved by our two expert witnesses and the Agency of Natural Resources, now testifying on our side. I had just enough time to get it into the mail and fax copies to CMC.

Stephanie was concerned that two of our key expert witnesses—Dan and Andy—would not be with us during the site visit. Dan had gotten a job in California and wouldn't be available for this next stage of our battle. Andy couldn't get away from New Jersey. Stephanie wanted to find replacement witnesses, experts in the fields of wetlands and wildlife biology and hydrology. She suggested one Mary Capkanis, a wetland ecologist and biologist from New Hampshire. For hydrology she proposed a Steve Revell from Lincoln, Vermont.

On the evening before the site visit, Mary Capkanis arrived, planning to stay for dinner and the night to be present in plenty of time for the next day's doings. It had been a wild day with rain pounding on the roof. The winds howled into the evening as we drank a bottle of sauvignon blanc and ate a large bowl of pasta with basil—still green in our garden.

Dawn was quiet. After the raging weather of the past two days, the quarry gods had given us a warm and gentle day with sunshine and no wind. In the early morning Mary Capkanis and I went out to the quarry, walking around each of nine stations which had been painstakingly negotiated in the previous weeks. Mary had a wonderful eye. "Oh look, there's a Northern Harrier. And this whole meadow could be habitat for snipe."

As we reached the grey and gold quarry field a lanky figure sauntered toward us. This turned out to be another of our new expert witnesses, hydrologist Steve Revell. He had already visited the quarry and read Andy's reports, but today had come early to check out the site again. It's hard to express the comfort I felt from both of them, as we all stood in the field early that morning.

The Chair of the Water Resources Board had told us that the parties should get together and conduct a "rehearsal" of the proceedings in the morning, prior to the official Site Visit with the Water Resources Board in the afternoon. At the allotted time of ten o'clock, Steve Revell, Mary Capkanis, Merrill and I walked into the quarry. We were surprised and disturbed to see six or seven pickup trucks parked on the quarry floor next to Turtle Pond. A number of men were standing about; several others sat in their trucks. CMC's biologist was there with rubber hip boots, pick up truck and barking black Labrador retriever. Very Vermont!

The parked trucks seemed to be part of a staged set designed to look like a working quarry site, instead of the beautiful wetland and wildlife habitat which we had described in months of testimony. Steve Revell who is tall and fairly rugged looking himself, murmured something about "the intimidation factor."

In a few minutes the Agency for Natural Resources/Wetland folks walked in, having parked their vehicles outside the quarry. These included Cathy O'Brien, Stephan Syz, Tom Willard, and Andy Raubvogel, ANR lawyer. It was a great relief to see them. Now they were part of our team.

This motley group waited a good forty-five minutes (I, at least, feeling a good bit of tension) for CMC's president and his lawyer. They finally arrived at quarter of eleven along with two members of the Vermont legislature who were cosponsoring Bill H266 as part of their campaign to exempt marble quarries from Vermont's environmental legislation (Act 250) and probably from Wetland Regulations as well. The Fisk Quarry was going to be their case study.

What was the next step?

Nobody had liked the admonition from the Water Resources Board Chair, Bill Davies, during the teleconference call the day before. "Choose one spokesperson for the entire site visit," he had ordered. We had all, South Shore Associates, Mary Jane and myself, ANR and CMC, wanted our own spokespersons. However it was quickly agreed that Cathy O'Brien would act as a neutral scribe and spokesperson. We decided that we would move from Station to Station of the Site Visit as per the negotiated agenda, and all the parties would indicate to Cathy what they wanted her to point out at the site visit in the afternoon.

Unexpectedly, this worked out. At Station One down by the scraped shoreline, our team pointed out features such as cattails, red osier dogwood, soft rush, water stains on the cliff, groundwater seeps, fractures in the rock, sphagnum moss, and what we argued were wetland violations by CMC which had started work on the site in 1995. We indicated the scrapings of dirt, vegetation, and rock which lay in piles along the water's edge of Big Pond.

Stephan Syz of ANR pointed out the different wildlife habitats of the area. CMC pointed out the man made aspect of the wetland features, and tried to figure out ways of demonstrating that the piles of scraped materials were very old. What they had not yet seen were photographs of the fresh scraped piles which we took right after the work was done. We planned to submit those as part of our pre-filed testimony.

So we went through all the stations and somehow managed to get a list which contained everyone's "significant" features. We barely finished this at 1:00. Everyone then rushed off for a quick lunch.

Our group went to Fisk Farm where our lawyer, Stephanie Kaplan, had just arrived. There ensued a rapid heating of chili, eaten standing up in the kitchen, while we discussed the morning happenings, then off we went to St. Anne's Shrine where a large room was the appointed site for a brief meeting among all the parties. After that we returned to the quarry for the main event. This time the five members of the Water Resources Board were present. The Board Chair had warned us not to speak with any of the Board members and nobody was to speak at any of the stations except for Cathy O'Brien, who was the agreed upon spokesperson.

There are outstanding memories. Station Three was Boulder Pond. We watched the opposition biologist wade out in rubber hip boots ostensibly to prove how shallow the pond was. "No more than six inches deep," he had said in his testimony, but in a moment found himself splashing about in water a good bit over his knees. Merrill and Stephanie were shaking with not very well suppressed laughter.

CMC had requested a station which took us back in the PSS1C Wetland just east of the quarry woods. They were challenging Cathy O'Brien's previous delineation of the area as a wetland. They had hoped to prove that that it was a dry area and the only reason that it was ever wet, was because of a blocked drainage ditch in the area.

Mary Capkanis and I however were quietly pleased. We had been back in the area earlier that morning where I had assumed it would look as usual with its marshy soil, sensitive fern, and other wetland vegetation. But in the early morning we discovered that the area had transformed into a veritable lake stretching eastward through the woods as far as the eye could see. This was due, we realized, to the uproarious rain during the previous two days.

As we hiked toward the area through the quarry woods, CMC's biologist started to say, "Can you imagine anyone thinking of this as a wetland..." And then we all came upon the great lake of shining waters. We looked at the ditch. The entire group was able to see water flowing merrily through the ditch, proving not only that the ditch was not blocked, but that if it weren't for the ditch the entire quarry woods would be a vast, shallow, and permanent lake.

We then returned to the quarry woods to the next station, a perc pipe that someone, perhaps from CNC, had once installed in the ground. The herd found themselves slogging precariously over mossy logs and through pools of water and mud, much to the dismay of CMC's expert witness and lawyers who had been testifying to dry conditions. The perc pipe in the woods was overflowing with water, quite close to the eastern boundary of the proposed quarry excavation. Then we headed to the quarry field--another proposed site for excavation--where three perc pipes were brimming over with water. The shoes of all not only squished but literally splashed as one walked through the meadow.

Since the representatives of ANR had never been on this part of the quarry property they were very interested in this as evidence of our wetland field theory. I told Andy Raubvogel, ANR lawyer that our wetland expert, Jeff Parsons, had done borings during his visit in May and had found hydric soil (a wetland indicator) throughout the field. Andy asked me if we were going to submit this in prefiled testimony. "Absolutely," I said.

Throughout the Site Visit, one of the legislators had been videotaping the proceedings, presumably as evidence to submit in support of his proposed bill. His colleague was forever wandering off on his own. As we approached West Shore Road and the end of the site visit we pointed out one of the beaver lodges which had been built where Big Pond borders the road. Suddenly and unexpectedly the legislator clambered down the roadside embankment, and made his way onto the beaver lodge. To our amazement he started poking at it with a stick, and then climbed on top--perhaps to be sure that it wasn't man-made? The sturdy structure of mud and sticks almost looked as though it were going to give way under the weight of the Vermont lawmaker. I wished for my camera.

As November unfolded, the world outside became soft and grey, trees black against a grey blue sky, grey blue lake; frosted grass, stiff and white, crackled underfoot: my foot, dog foot, cat foot. In the November days sunrise had migrated from the northeast fields to the southeast quarry, painting quarry sky with stripes of rose. A skim of ice covered Big Pond, all quarry life gone into or under and out of sight. Five leftover geese rocketed across the sky heading south; their rackety cries momentarily breaking the silence of the early morning world.

With the site visit behind us we turned to our next tasks. This was the submission by all parties and witnesses of pre-filed and rebuttal testimony. Initial testimony was to be submitted by CMC by 4:30 on the 17th of December. Following that, the deadline for our first round of testimony was January 16. Then would come rebuttal testimony first from them on January 30 and then from us. on February 13. Evidentiary objections were due on February 23 and a second pre-hearing conference would be held after March 3. Much typing lay ahead.

With the coming of December I remembered the extent to which the Main House on the property is not tightly bound together. Heat sifts happily to the great out of doors through the walls, the roof, the windows, drawing in the frigid air of Vermont winters. Nights of sleeping in altogether unheated bedrooms are made barely possible with electric blankets. Allow a few minutes of electric heater to take off the chill while one dresses or undresses. Dive into bed. Read a little while though the fingers start getting stiff with cold. Then turn off light and sleep in warm bed albeit with cold nose.

One day it snowed heavily. I had been shopping in Plattsburgh, NY across the lake and it was with some difficulty that I drove through blinding white, and made it back to Isle La Motte without driving into the lake. It seemed that for now, I should go back to Princeton. There I could start to work on sorting out the innumerable tasks that lay ahead.

Back in Princeton were signs of Christmas. Red velvet bows were tied on the lampposts of downtown Palmer Square. In my favorite coffee house, a toddler in her pink snow suit was chewing on a gingerbread cookie and "We Three Kings" issued forth from the cafe sound system. An older man hobbled in with cane and solicitous wife. He sat down and reached for his leg, picking it up and tucking it under the table while his wife went to order two caring coffees and a glazed doughnut to share.

We do have our moments when the light shines, it seems. Perhaps it is all we have. I think of Vermont nights that are so black that stars, most times invisible, are revealed in wondrous skies that stretch beyond our seeking

"We Three Kings" ended. "There are times," someone was saying on the radio, "when a little bit of light can ignite everything in the world."

17. Where the Wild Things Are

"Birds should be saved for utilitarian reasons; and, moreover, they should be saved
because of reasons unconnected with dollars and cents...
The extermination of the passenger-pigeon meant that mankind was just so much poorer...
And to lose the chance to see frigate birds soaring in circles above the storm,
or a file of pelicans winging their way homeward across the crimson afterglow of the
sunset, or a myriad of terns flashing in the bright light of midday as they hover
in a shifting maze above the beach--why, the loss is like the gallery of the
masterpieces of the artists of old time."
Theodore Roosevelt, "A Book-Lover's Holidays in the Open" (1916)

ROOSEVELT'S TERM OF OFFICE ENDED in 1908, upon which he was succeeded by his friend, William Taft. TR had every confidence that his hard won conservation policies would continue. Roosevelt's friend Gifford Pinchot, passionate defender of conservation and the first Chief of Roosevelt's newly constituted United States Forest Service, continued on under Taft. However he soon found himself working in an administration whose ideas were increasingly hostile to conservation, especially of the great western forests.

For Secretary of the Interior, Taft replaced conservationist James Garfield with Richard Ballinger, friend of the business elite whose ideas might be summarized in one of his speeches: "You chaps who are in favor of this conservation program are all wrong. You are hindering the development of the West. In my opinion, the proper course is to divide it up among the big corporations and let the people who know how to make money out of it get the benefits of the circulation of money."[40] Eventually Pinchot himself was fired by Taft. The grand dream of conservation, one of TR's greatest legacies, was endangered.

The battle of Hetch Hetchy continued through the Taft Administration and was lost, in Muir's eyes, in 1913 under Woodrow Wilson's presidency. Congress voted 43–25 (with 29 abstentions) to allow the Hetch Hetchy dam on federal land. John Muir died the following year, believing that he had failed in his life's work.

But on August 25, 1916, President Woodrow Wilson signed the act creating the National Park Service, a new federal bureau in the Department of the Interior responsible for protecting the 35 national parks and monuments then managed by the department and those yet to be established. It protected over 90 million acres as wilderness areas. John Muir would never know that his legacy had survived him.

January 1998

THE GREAT ICE STORM OF JANUARY 1998, stretched from northern New York to central Maine. The national press reported that massive damage resulted in millions living in the dark and cold for days and weeks. Throughout the night people were trapped in their houses without power, without heat, without water. Huge trees encased in ice were toppling over—on houses, roads; it was like an ice war. Isle La Motte, Vermont was Ground Zero.

"What's going on? We're hearing all these terrible reports in the news." I called Merrill from Princeton. Here in Princeton the early part of January had been mild, with grey skies and light drizzle.

Merrill, living in the Main House at Fisk Farm, still had phone service on Isle La Motte. "It's just this amazing natural disaster. First it started raining and then the ice started freezing around the trees. Pretty soon the entire island was just...all the trees were covered with this heavy, heavy ice. They started breaking. It sounded like gunfire Almost every single tree was topped off. All kinds of trees went down. There was even lightning. I got my pickup truck started and I tried to go around the south end but by Turners' driveway there were trees down every which way. I had my chainsaw and kept trying to get the trees cut away so I could get through. But there was constant crashing. Like explosions of sound. Branches and trees were falling in front of me and in back of me so I couldn't go forward or backward. Finally I just tried driving across the fields and coming in through the back fields, without even going on the roads. There wasn't much snow. Just ice.

"There's a whole tangled mess of trees and ice around the quarry," he said. "The sumac grove on your property next to the quarry was leveled. And the power company guys have cut so many trees when they were reinstalling telephone poles, you can see right into the quarry. Of course it's great to see the quarry but any arguments CMC had about vegetative screening are out the window."

"What about the view from West Shore Road," I asked.

"Lots of broken trees. If these trees die and it seems almost impossible that they won't, then the view will be completely open to the public. I think we'd better contact the Water Resources Board on this. It's going to change something. Anyway, I'm going to drive down to Connecticut to buy a lot of generators. You can't get any around here and the power is going to be out for a long time."

As Isle La Motte struggled with this emergency, I alternated between the telephone seeking news and my paper covered dining room table in Princeton. CMC had submitted their prefiled testimony and list of experts in December as ordered. I needed to get all the prefiled testimony from our witnesses and experts typed up, formatted and mailed to Vermont.

Also on my list of worries, my little dog Shasta had, at the age of 13, developed a large lump on her body. A stalwart Qwarrior herself, she was now spending her days curled up by my typing chair, occasionally looking up anxiously as my fingers flew over the keyboard and I tried to absorb what it was that I was typing.

Mary Jane and I had received Party Status to represent ourselves. South Shore Associates, to be represented by Stephanie, had received Party Status over the initial objections of the opposition lawyers. Anyone who submitted testimony had also to be at the final Hearing. We had lost our Motion to allow Dan, who was now working at Point Reyes, a National Park and Bird Sanctuary in California, to testify by teleconference, so in essence we lost part of our marvelous bird list. But Mary Capkanis was now with us, so with Mary Jane, Merrill, and Mary, wildlife habitat was pretty well covered. Andy Mills said he would come from New Jersey to testify. But just in case, we had Steve Revell to cover hydrology. Otherwise, all the original Qwarriors were ready to go.

Merrill called again. "It snowed the other day so the ground is pretty white. But you won't believe what just happened. I was working at my job in Alburgh and I came back to Fisk Farm for lunch. I noticed a car went by as I was having lunch. Of course I'm always looking out to see if anything is happening at the quarry. So when I finished lunch I drove south so I would pass the quarry entrance on my way back to work. So then I see that there's two vehicles parked there and some footprints in the snow. I looked in and there's these two guys walking over toward the Boulder Pond area. They had several ice augers...you know...for fishing...where you drill a hole through the ice? I knew immediately what they were up to. You remember that their wildlife expert stated in his testimony that Boulder Pond freezes solid in the winter. They were going to drill through the ice and try to prove there was no water under the ice and so no fish could live there.

"So later after work I came back and snuck into the quarry. I followed the tracks to Boulder Pond. I saw that they had drilled some holes in the ice...their footprints were all over the place. I saw a disturbed area in the snow on Boulder Pond - about maybe the size of a dining room table. And so I sort of brushed the snow aside and saw where they had drilled some holes in the ice and I saw where they had filled in the holes with snow. I dug the snow out of the holes and I had my tape measure with me. I measured the depth of the ice and how much water there was under the holes. Every single hole had water. It's been really cold this winter but each hole had water in it. So then I made a little diagram as to where the holes were and I'll testify to that. And I took pictures. What can they say? The only thing they can say is that I was in there illegally. But they still haven't put up 'no trespassing' signs."

As I received copies of testimony from everyone, both faxed and verbal, I typed everything into the prerequisite format. It had to be typed with numbered lines; on the first page in the right corner you had to type Water Resources Board / in Re: CMC/Docket no. CUD-97-06/ Exhibit # LF #1 or 2 or whatever. Thousands of words. Thank goodness for computers. Even those in 1998. A great advantage for me was the opportunity to assimilate much of the testimony.

Princeton was cold and grey, but Isle La Motte was buried under ice. My plans for going to Vermont to finish up with all the testimony, exhibits, and CVs for our witnesses, were going down the tubes.

"What am I going to do?" I said to Stephanie over the phone. "Our deadline for getting all this stuff in is January 16 and it's now the 12th. Also, Merrill says that the ice storm has knocked out trees and branches which has made a big change to views into the quarry. We really need to deal with that somehow."

"Well, it's hard to see how you can finish up the work on Isle La Motte," said Stephanie. "I'll file for an extension of time. Keep your fingers crossed. Also, why don't you add a letter to your pre-filed testimony asking that the ice storm damage be considered."

Stephanie requested an extension "due to last week's devastating ice storm during which much of the power on Isle La Motte has been knocked out thereby impeding contact with witnesses and also travel to the island to complete work needed to prepare testimony." We were granted an extension of a week.

By January 21 my dining room table was covered with great piles of testimony--typed, copied, collated and ready to be driven to Vermont. It was due in Montpelier at 4:30 on the 23rd so I decided I'd better drive it to Vermont and deliver it all by hand.

Shasta was looking worse and worse. The bump on her stomach had turned into a large oozing sore. I took her to the vet. He shook his head. "It's cancer and nothing can be done about it. The kindest thing would be to put her to sleep." He had told me this previously but I had been putting it off as long as possible. I stood next to her while the vet gave her an injection. I watched her fall asleep, peacefully, on the table. And wept all the way to Vermont.

February 1998

Back in Princeton. Sunny. Crisp cold. Snow crackle cold. The cat padded down the stairs, entering the living room checking on my state of being, checking perhaps to see if I was being calmly catlike or did I, as per usual, have unnecessary mental energy streaming out of my being, clouding the living room with a kind of grey smog, screening the present moment from all my senses. No comforting small dog at my feet.

The writing of Direct and Rebuttal Testimony was, in essence, a duel if not a battle. Testimony was in the form of questions and answers. Written arguments flew back and forth between the parties and the expert witnesses as in warfare of old. This time around, of course, the Wetlands Office of the Agency of Natural Resources was "on our side," arguing in support of their decision not to grant a wetlands permit for CNC's current operation plan. John Austin, wildlife biologist from the Vermont Division of Fish and Wildlife also submitted testimony. For us, every glimmer of support felt like the cavalry charging over the brow of the hill to the rescue.

CMC had fired its guns first with Direct Testimony in December. CMC's biologist and wetlands expert focused on two small wetland areas, Boulder Pond and Beaver Dam Woods.

"I am not a casual observer of wildlife," he wrote in his testimony. "I am a Certified Wildlife biologist with a Professional Development Certificate and certified in habitat evaluation procedures by the U.S. Fish and Wildlife Servoce. These are not wetland areas of any value." He "had never seen great blue herons, green backed herons, deer, resident muskrats. ...We neither caught nor saw any fish or minnows on either occasion. ...There is no fresh sign of beaver. The affected portion of the wetland has several tiny abandoned beaver dams on it. Since they were abandoned, approximately a decade or more ago, it is impossible to say whether they supported beaver activity for two or more consecutive years. In the two years of our observations, no fresh beaver sign has been observed. The tadpoles which enter the fall all die from freezing for the same reasons that minnows die in the area. As demonstrated in my site walk on November 4, 1997, there is no soft substrate for amphibians to burrow into; hence they all freeze solid and die in the winter."

The beaver dams to which he referred were those which Cathy O'Brien had pointed out to me in 1995 when she visited the quarry for the first time. At that time she had also pointed out fresh "beaver chew."

CMC's biologist continued. "At its best the opponents grossly overstated the value of the fisheries in this portion of the wetland. At worst they purposefully misled the Agency of Natural Resources. Either of these outcomes leads one to question the rigorousness with which the project opponents deal with all other scientific facts regarding this site and the application of ecological principles to their analysis."

We all shot back with our testimony. There were hundreds of pages from all the Qwarriors, along with photographs, reports and letters serving as exhibits. The following are brief samples from the outpouring of laboriously typed words.

In my initial testimony I wrote: "Family, friends and guests at Fisk Farm, often start the day by sitting in the early morning on the quarry cliffs that border our lawn and meadow. We have frequently seen ducks swimming on Big Pond, flying in and out of the quarry, and hiding in the shallows. I have also seen them in what is known in the neighborhood as Turtle Pond. The most spectacular bird for me is the Great Blue Heron. Throughout the spring, summer and fall you see herons flying in and out of the quarry a number of times in any one day. I would say that if you approach very quietly more often than not you can see one or two herons feeding in Big Pond. They are easily startled, and fly away when they become aware of human presence. Over the years neighbors as well as guests, tourists and cyclists along the West Shore Road have all watched with great delight the beavers which have inhabited the quarry property. Big Pond is the site of two lodges. In the summer and fall evenings of 1994 and 1995, Merrill Hemond and I watched six beavers swimming in a kind of wonderful dance through Big Pond. The trails of moonlight in the wake of their paths was a magical sight which I will never forget."

CMC's expert witness was having none of it. "With regard to the testimony, for example, of Ms. Fitch, I believe this is yet another attempt to avoid the scientific facts by painting an emotional view of the significance of the affected wetland. However heartfelt to her, I believe her testimony distorts the real values which are affected by the proposal under appeal...The beaver lodges observed are old and abandoned and are in the Class II open water wetland which the applicant is going to great pains to protect (as already described in the revised mining plan). The abandoned, failed beaver dams in the

AFFECTED wetland (that which is to be impacted directly) are nonfunctional."

"From the time I was old enough to remember," wrote Mary Jane, "we trapped and netted and fished for minnows in the Fisk Quarry. There are shiners, Johnny roaches, sticklebacks and catfish in the Big Pond. Also I've seen some kind of minnows in Boulder Pond. I spent hours in the quarry each day watching frogs, snakes and salamanders. After I was grown and married I would take my daughter to the quarry. When she stayed for weeks in the summer with my parents she would spend hours in the quarry as I did observing wildlife. There are large bullfrogs whose call you can hear resonating off the rock cliffs, large green and brown frogs, leopard frogs, tree frogs and peepers. There are huge garter snakes and milk snakes living in the quarry.

"Once while I was looking at the minnows in Boulder Pond, that would have been in September or October, I suddenly saw what I thought was a rock that I could actually step on, except that suddenly it moved. I picked up a stone and dropped it in the water and then I saw that it was a snapping turtle which then swam out into the middle of the pond."

Neil wrote, "Everyone went in there to get minnows to fish, the Grants, the Masaleks, the Williams. There was one place in there called Billy Goat Hill; people would throw their minnow nets out and collect their minnows."

CMC's biologist was incensed. Fish in Boulder Pond? In his rebuttal testimony he wrote, "I believe people placed minnows in the pond at least last year. They put the fish there for fishing purposes or to confound regulators; or they may do it innocently, as children would. The pond freezes solidly, in my opinion, every winter. I do not believe the pond or the down gradient woods are even remotely associated with fish spawning, nursery, migratory, feeding or other habitat."

How did minnows get into the pond then?

Mary Jane had written, "My assumption is that they work their way into Boulder Pond from Big Pond in early spring at times of high water. The water is actually flowing through from Boulder Pond to Big Pond at certain times of the year."

"Do you mean," the biologist responded in rebuttal testimony "that 2 to 3 inch long minnows power their way 6 to 8 feet up gradient to elevation 108 at the wet pond?"

In his rebuttal, Merrill responded. "He's wrong about the gradient. In high water it is more like 1 to 2 feet. The elevation of the surface water of Big Pond on June 6, 1996, was reported by Cross Engineering to be 102 feet. High water levels reach at least the 104 elevation in the spring of the year. In Exhibit LF-11 Figure 7, you can see water extending into the 1995 illegally quarried pit to a level which approximately coincides with Elevation 104 feet on the CMC Operation Plan.) The surface water in Boulder Pond as reported on the Operation Plan seems coincidental with the 107 or 108 foot elevation. I measured the depth of water in Boulder Pond to be two feet. That would put the bottom elevation of Boulder Pond at 105 or 106. This would mean that fish would have to swim uphill a total rise of one foot or a maximum of 2 feet—which is a lot less than the 6 to 8 feet suggested."

John Austin had sent in prefiled testimony which stated of the old quarry, "Its relationship to Lake Champlain and surrounding undeveloped landscapes seems to make it very attractive to a host of wildlife species including waterfowl, wading birds, and mink. I have observed, heard or seen evidence of mallards, mink, midland painted turtles, garter snake, green frog, eastern phoebe, chipping sparrow, common snipe, American woodcock, northern oriole, song sparrow, and loggerhead shrike. These observations were confirmed by Steve Parren, Coordinator of the Department's Nongame and Natural Heritage Program." CMC's biologist "states that he noted no threatened or endangered species or suitable habitat for such species. However on April 15, 1996, I observed a loggerhead shrike (a state-endangered species) perched in a small tree above the wetland area proposed for impact."

In response to John Austin's testimony regarding frogs in Boulder Pond CMC's biologist wrote, "I guess John and I are going to have to agree to disagree about the frogs. I continue to believe that for all intents and purposes, the vast majority of them will be killed every year due to freezing for reasons that I abundantly outlined earlier and in my pre-filed direct testimony (lines 237-252). The appellant's photographs in his present rebuttal testimony show the water and substrate, into which frogs would attempt to burrow is frozen solid."

He continued to discuss his credentials. "I have commented and testified extensively on my professional opinions of the wildlife value of this site as a certified Wildlife Biologist with over 27 years of post baccalaureate professional experience in wildlife ecology.

"In my opinion," he wrote at another point, " the Vermont Agency of Natural Resources does not want to have the WRB reverse their denial because they have been hoodwinked into believing that real, serious ecological harm could (not would) come to the slender .21 acre affected wetland AND the higher quality down gradient ponded quarry. Like most organizations and many people, the VANR doesn't want to be proven wrong, nor do they want to have to change their written institutional position."

By this time we were all furious. In response to the question, "Would you comment on the suggestion people placed minnows in the pond at least last year, possibly to confound regulators?" I wrote "I must say that this strikes me as a smear tactic. If it is really believed that any of the parties put minnows in the pond, I am amazed by such assertions. I am sure that everyone involved would be willing to provide sworn affidavits that this did not occur. I enclose photos of minnows in Boulder Pond recently given to me by Mary Jane Tiedgen."

Mary Jane was pulling no punches. The question had been asked: Do you know where the information came from regarding the kinds of fish in Big Pond? She wrote furiously. "In answer to the insults as to the lack of knowledge of us 'lay' people, much of the fish information came from us. I have trapped, netted and fished for minnows in the quarry for over 40 years. I do not need a degree in biology to tell the difference between a Johnny Roach, Pond Shiner, Stickleback or Bullhead. Furthermore, I can tell the difference between a beaver, mink, otter, and muskrat. I know a blue heron, kingfisher, killdeer and many songbirds. I don't need a degree in biology to identify these birds or mammals either. Some of the most ignorant people I know have many degrees and titles after their names. Many of the most intelligent have none."

She continued, saying that she didn't care if "their biologist scientifically figured out that 'the beaver lodges were abandoned 10 to 12 years ago.' I know a beaver when I see one. There have been beavers there for all these years. There are currently beavers in the quarry. Our pictures, in answer to his question, were taken in 96 and 97. I'm getting very tired of being called a liar, no matter how pleasantly or insultingly it is phrased. Our groups are not the ones who stated (in the Act 250 Application) that the Big Pond dries up in the summer, hoping to slide the paperwork through with no outcry from concerned people. The people in our group were not the ones who deliberately misquoted Cathy O'Brien about wetlands in the Act 250 application hoping that no one would notice. It was that behavior that certainly set the stage for the ethics of the people we were to begin our battle with."

John Austin picked up the discussion in response to the contention that the wetlands had no value to amphibians due to the potential for winter kill resulting from freezing. He wrote: "Successful species taxa such as frogs would not have survived long if they did not develop behaviors for overwinter survival as adults. Adult amphibians are able to move between habitats on a seasonal basis and will locate suitable winter refugia. Larval forms of amphibians are at risk of freezing and a quick deep freeze can be a problem at times. However, most larval amphibians metamorphose and leave breeding sites within a single season, an adaptive behavior that saves them from ephemeral water levels. For example, leopard frogs metamorphose in a single season and migrate to upland areas and find other sites for winter habitat. Department biologists and others have observed a variety of amphibian species associated with these wetlands."

But Merrill called into question whether the pond froze to the bottom in the first place. In his rebuttal testimony he wrote, "It is claimed that that fish can't live in Boulder Pond because it freezes solid. It appears that the basis of this belief was the visit on January 27 in which holes were drilled in the ice in Boulder Pond."

He elaborated. "On January 27, 1998, I had just finished lunch at Fisk Farm and was returning back to my building job at around 1:30, heading south on West Shore Road. As I passed the Fisk Quarry entrance two men were coming out of the entrance with a shovel and an ice auger. I recognized a person who works for the company and another quarry worker from the Goodsell Quarry. I immediately guessed that they were checking the depth of the ice in Boulder Pond since it has been stated in previous testimony that this pond freezes solid in the winter.

"That evening after work I followed the tracks to Boulder Pond. In a small area, about the size of a dining room table, I saw that they had drilled some holes in the ice. I measured the depth of the holes with a tape measure. One hole was 8 inches of ice deep and I could not tell whether this ice reached to the bottom or not. The second hole was about 7 3/4 inches deep. It had some water in it. The third hole was 24 inches deep altogether with about 8 inches of ice and about 16 inches of water below the ice." He concluded, "I would say that there was 16 inches of water under the 8 inches of ice within a small grouping of holes, indicating that there is a great deal of water beneath the ice, rather than water frozen to the bare rock bottom."

ANR's Cathy O'Brien wrote: "There is no doubt that he [CMC's biologist] is a qualified wetland and wildlife biologist. Throughout his testimony, both direct and rebuttal, however, he cites his credentials as proof that the wetland functions do not exist (in these areas). As the Wetlands Board has previously stated, mere assertions of fact, despite professional credentials, do not provide evidence with respect to the criteria of Section 5.

"A professional opinion is not a match for clearly documented evidence to the contrary. ANR found during the CUD process, and again the Board's appeal process that there is overwhelming evidence provided by Linda Fitch, Mary Jane Tiedgen, South Shore Associates and their witnesses, that the wetland does provide wildlife habitat. This is documented by pictures and numerous hours of field work and observation. This documentation includes the specific area to be directly impacted, as well as the wetland as a whole."

18. It's All About Water

"The conservation of natural resources is the fundamental problem.
Unless we solve that problem it will avail us little to solve all others."
Theodore Roosevelt,
Address to the Deep Waterway Convention, Memphis, TN, October 4, 1907

SEVERAL YEARS AFTER ROOSEVELT VISITED the Fisk home on Isle La Motte, the Glory Days of Fisk Farm had begun to fade. The quarry business took a downturn as the introduction of reinforced concrete and then the invention of concrete blocks cut into the market for building stone. The demand for the beautiful limestone on Isle la Motte plunged. In 1905, in an effort to salvage his quarry business, Nelson Fisk installed a large stone crusher to use up the waste from the Quarry in hopes of selling it for use on the roads. To no avail.

In 1918 the Fisks mortgaged their property–land, quarry, their barns and the big house. An old deed shows that in 1919 Nelson Fisk sold his quarry to the Vermont Marble Company. Indeed, most of the old island quarries, no longer prosperous, went silent. The only one that continued on was the Goodsell Quarry on the east side of the island. Without the continual pumping, an integral part of many quarry operations, ground water filled the deepest parts of the old Fisk Quarry.

Fascinating and contentious as the discussion in testimony on wildlife was, the corner was turned on the subject of water. Every one of us who lived near the old Fisk Quarry could testify about wildlife, about what we, our parents, our children, had seen and heard over the years. And to a certain extent we understood the water. Basically we knew where the water was on the surface. We could see and catch fish in Big Pond, walk along the little stream in "Beaver Dam Woods" which hugged the northern rock face of the old excavation, explore the shallow, marshy area of Boulder Pond. Back in October of 1995 we found the brown fronds of what we learned was "sensitive fern" in the woods east of the quarry property. We knew about the stream in the east, and that the meadow to the north and east of the quarry was wet throughout the year. Given what seemed to be the year round wetness of the surface soils and plants like sedges, red osier dogwood and even, in a few areas, cattails, we believed that the entire field would qualify as a Class II wetland, though it had not been officially delineated as such.

However at a certain point, water goes underground. There are technical concepts regarding water which were, for the most part, beyond our—or certainly my—lay powers of observation; these required genuine expertise in the field of hydrology or "geo-hydrology." We needed an idea of how water worked on the land. And we needed to know how the Engineering Plan, if put into practice, would impact the water on, in, and under the land.

Andy Mills had stayed at Fisk Farm during the period of April 3 to April 16 in 1996. During that time he performed a field investigation in the site area. In preparation for the Act 250 Hearing in April of 96 he wrote up a report.

> "The work involved site reconnaissance, surveying, static water-level measurements, slug and pumping tests of the neighboring Fitch domestic well, and water sampling and analysis. Site Reconnaissance included inspection of the quarry ponds, the marshy lands adjacent to the excavated area, and a spring located between the main quarry pond and the lake. Bedrock fractures in the quarry wall and quarry floor were inspected and their dip and orientation measured where possible, as was the bedrock dip evidenced in the quarry wall there. Stations were established for the measurement of static water levels and for water sampling at the main pond."

The appendix of his impressive report was filled with charts:

Table 1 Static Water Level Data showing comparisons between Lake Champlain, the Big Quarry Pond, the small Quarry Pond and the Fitch Well
Table 2 Results of Slug and Pumping Test in Fitch Well,
Table 3 Results of Chemical Analysis of Water Samples.

The Act 250 Hearing in the spring of 1996 had been recessed and Andy's detailed report with charts was not used at that time. But the rigorous appeal process to the Water Resources Board, demanded every ounce of expertise that could be summoned from our lay and expert witnesses. Particularly from Andy. Like the rest of us he now submitted his findings in the form of testimony. And like the rest of us, Andy broadened the discussion from the two relatively limited wetland areas (Boulder Pond and Beaver Dam Woods) on which CMC witnesses focused, to the larger hydrological picture of the proposed project. How would the excavation of an ever growing pit some 28 feet in depth in the deforested woodlands and fields surrounding the old Fisk

Quarry, impact the distribution of water throughout the quarry property and surrounding land?

It would have a substantial impact, Andy argued.

How so?

Fisk Quarry Land

Boulder Pond

Beaver Dam Woods

Fisk Farm

Big Pond

West Shore Rd

Aerial photo by Bob McEwen

In a number of ways, he wrote. "Many of the soils bordering the quarry on the north and east side are poorly drained. This results in a seasonal to perennial perched water table. In early April 1996 the woods immediately east of the excavated area of the quarry were marshy throughout, and this after a winter and early spring with lower than normal precipitation. The open, unwooded portion of the land northeast of the existing excavation had a high water table in early April 1996 in two percolation standpipes which had been set into the surface soils in that area. The water levels in the standpipes were close to ground level.

"Based on my preliminary assessment, it appears that two water tables or potentiometric surfaces exist beneath the site area. The lands surrounding the old quarry have two water tables. The upper water table is due to the poor internal drainage of many of the surface soils, which results in an almost permanent perching of water within 0 to 2 feet of the ground surface over most of the un-excavated portion of the quarry property.

"The lower water table or piezometric surface may occur some 10 to 15 feet below the top of limestone bedrock, based on static water levels measured in the nearby Fitch well. The water of this bedrock aquifer is fed by the percolation of water from the overlying soil through vertical fractures in the rock, and is believed to exist under more or less confined conditions.

"Where the upper water table exists, it is believed to serve as the source for the replenishment of the bedrock aquifer. The rate of downward percolation from the upper zone to the lower one is quite slow, but given the large aerial extent of poorly drained soils in the vicinity of the quarry, they represent a significant recharge source for the bedrock aquifer."

I had a hard time grasping this. An "unconfined aquifer" I learned somewhat reluctantly, is sometimes called the water table. The term "perched water table" refers to ground water which gathers above soil with poor drainage such as a clay soil. A confined aquifer is where water is sandwiched between "confining" layers such as bedrock.

"Ok, so there's wet soil on top because of poor drainage" was a concept I eventually came to understand. This simply supported our own observations of the land surrounding the old quarry: our observations of what we saw growing, what I felt when I walked barefoot through the damp fields, from the shine of water as we peered into the white plastic perc pipes standing in the field owned by CMC.

"Then there's a layer of bedrock. Then below that—maybe 10 or 15 feet—there's a water table below. So the upper water table...those wet soils and all—feeds this lower water table?"

"Very slowly," Andy had explained one night over dinner. "But it's a very significant source of recharge."

In his testimony Andy then turned his attention to the old quarry excavation itself? Where does the water in Big Pond, Beaver Dam Woods and Boulder Pond come from?

"Big Pond," Andy wrote, "is fed by ground water from the several water tables seeping through the fractures in the rock. One year round resident "reported that his father had said that that the reason work was stopped in the Fisk Quarry many years ago was that they found a 'black marble' zone that went deeper, but that as they excavated deeper the water seeped into the quarry so fast they could hardly keep up with it."

That was news to me. I had always thought that the quarry business had failed because there simply was no market for the stone. Perhaps both were true.

The Engineering Plan which Joe Bivins and Merrill had pored over for weeks during the previous winter had called for three phases—basically three areas of excavation to be accomplished over time. The first phase would in-volve the excavation of the woods just east of the existing quarry—all the woodlands up to the quarry property boundary.

What, from Andy's perspective would happen if you dug such a pit? He wrote, "Groundwater and surface water will tend to move from the east to-ward the excavation, probably at a rate greater than is presently happening. This additional water, probably both water seeping within the overburden soils as well as deeper groundwater, will be taken largely from the Class II wet-lands located immediately east of the quarry property."

We knew that was where the sensitive fern grows. That's where Jeffrey Williams hunted woodcock for years. That's where, during the November site visit, we found (to our not so secret delight) that a great lake had formed after several days of rain.

Andy's report continued. "At the same time, groundwater in the bedrock will tend to move from all other directions as well, until the water in the Phase One excavation reaches its static level. I would estimate that the final "static" depth of water would be likely to range from o to 3 ft over this area."

I visualized the woods gone, all the trees clear cut, the soils removed, all replaced by a pit. Water would collect from seepage from the wet soils, from the deeper groundwater, and directly from rainfall. The pit would, of course, have machinery in it—excavation equipment, jackhammers, loaders, genera-tors...

"The water in this pond will tend," continued Andy, "to feed fractures in the underlying rock and move as groundwater toward the west, discharging finally into nearby Lake Champlain."

What about Phases Two and Three of the Operation Plan? The second phase called for extending the pit northwards toward the land I had bought from the Halls in 1994. Phase Three was designed to reach to the boundary of our field.

"In both phases," Andy wrote, "ground water, seepage from the wet soils, and rainwater would fill the pit to its static level, then would move through fractures in the rock as groundwater in a westerly direction toward Lake Champlain and finally discharge into the lake."

"I would estimate," Andy continued, "that the 'final' static pond level would be likely to range between 103 and 104 ft elevation. Thus, the final depth of water would be likely to range from 1 to 5 ft over this area, assuming that it will not be possible to prevent runoff and seepage water from accumu-lating at the bottom of the excavation."

So what was supposed to happen with the water in these pits?

"CMC is proposing to construct a detention basin north and east of the present quarry wall. This basin presumably would receive all the water pumped from the excavations. The detained water would be released by a sluice pipe onto the land north of the quarry."

The land north of the quarry was my land, the land I had bought from the Hall family in 1994 along with the old Horse & Carriage Barn. So according to their current plan, all the water from the pit would be discharged through a sluice pipe onto my land. Way to go, CMC!

And what will happen to the water levels of Big Pond through all of this?

"If substantial groundwater is collected in the new pond(s) associated with the excavation in Phases One through Three and then disposed of by pumping to a proposed detention basin, there would then be some reduction in the bedrock groundwater flow which replenishes Big Pond."

Ok. So water sources in Big Pond would be reduced. What about possible pollution of Big Pond?

"It's possible and indeed likely that water which will collect in the excavations could pass through fractures in the bedrock and into Big Pond, transporting contaminants such as oils and hydraulic fluids. And along with that, water pumped into the detention pond could do the same thing...seeping through bedrock fractures and carrying with it any of its contaminants."

What about our wells?

"It's entirely likely that a hydraulic connection exists between the water in Big Pond, the proposed quarry excavations, and the bedrock aquifer that I've mentioned earlier." Back in early April he explained it to us over one of our many community dinners.

"Remember, we've observed and we have those pictures of seepage though fractures in the quarry walls. Furthermore, the dewatering of the excavations will drain fractures in the aquifer, reducing the available drawdown in the wells, resulting in lower water in the wells. This could be a problem."

How so?

"For your well, in particular, according to the lab analysis that we had done, the water pumped from the deeper geologic units contains more sodium.

A salty well? Neighbors to the north had a well with too much sodium.

CMC's several geologists had a different view of things. One of them who had visited the site for several hours back in 1996, argued that "there is no evidence of ground water discharging into the quarry area and many of the ponded water areas in the quarry simply dry up during the summer months."

We were amazed. So much testimony had already been provided as to the fact that the quarry ponds NEVER dry up. Once again the question arose! Did the expert witnesses hired by the company have no access at all to previous testimony? Previous documentation? If not, what a waste of time and effort for them, for us, and for the whole process.

This particular geologist also wrote "During my site visit, I did not observe any fracture or fractures along the existing northern quarry wall of the wetland which could serve this purpose." The purpose to which he referred was the replenishment of the quarry ponds via ground water from upper and lower water tables. No particular cracks or crevices. No karst.

What was "karst?"

We learned that karst is a phenomenon in which water dissolves "carbonate bedrock" such as limestone, dolomite or marble. This can result in the enlargement of cracks and crevices, as well as forming sink holes and caves. Based on his review of the literature and his observations of the site, CMC's geologist wrote, "I am of the opinion that...the limestone found at the Fisk Quarry does not have any particular tendency to develop karst-type features...Therefore, other than minor fracturing...I am of the opinion that there are not other significant mechanisms for groundwater movement on the site."

Andy disagreed.

"Both bedding-plane fractures and vertical fractures are clearly apparent in the north wall of the existing quarry excavation. And the surface expressions of vertical fractures exist in the quarry floor and on the rock ledge just north of Big Pond, and these fractures occur at intervals ranging from 30 to 100 feet."

Neil Hanna had also made an interesting comment in his testimony. "They talk about karst and sink holes in the area. One of the things I encountered, maybe twenty years ago, was when several men were digging in the ground behind our house as they were putting in a septic system. They unearthed a large stone and when they moved the stone they uncovered a cave they could actually walk in. They ended up filling it up with crushed stone. Since then, every so often, especially in the springtime, a hole will appear and take the earth right down with it. I've had to plug these holes up with rocks and stones so that the garden wouldn't disappear. One year we got a tremendous rainstorm in the fall; water filled up the cavern and some of it leaked into my basement. In that same rainstorm a big sink hole developed in the yard of Dick Jarnot, my neighbor. I would say it was eight by six feet deep. Eventually we had to get rocks and I filled it in so people would not fall into it."

Lyle came up with a dramatic photograph of a 6 to 8 inch diameter channel in the northern quarry wall showing water pouring out in a veritable stream. "Any kid who has climbed around on the quarry walls knows about this hole," he said to me.

Another geologist for CMC stated that because the quarrying operations would take place within 30 feet of the present ground surface, there would be no adverse effect on the underlying ground water in the bedrock. Only the deep geologic layers supply water to the bedrock supplies of the area.

"I don't agree," said Andy in his testimony. "The bedrock groundwater system at the site is deep and complex. Ground water is available from the deeper geologic units (100 feet and deeper) but evidence indicates that superficial ground water also provides water to local wells. During the second week of April 1996 after two to three rainy days, the static water level in the Fitch well rose by 0.73 feet and in Big Pond by .3 feet, demonstrating a hydraulic connection between the well and water recharging through the soil and underlying fractured bedrock. The water available in the Fitch well, for example is clearly a combination of water from the deeper horizons and water seeping in from fractures in the upper bedrock."

"There are no neighbors who get their drinking water solely from wells," wrote one of CMC's geologists.

"What?" we exclaimed, upon reading this statement.

Andy responded. "In his report dated November 11, 1996, the witness himself implies that all ten of the wells located within one mile of the quarry and for which he obtained information are used for water supply purposes. The Fitch well and the Grant/Garinther well are solely dependent on well water for drinking water supplies. Linda Fitch's state license for lodging depends on satisfactory well test results taken every year at the beginning of July."

"Poorly drained soils would probably contribute only a minor percentage of the overall recharge to the bedrock aquifer," said the CMC hydrologist.

"I disagree," responded Andy. "Saturated, poorly drained soils can contribute a substantial amount of recharge to an underlying aquifer. If, on the average, only 0.05 inches of water per day seeped below the root zone of such a 'wet' soil and moved toward the bedrock water table, this would amount to 18.2 inches of recharge annually, not a low recharge rate."

"Most of the quarry operations," a CMC witness stated, "will be completed above the standing water elevation, so that dewatering will not be required during most of the quarry operations."

"I assume," said Andy in response, "that he is referring to the standing water elevation of Big Pond. There is another standing-water elevation of significance here—the water level elevation in the Class II wetlands just east of proposed quarry operation areas. The water-level elevation is at the current land surface and will provide a significant head and resulting gradient in the direction of the proposed excavations. As I have previously indicated, I would expect that operations will require some kind of regular or ongoing dewatering due to flow from this wetland area."

I was beginning to understand terms like "head" and "gradient." "It's all about water moving from a higher place to a lower place," Andy patiently explained to me. "Differences in 'hydraulic head' cause water to move from one place to another. 'Gradient' is the slope of the water table or stream."

Direct and Rebuttal testimony went on in this vein.

"Since the site is located at the low point in the regional groundwater system," argued one hydrologist for CMC, there is no gradient to drive downward movement, and therefore," he implied, there could be no such thing as an upper water table serving to recharge the bedrock aquifer. "Rather, the shallow water table is probably recharged by precipitation and upward movement from ground water in the fractured-bedrock aquifer."

"I disagree," wrote Andy. "The evidence indicates that in the vicinity of the site, the wetlands and the adjacent saturated hydric soils serve as the source and conveyors of groundwater recharge to the underlying upper bedrock. I believe it is unlikely that the bedrock ground water is recharging the perched or shallow water table as has been asserted. For example, the static water level in the Fitch well in the spring of 1996 was approximately ten feet below the top of bedrock. Since the static level didn't come close to the overlying overburden soils, I conclude that the bedrock ground water does not move upward to "feed" the shallow water table."

The volley continued.

"There is no basis for the detailed comments in Dr. Mill's testimony regarding the probable impacts to groundwater and surface water flow regimes during various phases of quarry operation. The reality of the situation is that groundwater and surface water flows and interactions are likely to be far more complex, and not nearly as directly connected, if connected at all, to nearby wetlands...I am familiar with sites in Vermont where very deep quarries coexist with adjacent wetlands where the differences in water levels can be 100 feet or more. There is simply no evidence to suggest that a direct connection via bedrock fractures will result in drainage or alteration of existing surface waters as a result of the proposed operation of the Fisk Quarry."

Andy replied: "I do see the site and environs as being a complex hydrologic system. This implies the possibility of hydraulic connections among the different water bodies and groundwater aquifers of the system. It also implies the impossibility of knowing precisely what portions of which water body or which aquifer is in hydraulic connection with other parts of the system on any given day. However, my experience with water over the years has taught me that you cannot assume the absence of a hydraulic connection between adjacent water bodies/aquifers, especially when pathways (fractures) are clearly present and when there is a clear gradient, which is the case between the Class II wetlands to the east and the proposed or existing quarry excavations."

So went the battle of testimony, and rebuttal testimony with regard to hydrology.

"We believe that CMC can run a clean quarry," declared extensive opposition testimony. In response, Merrill and Joe Bajorski both testified about contamination of water from machinery used in the quarrying operation.

Merrill wrote, "I've worked on job sites that use excavators, generators, pneumatic drills, gasoline engines and water pumps, dump trucks, and a variety of diesel powered engines. All this equipment needs to be greased, oiled and refueled daily on the site. Certain equipment requires greasing several times a day if it has any kind of track system or metal parts which work against each other as is in the case with the bar saw which CMC will be using to cut the stone. It's like a giant chain saw needing to be constantly oiled. Also, they run water over the chain which means that the grease and the water would be constantly mixing together."

The opposition biologist scoffed.

"Mr. Hemond emotionalizes about his relationship to things natural and his construction work experience. If every construction site were as awful as those sites described by Mr. Hemond there should (in his logic) be no construction unless, presumably, it suits him. He states that there is a large potential for spillage and leakage on the site. This is not true for reasons outlined below under my response to Dr. Mills' testimony. CMC has vigorously tried to anticipate every potential problem of the proposed project and to act in an appropriate manner, given regulatory standards in place for such activity."

Merrill replied. "Daily spillage and maintenance problems are a given fact of construction sites. They are not an unusual occurrence. In the Goodsell Quarry you can see cans of grease, open cans of oil, leakage from the giant refueling tank which is constantly leaking fuel on the ground, etc. On other job sites I have also seen hydraulic hoses which burst under pressure spewing hydraulic fluid under pressure over a fairly wide area.

"CMC's biologist says 'it would take a major accident for any damage to be caused to the ecosystem.' As far as major accidents are concerned, these are more frequent than you might imagine. For example, just last year, on November 8, 1996, a violent rainstorm occurred on Isle La Motte. The Goodsell Quarry filled with water from rain. Equipment, cables and machinery were submerged by water which filled the quarry to the top. An oil slick covered the muddy water.

"A great deal of dirt and soil was washed into and deposited in the quarry as a result of this storm. Rainwater runoff flowing through mounds of dirt (overburden excavated by earth moving machines) both contributed to the sedimentation. The flood waters mixed with fuel oil, lubricants, and hydraulic fluids spilled on the quarry floor during quarry operations.

"The operator of the quarry immediately began to pump the quarry down and discharge the heavily sedimented water, which was covered by an oil slick, into a ditch (drainage way) which in turn discharges into Lake Champlain. This pumping operation lasted from November 9 until well into December when a second storm refilled the quarry. At that point the operator closed down the operation for the winter."

The Engineering Plan had other questionable features. Merrill wrote, "In response to concerns expressed by the Wastewater Management Division from which CMC is also required to get a permit, CMC has proposed the creation of a detention pond and sump for this operation. All water that collects in the working pit area during operation and off season will be pumped into the detention pond/sump area...The sump will be a 280 foot long pit, 5 feet deep bordering the Fitch property and Big Pond. A berm 3 feet high and 20 feet wide will hold the water in the detention pond. The drainage area from this pit includes the field to the north owned by Linda Fitch."

"There are problems with this plan," Merrill asserted. "The proposed sump hole will become eventually filled with mud and stone sludge and the water exit could become clogged. In the event that the outlet becomes clogged, the water pumped into the Detention Pond will overflow the berm, going into Big Pond and directly into the Fitch wet field. Petroleum based pollutants would have a tendency to float on the surface of the water and be the first to exit over the top of the berm onto the Fitch fields and to Big Pond (a protected Class II Wetland which CMC describes in their CUD application as having valuable wetland functions) a few feet away."

He continued. "The location of the proposed detention pond could be a problem because I believe that the wetland delineation line which Cross Engineering has drawn running across the middle of Big Pond is inaccurately located. The quarry pond is shallow in many places north of the wetland boundary line drawn by Mr. Spear, CMC's Wetland Consultant. If the wetland boundary line is further north than presently drawn, then the present 50 foot buffer zone is also further to the north. The proposed location of the detention pond would then be in a wetland buffer zone."

The opposition biologist shot back. "Mr. Hemond also seeks to discredit my wetland delineation of the deepwater habitat. As he pointed out himself this is a deep pond (he claims up to 30 feet). That means some of it is lacustrine habitat and not jurisdictional under the Vermont Wetland Rules. My 27 years of continuous post-baccalaureate professional experience in wetland/wildlife ecology speaks for itself, as do the credentials of Ms. O'Brien of the VANR. She concurred with me on the edge of all wetland areas prior to the application finalization. What are Mr. Hemond's credentials?"

"My credentials in this case," Merrill responded, "are my ability to read plans and take measurements, my good eye sight, my common sense and my day to day familiarity with this land for the past four years."

"Wait, look at this!" said Merrill on one cold March day as he read testimony from CMC's geologists. "Yes, yes, yes!" Both his thumbs were in the air.

"What's yes, yes, yes?" said I. Weary.

"Wait until you read this. Here, read it!"

I picked up the 16 page report and on page 21 read the following: "I have recommended, and CMC has agreed to amend, the project plans to direct outflow from the ponds to the old quarry rather than overland. The revised pond design incorporates a vertical riser which would be open on top to allow for the outflow of the clearest water in the pond."

"Wait...this is..."

"A new plan! A revised plan! Not part of the original plan. They said they would conduct their appeal on the basis of the original plan!"

"So they changed their minds about pumping millions of gallons of water onto my land?"

"Yes and it means..."

"So this is a change. They can't change their minds can they?"

"Nope!"

"So this means...?" I said. Light had begun to dawn.

"Motion to dismiss. Just what Joe Kennedy was talking about last summer. Motion to dismiss. Where's Stephanie? Where's her phone number? Call her right now for God's sake!"

19. Motion to Dismiss

"Believe you can and you're halfway there."
— *Theodore Roosevelt*

On JANUARY 6, 1919, NEWSPAPER HEADLINES ALL OVER THE COUNTRY delivered the news: "Theodore Roosevelt Dies Suddenly At Oyster Bay Home: Nation Shocked." Though he died of an embolism, many speculated that Roosevelt had never really recovered from the death of his son Quentin in aerial combat over France the year before. He was 61.

Nelson Fisk, the man who had hosted Roosevelt during his visit to Isle La Motte in 1901, died four years later on October 1, 1923. He was 69. His grieving wife closed up the big house and went to New York for the winter. For Elizabeth, tragedy mixed with triumph when, in November, *The Ladies Home Journal* published a long article with pictures about her illustrious weaving career. "Color and Beauty from Village Looms" it was titled.

But in December Elizabeth received a telegram with more horrifying news. An article in the December 9, 1923, edition of *the Burlington Free Press* described it:

> "The historic old home of the late Nelson W. Fiske was completely destroyed by fire of mysterious origin shortly before midnight last night. The house was unoccupied, Mrs. Fiske having closed it and gone to New York for the winter. Mrs. Fisk has been notified by telegraph...All the historic and valuable contents of the home were destroyed

> "The property could not be replaced for $15,000...This wonderful old stone home, two and a half stories high, built by the Fiske's great grandfather over 100 years ago from stone from his quarry, contained much valuable furniture, heirlooms, curios, paintings, weavings in linen in color, done by Mrs. Fiske, the only woman in the world, so far as known, to do such unique work. Now the valuable property, valuable in a material way and valuable because of historic associations, is reduced to ashes."

The Fisk home destroyed by fire

March 1998

Montpelier, Vermont is the smallest capital city of all the states in the US. The earliest settlement may have been established in 1787 or 88, at the time Ichabod Ebenezer Fisk came to Isle La Motte, some eighty miles to the north. At the time, Vermont was still an independent Republic. Within twenty-five years or so, by the time Vermont had become a state, Montpelier had grown from around one hundred to a thriving population of twelve hundred. Nowadays, with a population of around 8,000, its Greek Revival State House gleams gold in the foothills of the Green Mountains; its marble floors contain a shining "black marble" and docents in the State House proudly point out the spiral forms of gastropods in the black polished stone from Isle La Motte.

Montpelier is an hour and a half drive from Isle La Motte, south of the gentle hills of the Champlain Valley and the lake. In the past few years I had become intimately acquainted with this tiny, picturesque city. Once again, now in the early spring of 1998, I was driving to Montpelier.

On March 9, Stephanie had sent out a "Motion to Dismiss" on behalf of South Shore Associates, Mary Jane, and myself. At a Pre-hearing Conference on March 12, Chair Davies brought up Stephanie's Motion to Dismiss. He set a deadline of 4:30 p.m. Monday, March 23 for the submission of any written memoranda in response to the motion, suggesting that any such filing identify pre-filed testimony and exhibits addressing the issue. He also indicated that oral argument before the Board would be heard with respect to the Motion at 10:00 am Tuesday, March 31. The dates for the actual Hearing were set for April 13 and 14, barely two weeks after that.

Stephanie's Motion was entitled Docket #CUD-97-06 and sounded, to us-- war weary, hard bitten veterans of all too many tours of duty--like the most lyrical of poetry. She stated that

> "Parties in the above-referenced action, South Shore Associates, Linda Fitch and Mary Jane Tiedgen, have received information concerning a change in the Operation Plan of CMC of May 19, 1997. The parties hereby move to dismiss the Appeal, Docket #CUD-97-06 on the following grounds."

She then noted that in September, the Chair had indicated that any change in the May, 1997 Operations plan would be grounds for return of jurisdiction to the Agency of Natural Resources. She pointed out that in his rebuttal testimony, one of CMC's geologists had proposed a change in the Operation Plan indicating that he "has recommended and the CMC has agreed to amend the project plans to direct outflow from the ponds to the old quarry" rather than overland to my meadow. She wrote:

> "And on line 66 Mr. Nelson restates, 'I am confident that the redesign of the pond as proposed will prevent the type of uncontrolled situation alluded to by Mr. Hemond.' On the basis of the foregoing and in accordance with Rule 21 of the State of Vermont Water Resources Board Rules of Procedure, the parties hereby respectfully request that the Appeal be dismissed and that notice of any hearings related to this Motion to Dismiss be delivered to the undersigned. Dated as of this 9th day of March, 1998."

Though Stephanie had filed the Motion to Dismiss there were, nevertheless, other filings which had to take place. All parties had the opportunity to file objections to opposition testimony if they so chose. And then to defend against the objections. The Water Resources Board had the authority to sustain or override the objections. I sent an email to all the potential witnesses who had to be at the hearing in April.

March 24, 1998
Linda to the Quarriors

Dear All,
Here is an update for all Fisk Qwarriors. All prefiled direct and rebuttal testimony has been filed with the Water Resources Board. We have almost completed the process of wrangling over evidentiary objections. (This was a process new to me. I really had no idea of what was admissible testimony and evidence and what was

not when I started out. I know now!) This last has involved not only the filing of objections by all parties to opponents' testimony, but a pre-hearing conference in Montplier held on March 12 for oral argument. CMC filed 18 pages of objections to our testimony and exhibits. Here are some of the things we won:

1. CMC tried to exclude Charlotte Merhtens' testimony on the basis that the relevant fossils would not be in the area of proposed quarrying. We took the position that the entire quarry consists of rock which constitutes part of the oldest reef in the world and is within the areas of proposed impacts and their buffer zones. We won our point and our distinguished paleontologist and her testimony are in!

2. They tried to exclude testimony of Merrill Hemond on the basis that he is not an engineer or hydrologist. They lost. Merrill is in with his keen observations and analyses concerning just about everything!

3. They tried to exclude Scott Newman for some reason that I can't figure out. They lost. Scott is in!

4. They tried to exclude devastating testimony from Merrill and Joe Bajorski concerning CMC's operation of the Goodsell Quarry (an unsavory operation at best.) They lost!

However, we suffered some losses as well. We lost:
1. Dan Froehlich's report and wildlife list. (Very disappointing!)

2. We are fighting for Mary Capkanis' Fish and Wildlife Table. If we lose it will be unfair but I don't think it's fatal, Mary, since so many of our witnesses are testifying about so much wildlife.

3. We've lost all of my photographic exhibits for lack of what Chair Davies calls proper foundation. We are fighting this since "proper foundation" is not discussed in any of the Water Resources Board Procedures or Vermont Rules of Evidence. This is potentially a big loss, but again not fatal since we have so much strong evidence on all fronts.

Other nice things to know are that ANR's rebuttal testimony was just as strong as their prefiled testimony. Cathy O'Brien of the Wetlands Office began, for the first time, to discuss the possibility that the quarry field is a Class Two wetland. District Wildlife Biologist, John Austin, continues to defend his perspectives. And it is so nice that Jeff Parsons keeps talking about seeing the beaver despite the opposition's "mathematical formulas" proving that THERE ARE NO BEAVER.

Everyone's testimony is outstanding and taken as a whole it seems to me (prejudiced though I may be) invincible. It's hard to imagine that we will not win, but I take NOTHING for granted. As I write our opponents are busily trying to get at least three pieces of legislation passed which exempt marble quarries from Act 250 jurisdiction and which destroy all wetlands legislation in the state of Vermont. Our best strategy, I believe, is simply to stay with this process, to be on-goingly alert to all legislative efforts, for Linda to catch up on her sleep, and for EVERY-

ONE to show up for the two day Hearing on April 13 and 14. We do not yet know where that will be. I'll let you know!

Let me remind you again that if you are not there your testimony cannot be used, and the testimony of each of you contains vital pieces to the case which we have developed. (Just as an example, Neil Hanna describes a sink hole in his back yard which is very important to our geohydrologist and hydrogeologist) in supporting their hypothesis that the geologic structure of the entire Fisk Quarry area is characterized by karst (with crevices and cracks throughout the rocks that potentially allow for unpredictable pathways of groundwater flow). So Neil...we need your sinkhole!!! Jeff Williams....we need your waterfowl and woodcock! Scullys...you have good beaver testimony! And so on.

Chair Williams Davies has told us that we need to be prepared to be at the Hearing from 8:30 a.m. to 9:30 p.m. on both days of the Hearing. I'm certainly hoping that it won't take that long. CMC has asked for six hours to cross examine. ANR wants three, SSA (via Stephanie Kaplan) asked for three, Fitch/Tiedgen asked for three to four hours.

Please tell me if you need to be fed, housed and otherwise sustained. I'm expecting that Andy Mills and Dave, Mary and the kids will be on Fisk Farm for the weekend. Joe Bajorski and South Witch—let me know what you need!

March 31, 1998

I drove up a winding road to the top of the hill where the National Life Records Center Building was perched, looking down from its lofty perch upon the town of Montpelier. It was the appointed place for the day's Hearing. There was a gathering of folk around a gleaming oval table in a conference room. This time it was all attorneys. And me.

CMC was represented by one of its attorneys. The Agency for Natural Resources was represented by two attorneys. South Shore Associates was represented by Attorney Stephanie. And Linda Fitch was represented pro se and on behalf of Violet Fitch. (She would have been the one shaking in her boots.) The Water Resources Board was represented by Chair Davies and six Board members.

Chair Davies explained that there would first be a discussion of the issues concerning the Motion to Dismiss and the Board then would deliberate on the Motion immediately after hearing oral argument from the parties.

Stephanie spoke first. "It is evident from CMC's pre-filed testimony that certain revisions were made to the Operation Plan, specifically to the design of the detention pond. Among the changes are modifications to the direction of outflow from the project, as well as a new location for the discharge. This is contrary to the company's assurance that this appeal would be based on the Operation Plan of May 19, 1997."

CMC's attorney was scribbling something on a pad of paper, then sat up straight in his chair. "I object," he argued. "We believe that the Board has discretion to admit additional evidence and to consider the proposed modifications because in the context of this de novo proceeding, the Board, rather than ANR, is the trier of fact, and the Board must formulate necessary conditions which may not be supported by the evidence admitted below." He cited a particular case in support of the argument.

"In addition," he continued, "CMC believes that the "futility doctrine" should, as a matter of fairness, compel the Board to retain jurisdiction in this matter, hear the evidence relating to the proposed modifications, and act on the CUD application."

The "futility doctrine." What was that?

What he meant, I learned later, was that they believed that the Wetlands Office (part of the Agency of Natural Resources or ANR) would simply look at the evidence previously presented by both sides and come up with their original decision. Denial of the permit.

"It is our belief," the lawyer stated, "that a remand to the Agency of Natural Resources will merely protract the process and will essentially require CMC to do a futile act. Because of the alleged futility of a presentation of evidence in support of the proposed modifications to ANR on remand, CMC requests the Board to consider the changes in the context of this de novo proceeding."

To my relief one of the Water Resources Board Members, spoke up with what sounded to my untutored ears like a challenging question. "I hear you saying that you feel that the proposed modifications offered, if they were to go back to ANR, would have no effect on changing ANR's mind; so my question to you is: why do you offer them?"

CMC's attorney shot back, "You people are the trier of fact, not ANR. You make the decision. That's why we offer them."

"And my understanding is," said the Board member with what I hoped was a trace of irony, "you are offering them to us to make it more palatable to us."

"That's right."

By the end of the conversation we were asked to wait outside the conference room while the Board deliberated.

It felt like the waiting room as you waited--holding your breath--to hear the results of major surgery being performed on a family member. A family member with some sort of life threatening condition. Finally we were called back in. We sat back down in the hard backed chairs to hear Chair Davies.

The bottom line?

The Board had decided that the case should be remanded! It would be sent back to the Wetlands Office of the Agency of Natural Resources where the proposed changes to the plan would be considered. Suddenly I could breathe.

No, it was not a final decision. No, we hadn't "won." But the heavy pressure to prepare for a hearing in April—scheduled to take place in two scant weeks with all witnesses present—had lifted. For the time being. For the first time in months we would have time to breathe. Time for us, certainly for me in my exhausted state, felt like the most blessed of gifts.

Some weeks later the official MEMORANDUM OF DECISION AND RE-MAND ORDER came in the mail with a detailed explanation by the Water Resources Decision.

"While the Board favors refinements to a project proposal that have the effect of mitigating environmental impacts, the appropriate time for such refinements is when the permit or conditional use applicant is preparing its application. It would be improper to allow the appeal to proceed where CMC, stated in a letter dated October 9, 1997, that it was not going to redesign the project but pursue the appeal based on the present design and where SSA, ANR, and the other parties prepared their testimony in reliance on this design.

The ANR conducts the initial review of a CUD application and the Board's role is to conduct a de novo review of CMC's application. While the law may allow the Board to consider new evidence and proposed monitoring requirements that were not reviewed by ANR, the Board's fundamental obligation is to review the merits of the same application that was reviewed by ANR..."

It continued to sound like poetry.

20. Hope

*"Hope is the thing with feathers, that perches in the soul,
and sings the tune without the words, and never stops at all."*
Emily Dickinson

1924

HER HUSBAND HAD DIED. The only remains of her beautiful house were fire blackened stone walls. But somehow Elizabeth Fisk picked up her life and determined to go on. She asked a young architect on Isle La Motte (Cedric Start married to one of the Hill daughters) to redesign the small Stone Cottage on the Fisk property where she proposed to live--at least during the summer months--and continue to weave. He built a balcony bedroom and added a small wooden shed to the back of the stone structure in which he installed a bathroom and kitchen. Elizabeth planted white currant bushes around the cottage and purple wisteria to wind over a trellis arching over her front door. A sign was hung just above the trellis:

ELIZABETH FISK LOOMS - WEAVING.

"If houses could talk," wrote one woman in an article about Mrs. Fisk, "then a small, stone cottage overlooking Lake Champlain might tell us of the busy weavers that once threw their shuttles and blended their beautiful hand-dyed yarns inside this small studio. They used yarns that matched the colors of the flowers, birds, and the beautiful countryside that surrounded them on the islands of Northern Vermont."[41]

"...These weavers were part of a remarkable enterprise that was started in 1910 and was extremely active for more than twenty years...Mrs. Fisk first started weaving when she went to live in her husband's home on Isle La Motte...She was fascinated by the looms that at that time had been relegated to the attics of the island homes...Eventually...she used a method whereby a complicated design could be woven into the linen the same time the background was being done. [42]

Visitors in front of Elizabeth Fisk's weaving studio

April 1998

Spring arrives about a month earlier in Princeton than it does in northern Vermont. After the Hearing I went back to New Jersey in time for the first early crocuses. CMC's appeal to the Water Resources Board had been re-manded to the Agency of Natural Resources. I wouldn't have to spend the month of April making sure that all our witnesses would be present for a Hearing on April 24. Working out our courtroom strategies with Stephanie. Preparing verbal testimony. Our responses to cross examination.

We hadn't won anything except time. A chance to rest. Or had we won a possible opportunity? After three years of unrelenting effort I felt that we were at a critical turning point. Perhaps the president of CMC felt that as well. Could we possibly negotiate a deal with him? What would a fair price be for the 20 acre quarry land? How could this be determined? And if so, who might be the best person to conduct negotiations?

Early on Scott had been saying, "You should contact Paul Bruhn. He might be able to be helpful somehow." Who was Paul Bruhn? A native Vermonter having grown up in Burlington, early on Paul worked with Patrick Leahy, States Attorney for Chittenden County. He managed Leahy's campaign for US Senator, and served as his Chief of Staff in Washington for several years. After that, back in Vermont he became interested in helping to preserve historic buildings and eventually founded the Preservation Trust of Vermont in 1980. The mission: "to help communities save and use historic places."

Well, the Fisk Quarry was kind of a city, an exceedingly historic city inhabited by citizens of an ancient ocean hundreds of millions of years ago.

"Just as we want to preserve the Egyptian pyramids, Mayan cities and early cities of North America, so must we also insure that Ordovician reef cities will be available for succeeding generations," one geologist would later write to us.

In the early days of the Quarry War I had tried without success to contact Paul Bruhn. It was a time when I was writing to everyone I could think of. Paul hadn't responded then. But one day, probably sometime during the summer of 1997, I saw a man walking across the lawn. Not unusual as Fisk Farm has many drop-by visitors, attracted by the old stone buildings and their history. I went out to meet him.

"I'm Paul Bruhn," he offered.

Ah. My mind worked quickly. I would take him to see the quarry from the cliffs in our back yard. And refreshments! What did we have handy? Carol was in the garden. "Scones and tea on the front porch," I whispered frantically.

The quarry was in a sunny mood, the pond clear, its many shades of blue sequined with sunlight gleams, the quarry cliffs opposite pale grey etched with the white curving forms of the stromatoporoids, the green of trees and plants growing, seemingly, directly out of rock. Spiral shapes of gastropods were everywhere in the limestone surface on which we stood. It is a dramatic view and I hoped that Paul felt that.

"It would be great to preserve it somehow," I said. "It's a great resource for education and science."

Right then and there he told me that if we ever got to the point of making a deal, the Preservation Trust would commit to a portion of the funds needed. We walked back to the Main House and sat on the front porch. Magically, Carol appeared with a tray of her fabulous lemon current scones and a pot of tea.

Several years later, after our case had been remanded to the Wetlands Office, I again called Paul Bruhn. "We don't know if they're going to reapply to Wetlands Office for a permit," I said over the phone. "But we're tired, they're probably tired and we're hoping that they might be willing to think about selling. It may be difficult to figure out a selling price."

Paul agreed to try to negotiate a deal with the president of the CMC. His subsequent "Qwarrior" title became "Chief Negotiator."

April 1998

Then there was an unexpected and unlikely development. It became known that the Vermont legislature was about to pass a controversial piece of legislation. This was Act 60. Known as the "Equal Education Opportunity Act" it would require "property-rich" towns to share their school dollars with poorer communities. Isle La Motte was deemed a property-rich town because--as an island--it has miles of desirable lakeshore.

Property-rich or not, the projected rise in tax rates worried people on Isle La Motte. Many were far from wealthy. Some had purchased lakeshore in the days when it was considered worthless--useful perhaps--for the watering of cows. Among the old families were the Spauldings who lived on the southeast end of the island. The Spaulding farm had been worked for generations but with the decline of farming, the family had turned a portion of their land into a vacation campground, especially popular with French Canadians from just across the border. It would have been hard to develop the land in any other way as the underlying bedrock made the installation of septic tanks impossible. The underlying bedrock was the reef.

The Burlington Free Press planned to write a feature article on the potential difficulties raised by the passage of Act 60. But when they heard about the particular challenge that the Spauldings faced, the article assumed a new focus. Ancient reef? That sounded like a story!

Back in Princeton I received a phone call from a reporter from *the Burlington Free Press*. She had some questions about the reef. And on April 26 a major article appeared in *the Burlington Free Press*.

World's Oldest Reef Threatened
Tax bite may doom rare VT. Find
by Nancy Bazilcheck
ISLE LA MOTTE ----
In her imagination, Charlotte Mehrtens is snorkeling over a 480 million year old coral reef in a waist-deep tropical sea. Never mind that the University of Vermont geologist is really standing in the middle of an abandoned cow pasture in Isle La Motte.

Underfoot is a treasure capable of transporting geologists into ecstasy: the Chazian Reef, the oldest known fossil coral reefs on the planet. The dull grey rocks bulging from the pasture are laced with curlicues and rod shaped streaks, fossils of some of the most primitive animals on Earth.

The thousand acre reef, covering property owned by a dozen people, survived the formation of the Green Mountains and the volcanic eruptions that helped shape New Hampshire's White Mountains. It has been studied by geologists from around the globe. Yet it might not survive property tax increases or development in the 1990s.

Act 60, Vermont's education funding law, might force some isle La Motte landowners to sell their land. A Proctor company is attempting to reopen a quarry in one section of reef, to grind up the fossil rocks for use as road fill. The state's land protection groups say they probably cannot protect the entire reef, which covers the southern third of Isle La Motte.

Half a billion years ago, the Isle La Motte coral was at the bottom of an ocean south of the equator, about where Zimbabwe is now. Vermont as we know it did not exist. Neither did Lake Champlain. The reefs formed in a tropical sea, with the Adirondacks to the west as an immense coastal range.

Eventually North America migrated to its present location and the reefs were preserved as fossils in a band of limestone that stretches along the East Coast from Virginia into Canada. The reefs in that band are almost as old as the ones in isle La Motte, but for reasons geologists don't understand, Isle La Motte is home to the oldest.

Aside from their age, the Isle La Motte rocks are important for geologists because they have a story to tell. The stretches of exposed bedrock that make up the southern third of the island represent about 2 million years of time. That's long enough for geologists to be able to see vast changes in the fossilized animals that make up the reefs. In most areas it's not possible to get that kind of complete picture. Instead, geologists have to content themselves with a picture here and there.

It's the difference between a photograph and a movie," Mehrtens says. "I look at this stuff and I say, "Oh, my God, there's so much to do." So much to find out. So much research."

Tax Squeeze
Debbie Spaulding knows her family's 450 acre fields and campground contain the unusual fossil reef. She has allowed people to view the rocks--everyone from students at Bellows Free Academy in St. Albans to a group of geologists from Toronto.

But Spaulding, and her husband Rustam, expect to see their property taxes jump this year because of Act 60, the state's education funding reform law. The law requires property-rich towns to share their school dollars with poorer communities. Isle La Motte is a "rich" town because the island has tens of miles of valuable lakefront land and relatively few students to educate. The town's tax rate is expected to rise from 2.85 per hundred dollars of assessed value to 3.90 next year.

The Spauldings used to farm the land, as Rustam Spaulding's father did before him. But it was difficult to make ends meet and eventually, after an unsuccesful try at raising beef cattle they turned 30 acres into Lakehurst Camp ground. Now their modest brick-red home with a breathtaking view of the lake is the office for the small campground. The trash bins and signs near their home office and on the drive down to the lake identify their chief customers. Everything is in French. Canadians come to spend summer weekends in tidy trailers with a lakeside view.

Even before Act 60 became law, the couple were worried about the viability of their business. The Canadian dollar's value is so low it makes it tough for the Spauldings' customers to afford to come. The Spauldings don't think they can even sell their land for development because all the bedrock--the ancient coral reef--makes it impossible to put a septic system on the land.

Because they operate the office for the campground out of their home, they won't qualify for the homestead exemptions that gives taxpayers with incomes less than $75,000 a tax break under the new law. They do qualify based on income, Debbie Spaulding says. "We feel like we are between a rock and a hard place," she said, laughing.

The Spauldings would like to sell their land to a conservation group, but calls to the Nature Conservancy, the Vermont Land Trust and the state haven't yielded much hope. Their place is not a working farm which makes it ineligible for some kinds of protection.

Nearby resident Linda Fitch has a little more hope. She is working with the Lake Champlain Land Trust and a coalition of neighbors to try to purchase a quarry that CMC wants to reopen northwest of the Spaulding property.

"This is a huge thing for the state of Vermont," Fitch said. "Very few people understand how important these reefs are scientifically. We would like to see them preserved."

My friend, Donald Gibson in Princeton, was a professor of English at Rutgers University in New Brunswick, New Jersey, just up the road from the town of Princeton. Intrigued by this article he suggested that we visit a colleague of his, a geologist at Rutgers, to show him the article and to ask his advice on how the community of geologists might be able to help preserve the reef.

The geologist turned out to be one George McGhee, a paleontologist whose work was focused on the analysis of ancient ecosystems and the evolution of life through time. He was immediately able to see what the stakes were.

"I'll send out an email to my colleagues," he said. "We may be able to muster some support."

Throughout May and June of 98 I began to get emails. I called them "paleo-alerts."

Robert J. Elias
Professor of Paleontology
Department of Geological Sciences
The University of Manitoba
Winnipeg, Manitoba
Canada R3T 2N2

Linda Fitch:

I wish to express my hope that efforts are successful in saving the Isle La Motte reefs from elimination due to quarrying. These 480 million year old structures, dating back to the Ordovician Period, are the oldest and finest examples of their kind in the global geologic record. They represent the earliest reefs constructed by communities of stromatoporoid, coral, and bryozoan animals in an ancient marine environment. They formed during the Ordovician evolutionary radiation, one of the greatest times of diversification in the history of the biosphere.

As a result of quarrying operations in the past, beautiful exposures of these reefs have been available for scientific study, education of students, and enlightenment of the public. I will never forget my visit to the famous Fisk Quarry, as a field trip participant during an international paleontology conference in 1986. It is essential that the most important reef sites be preserved in their original geologic context, in perpetuity. Future quarrying operations must not eliminate this unique record of our natural heritage!

Sincerely,
Robert J. Elias

Robert N. Ginsburg
Professor of Marine Geology
Rosenstiel School of Marine and Atmospheric Science
University of Miami, Miami, FL 33149

Dear Linda Fitch,

I write in support of all efforts to preserve the magnificent fossil reef communities on Isle La Motte.

I am a Professor of Marine Geology with decades of experience studying both living and fossil reefs. The Ordovician reefs on your Island are a scientific resource of extraordinary value because they are a time capsule of the beginnings of reef building. Reefs have played a key role in the history of life and the formation of calcareous rocks and having access to the nearly unique exposures on Isle La Motte contributes both to research and teaching. Moreover, reefs are major reservoirs for oil, gas and metallic ores in many different parts of North America and the rest of the world. Understanding Ordovician reefs is valuable in exploration and development of reefs of other ages elsewhere in the world in the same way that understanding ancient societies guides our thinking and analysis of modern examples...

Last year I chaired the International Year of the Reef, a worldwide effort to raise awareness of the value of living reefs to science and society. One of the central themes we used in that effort was that reefs are like cities in that they have the same functional elements: organisms that are builders, some that serve as water purifiers, others that handle waste disposal, and even some who keep the reef cities tidy. Just as we want to preserve the Egyptian pyramids, Mayan cities and early cities of North America, so must we also insure that Ordovician reef cities will be available for succeeding generations.

I do hope that you and your fellow residents of Isle La Motte can insure the survival of those splendid examples of ancient reefs.

Frank R. Brunton
Dept. of Earth Sciences
Laurentian University
Sudbury, ON P3E 2C6

Just received an email warning of possible destruction of the Isle La Motte coral sponge reefs in Vermont. I would like to help prevent this. I collected some material from these reefs in fall of '96. I am a ancient reef paleoecologist, interested in evolution of these Middle Ordovician reefs and they hold much more information than is found in Max Pitcher's classic papers. I am hoping to begin a re-examination of these structures in the next year, so this news is devastating both from personal perspective but more importantly from an evolutionary, geo-historic perspective. I will look into what I can do from this end, but would like info on what steps are being taken to make this a protected geo-historic site or something along those lines. I am not familiar with US laws and regulations in how to fight such exploitation

Ken Tobin
Dept. of Geosciences
Princeton University
Princeton, NJ 08544

I am a geologist who interprets the paleoclimatic conditions associated with the formation of carbonate rocks during the period (505 to 439 millions of years ago) when the reefs on Isle La Motte were formed. The reefs on Isle La Motte formed during a particularly interesting period in earth's history when the carbon dioxide composition in the atmosphere was 14 to 16 times that of today. In my opinion the most pressing environmental concern that faces our society today is that of global warming associated with raising values of carbon dioxide caused by the burning of fossil fuels. The rock records case studies of climatic conditions, which with patience can be accessed. This "warehouse" of knowledge can provide examples of what happens to the earth when carbon dioxide values are elevated. Research I have completed on the chemical composition of components within the reefs on Isle La Motte provide keys to unraveling what sea water chemistry was like back during this period. This information when integrated into a global web of data can start to address oceanic-atmospheric interactions during this period. It would be a shame if such a valuable resource was lost to the wheels of progress.

Dr. Stephen Kershaw
Dept of Geography and Earth Sciences
Brunel University
Uxbridge,
Middlesex UB8 3PH
United Kingdom

Dear Linda Fitch,

I am a stromatoporoid specialist, based here in the UK, with a 20-year publication record of work on stromatoporoids. Because most of my work has been on the Silurian and Devonian, I have had no opportunity to visit Isle La Motte, but would like to do so in the future; therefore I have only seen photos of the reef site.

This site is, as is well-known amongst fossil reef workers, one of the most important sites in the world for the study of fossil reefs. This is because it is not only beautifully exposed, but is, critically, the oldest of the Palaeozoic reef systems which contain certain fossils (stromatoporoids and corals), that later in evolution, developed into the widespread and well-studied reefs of the Silurian and Devonian around the world. Importantly, also there are very few examples of these Ordovician reefs, and that makes the Isle La Motte site of special importance.

If the reef is destroyed, it will not be possible to test out ideas of reef ecology and evolution that are being developed by workers at present. For example, it has long been supposed that reef systems always developed in environments involving sea level fall, but more recent ideas are overturning this notion, and that reefs may instead be features of rising sea level, and therefore are important in developing models of ancient sedimentary systems that goes beyond the study of reefs. This is one aspect of a large review paper on stromatoporoids that I have got in press, to be published later this year (in the journal called "Paleontology"), the first comprehensive review on stromatoporoids for many years. That same paper reviews the current knowledge of stromatoporoids in the Isle La Motte reef, because of their importance in the geological history of both the reefs and the stromatoporoids. Loss of the reef would therefore deprive science of the material with which to test ideas on evolution of reef systems, and it is to great advantage to preserve the site.

This letter is intended to provide perspective on the importance of the site, and I therefore hope that it is of value to non-geologists who are assessing the site. I would be pleased to supply any other background information about the nature and evolution of fossil reefs and the fossils they contain, so that prospective developers are in full possession of the facts of this key locality before decisions are made about its future.

Personally I envy the location of your home right next to this place. Working in London, England, I am some distance away from such gems."

The Qwarriors

Reef Builders
Stomatoporoid mounds in the walls of the Fisk Quarry.
Now extinct they are thought to be related to sponges.

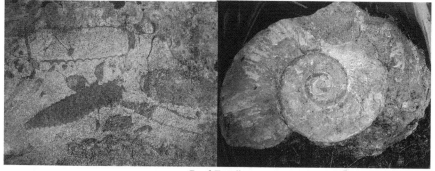

Reef Dwellers
Cephalopod fossils. Cephalopods were the ancient ancestors of the modern squid.
Their earliest forms were straight-shelled but over time they evolved coiled shell shapes.

Artist, Michele Ratté, daughter of former VT State Geologist,Chuck Ratté,
makes tracings of fossils in the rock.

21. The Deal
"Keep your eyes on the stars, and your feet on the ground."
— *Theodore Roosevelt*

ROOSEVELT'S TRIP TO YOSEMITE WITH THE GREAT NATURAL-
IST JOHN MUIR in 1903 has been described as "the most significant camping trip in conservation history."[43] It is probably on this occasion that Roosevelt was convinced that land should be set aside by the US government and
conserved in perpetuity. "The third night of camping was at the edge of Bri-
dalveil Meadow in Yosemite Valley, where President Roosevelt was Muir's cap-
tive audience to hear a convincing plea for Yosemite wilderness and for setting
aside other areas in the United States for park purposes."[44]

Roosevelt later wrote, "The first night we camped in a grove of giant sequoias. It was clear weather, and we lay in the open, the enormous cinnamon-
colored trunks rising about us like the columns of a vaster and more beautiful
cathedral than was ever conceived by any human architect."[45]

It is the healing capacity of nature, of beauty, of solitude that fueled all of us in
our struggle to preserve the quarry as we knew it. A quarry is not exactly a
pristine wilderness. But the Fisk Quarry embodied the story of how nature
can re-create itself, restore itself after a period of many years. We were fighting for a place which, over the years, had healed not only itself, but us and our
spirits, had brought us, our children, and our grandchildren closer to nature.
Over the years it had slowly transformed from a busy place of men and machines in the nineteenth century to a water filled wonderland for animals,
birds, exploring children, and adults seeking respite and solitude.

We had worked for three years, attempting to make our case. "The only
way that you can really conserve land," we had been told, "is to buy it. Put
conservation easements on it."

Spring/Summer 1998
Carol and I took a moment from the morning tasks to sit on the front porch,
to drink more cups of coffee made with fresh ground organic French Roast

beans. With coffee we savored wind off the lake from the south, a phoebe singing in the apple tree, the washing machine rumbling clean the queen sized pink and green flowered sheets for the Stone Cottage because B&B guests were expected shortly.

It was somehow a relief, the getting lost in the details of living; the concrete, hands on, down home reality of hanging sheets out to dry on the line, the clatter of red winged black birds in the field, the blooming of pale pink astilbe by the stone wall, the pleasure of walking by the old green velvet settee in the living room, the matter of the fact of a cat destructed mole on the garage floor next to the garden cart—the infinitely comforting, grounding universe of physical reality. Such a relief from the inexorable deadlines for testimony, rebuttal testimony, objections, motions, newspaper articles, negotiations and ongoing and miscellaneous worry.

For the third summer we hosted our "Tea Gardens" on Sunday afternoons. Carol made scones and decorated cakes with fruits and flowers. We made tea sandwiches. Cream cheese with cucumbers and dill from the garden. Folk singers and other musicians sang and performed on the lawn. Artists from all over Vermont brought their work and exhibited in the barn.

One of the artists was Merrill Hemond, builder and Master Scout, whose paintings were another and unexpected talent.

Paul Bruhn as Chief Negotiator was working on making a deal with the president of CMC. The problem—or so it seemed—was price. When one purchases land through a land trust for conservation purposes, there is a ceiling on the price that the land trust can pay. That price has to be justifiable to sources such as foundations or government funders. The value should be determined by a qualified appraiser. Should such a price take into account the mineral rights of the quarry? Do you appraise land on its quarrying value? But what if the quarry does not qualify for the necessary permits?

"They bought the two quarries (Goodsell and Fisk) back in 1995 for $90,000," I said to Paul early on. "Taxes for the Fisk Quarry, interestingly, were $64 a year. Just for the sake of argument, if you divided the $90,000 by two you could say that the market value of the Fisk Quarry then was $45,000. Ok, so make it $50,000."

That figure had once been mentioned informally to the president of CMC president. "$50,000," he had said. "Well that's nothing. $50,000 for 20 acres is less than land like this goes for around here. You people should get together and name a realistic figure."

Paul looked for an appraiser who could come up with a viable appraisal for a quarry. "We will try to argue the case that it would be to Oliver's advantage to make a 'bargain sale,'" he explained to me. He said that if the sale is to a nonprofit with tax exempt status, the difference between the appraisal and a lower price would be considered a donation to the nonprofit which, as a deductible contribution, could be a big tax advantage.

Fearful that CMC would bring the case back to the Wetlands Office, we continued to prepare for the possibility of renewed legal activity. We focused on the possibility that the quarry field and the entire stretch of land called Fisk Flats, of which I owned some 10 acres, might all be wetland.

Stephanie visited frequently. "It's hilarious," she said. "Linda is always walking through the field barefoot so she can feel whether it's wet. Always sticking her finger into the ground saying 'See? It's wet!' "

In the meantime Paul continued to work on getting an appraisal for the quarry property. He found an appraiser who did a complex analysis of the value of stone, amount of stone potentially to be quarried, and a thousand other details. Using complex formulas a Vermont appraiser finally presented us with a thick bound document which calculated that the working quarry could be worth as much as $400,000. This would provide the justification of some kind of price—yet to be worked out between Paul and CMC's president, for the purchase of the quarry.

August on the island is marked by the ripening of apples in Hall's Orchard.

In those days Mina Hall, matriarch of the family, would walk across the road from her old stone house--the Halls' ancestral home since the early 1800s--to greet us at the roadside stand as we stared at the rows of apples in great wooden boxes and smaller bags. It was hard to choose. Yellow Transparents, Macs, Cortlands, Empire. They had names like poetry, fragrance like harvest.

Carol left at the end of August to go back to her home in New Jersey and to her job as a school counselor. Merrill was elsewhere on a building job. Mother had gone back to her retirement community in New Jersey. I would stay. We had gotten through the summer, and despite our fears there was, as yet, no indication that CMC had filed another CUD application.

The days cooled. Clouds of birds would gather in this tree or that chattering excitedly about which southern route to take. "Let's go over Albany, no, that's all city, I say we fly over The Thousand Lakes." Chatter chatter talk talk. Sky sometimes blue, often grey, the land now shaded in the reds, golds, browns, of sumac, maple, oak, the black branches of lilac, the cold, wet, still green grass of early mornings.

Though there was much to do during the day, with the onset of evening, with everyone gone, it felt like a lonely world. I went out into the last edge of sunset one night and jogged past the quarry--stopping in utter delight to the sound of a screech owl. I heard it twice and went into the quarry to pursue it but found only autumn silence. I came back after a mile of walking in the deepest blackness of what seemed like midnight and saw, to my great surprise, that it was only 8:00 p.m. No wonder farmers and peasants and all such go to bed at sunset. So goodnight from the peasant woman (mixed with bits of warrior).

In early November Paul called me and said, "Good news! It looks as though there might be a Christmas present. I think I've worked out something with the president of CMC." Paul said that he had verbally agreed to sell the Fisk Quarry for $200,000. I'll meet with him in Rutland tomorrow and hopefully will come away with a signed agreement."

But somehow, it didn't happen. "I don't know what's going on. It seems as though he's stalling for some reason." Paul was completely frustrated but he wasn't ready to give up. However, if there were to be an agreement, and if by some miracle the money could be raised, it was time to work out the possible future ownership of the quarry. An old friend in nearby Alburgh, Pat Elmer, gave me the name of a lawyer in St. Albans, who might be able to help us form a nonprofit organization with 501(c)(3) tax exempt status. I went to see one Lawrence Bruce who turned out to be very much interested in environmental issues. To my delight he agreed to serve, pro-bono, as our lawyer in setting up the trust.

The new nonprofit was to be called the Isle La Motte Reef Preservation Trust. I walked around the neighborhood rounding up a potential Board of Directors. I would be President. Mary Jane agreed to be Vice-president. New Isle La Motte resident, Bob McEwen, agreed to be Treasurer, Larry Bruce agreed to serve on the board as Secretary. Also on the board were to be Neil Hanna, and a new friend--Michael Cohen--Rabbi of the Israel Congregation in Manchester Center, Vermont and founding member of the Arava Institute for Environmental Studies in Israel. He had called after reading *the Burlington Free Press* article--fascinated with this amazing geological phenomenon in Vermont. An activist environmentalist, he had good ideas and contacts for us, not the least of which was Tom Benson, then President of the environmentally oriented Green Mountain College. Tom also joined the Board.

Though the fledgling organization was quickly registered with the state of Vermont as a nonprofit, we had yet to receive the all important tax exempt status from the federal government. "This will take some time," warned Larry Bruce.

The new Executive Director of the Lake Champlain Land Trust, Peter Espenshade, was very supportive of the project. He agreed that if the purchase of the Fisk Quarry were to take place soon, ownership at the closing could be transferred to the tax exempt Lake Champlain Land Trust until such time as the Isle La Motte Reef Preservation Trust received its own tax exempt status.

I wrote to Charlotte Mehrtens: "I don't have to say that your help during this past three years has been invaluable. In fact, without you none of this would have been possible. I'm hoping that you will continue to be the central guiding light of this project and chief advisor concerning its use as a scientific and educational resource. I'm also hoping that this all works and that we don't find ourselves back in some form of permitting process, spending night and day providing testimony in response to a new Operations Plan submitted by CMC to the Wetlands Office."

I went back to Princeton just long enough to create Thanksgiving for my family. There I saw an ad in the local paper, Town Topics. Mini poodle puppies I read. From a litter I chose a tiny cream colored ball of fur who showed all the signs of becoming an energetic little character who would do just fine in Vermont. Together we returned to the island. By the end of November Dido (her Greek human family of origin and I wanted to give her a Greek kind of name with no more than two syllables) and I were sleeping in the Doctor's Office, the only warm room in the house.

Early mornings were a composition of grey and white light, the lake dark and still. There was no wind just quiet snow and the sound of the furnace, humming in what might have been the key of A flat. Now it was lighter and I could better see snow in the air, snow rimming the quarry, snow transforming our summer world into a new place, turning the summer state of mind upside down.

"Let me know if you want me to plow you out," said Dave Rowe the other day...Dave whom I associate with summer...with lawn mowers and weed whackers.

Life here in winter demands a kind of focus having to do with survival. The weather is so important. Being warm is so challenging. It is a matter of intense interest how you heat your house. How your neighbor heats their house. Whether one has wood. Where it's stacked. How it's stacked. Is it dry? Or propane? Fuel oil? Electricity? Everything so expensive. Warmth so hard to come by.

And it was rifle season for deer. The pickup trucks equipped with gun racks were out and I knew enough to slow my car down when I saw the guys gathered around one parked truck with a six point buck lying in the truck bed, its heart stopped and its eyes open, and to offer congratulations. To the guys. A silent prayer for the buck. They (the guys) and I are allies in one important sense: we all want the open space; we want the woods; we want the habitat. We want the deer to thrive...if for different reasons. Community. Getting along. It's all about finding common ground. (Is that Gifford Pinchot speaking?)

Dido was a source of comfort. She spun around the house with joy, frolicked with the occasional ant traversing cold floors, and celebrated the coming of each new day by wagging herself out of her little basket and around, under, and between my legs. Comfort indeed!

In early December I got another call from Paul Bruhn. "Ok," he said. "I've got another appointment with you know who tomorrow afternoon at around 1:00. Keep your fingers crossed." "Tomorrow" was December 5th.

On the Day, as afternoon approached I was pacing the floor. I continued to pace, watching the clock, looking at my watch, listening for the phone. 1:00 p.m. came and went. 1:30, 2:00. 3:00. Finally it was 3:45 and the phone was ringing."

"Ok," said Paul on the phone. "I guess I'm ok."

"What happened?"

"The police just left."

My heart started to pound. "What?"

"Well, you know how it is. He started stalling again. Finally I got so mad that I guess I just got carried away. I broke something...I don't know what it was ...some vase or something. I guess it was kind of valuable. Anyway he called the police and I got taken down to the station. I had a lot of explaining to do but they let me go...I guess there will be a hearing or something."

A great stillness came over me. We had gone through so much...the terrifying hearings, Joe's death, and now this. I could see the headlines. I took a deep breath and forced myself to be calm. We will get through this--even this --as well.

And then...and then...Paul started laughing. It suddenly dawned on me. That wretch! He was having me on with his warped, insane sense of humor. In the next sixty-seconds he heard language from me that, I imagine, he couldn't imagine that I even knew. When I finally let him get a word in edgewise there was an unapologetic remnant of chuckling in his voice.

"Ok, ok," he said. "There was no police. No broken vase. He signed an agreement to sell the quarry for $215,000. He wants to close on December 31st. We've got until then to raise the money."

A few more moments of profanity from me. And then, "This is December 5th. We're supposed to raise the money by the end of the month? In three weeks?"

If you live in Vermont and you have no time at all in which to raise a great deal of money and you have to find the perfect fundraising partner...well, that would be Paul Bruhn. Throughout December, we were both on the phone. I wrote letters. Paul went after his vast network of contacts.

At this time of year I did not like being away from my Princeton home, my mother and my sons. My new daughter in law. I hated not being able to do any Christmas shopping. No Christmas cards. No cookie baking. No getting the traditional ornaments down from the attic. The little island felt desolate and austere and lonely, with one car going by the house each day. How could we ever make the goal? It seemed possible that the quarry war would stretch on into the new year, depleting my finances and time and energy, world without end.

But Paul and I talked on the phone every day. Among other things he was instrumental in inspiring press coverage. On December 15, the first piece appeared as an editorial in *The Burlington Press*.

"Fossils to Keep"

It took 2 million years for the world's oldest coral reef to form, but it's the next 11 days that really matter for this unique geological resource in Isle La Motte. The effort to conserve the 20 acre Fisk Quarry and its priceless fossil outcroppings is $60,00 short of the $200,000 needed to close the deal by December 31.

For Vermont and for science everyone should hope the contributions come in quickly. The preservation of this strategic piece of bedrock would safeguard a precious natural resource that shows and tells the story of the earth's formation

The owners of the quarry, Oliver and Mary Danforth of Rutland, are to be commended for agreeing to sell the land to conservation groups at a price well below market value.

They made the decision after initially setting out to seek Act 250 permits to actively quarry marble from a site long dormant—an operation that could have destroyed reef with priceless scientific value. The collaboration is a fine example of conservationists and landowners working together for the greater good.

The Preservation Trust of Vermont, the Lake Champlain Land Trust and the newly founded Isle La Motte Reef Preservation Trust deserve praise for pulling this nearly successful deal together.

The 480 million-year-old reef in question stretches over 1,000 acres of Isle La Motte. In its entirety, the reef has been compared to the Egyptian pyramids and Mayan cities in significance. If the funds cannot be raised, the Danforths say they will likely go forward with their effort to quarry the site. This would jeopardize an important scientific site and unravel a healthy collaboration.

It's not too late to give toward a conservation deal that represents a victory for science and for Vermont."

Day by day, bit by bit, we inched toward the goal. Some money came from neighbors; other from family; but it was Paul with his lifetime of contacts and influence in Vermont who made it happen. After the first editorial in the Free Press came another article. A slow trickle of funds turned into a steadier stream and checks came pouring in from all over Vermont. A very substantial contribution from the Freeman Foundation came via the influence of Paul and the Preservation Trust of Vermont.

On a wintry evening just before Christmas, I decorated the house. I set red candles and a bowl of red glass balls on the dining room table, a string of white lights over the front porch, a Christmas arrangement of garden squash, rosemary and sage still alive in the herb garden, and pine boughs by the front door. In the evening, friends and some Qwarriors gathered in the living room.

"We're almost there, thanks to Paul," I said. "But we're $20,000 short. The question is, can we find $20,000 in the next six days? We need an angel to deliver just enough money so that I can get to Princeton in time to get a tree, deck my house, shop, and have a traditional family Christmas."

At that moment the phone rang. Five minutes later I returned to the living room in an ecstatic daze. "It was Richard Rachals. I don't think you know him but I met him at a Citizens Participation Network meeting...you know...the organization that Joe Bivins set up. Anyway he asked how much we needed and I told him. He said he could make a bridge loan for the $20,000 so we can close by the 31st. He said he was doing it for Joe."

On December 30 my mother sent an email to her three sisters. Scattered across the country from Oregon, to Colorado, to Arizona and New Jersey, all of the sturdy Octogenarian sisters stayed in touch via email. This one was entitled "Joy on an Arctic Night."

> Dear Sisters,
> I have just received a joyful call from Linda who said she left Fisk Farm this morning at 6:00 am, arrived in Rutland at 9:00 am, had breakfast, located CMC's office, bought paper cups for the champagne she had stored in her car, and was ready for the Fisk Quarry closing at 10:30. After the papers were signed, there were champagne toasts and warm expressions of friendship and good wishes for the future of the new Isle la Motte Reef Preservation Trust.
>
> On this subzero night Fisk Farm is full of warmth and joy as neighbors and friends gather to celebrate the end of more than three years of struggle and the preservation, not only of the ancient reef, but the peace and beauty of Isle la Motte and particularly the neighborhood next to the Fisk Quarry.
>
> Thank you for three long years of empathizing with the Quarry Crusade which sometimes seemed destined to go on forever, and thank you for joining in the rejoicing.
> Love, Violet

It's early morning darkness; the ground, I see from the bedroom window, is white. Heavy frost? Light snow? I leave my warm flannel sheeted bed for the frigid world and hastily put on warm pants, three layers of shirts ending with red sweatshirt and the warmest of socks. Turn up furnace to heat only the Doctor's Office--a little island separated from other rooms by a red and black woven bedspread hanging over the door. Grind coffee beans in the icy kitchen, feed the cold cat and warm pup who then ask to go outside. The smell of freshly ground, French roast, organic coffee fills the kitchen; my cup, steaming, heavenly.

I step out into the world; outside is soft and grey, trees black against a grey blue sky, grey blue lake; frosted grass is stiff and white and crackles underfoot: my foot, dog foot, cat foot. Sunrise has migrated from over the northeast fields to the southeast quarry, painting quarry sky with stripes of rose. A skim of ice covers Big Pond; all quarry life has gone into or under and out of sight. Five leftover geese rocket across the sky heading south; their rackety cries momentarily break the silence of the early morning world.

I know again, that this small island and every small place, all contain all the elements of the larger world. Transcendence and anguish abound; there are celebration, connection and deadly events. Light interweaves with shadow. Here we are, this island—a grain of sand, with all things contained herein.

And here I am, still, in the cold season of my Vermont world. We have managed to preserve a small patch of rocky land on this northern island; a gravesite of our ancestors: our ocean going, hardshelled, reef building ancestors who once created a great underwater civilization in this place. For those of us who live or visit—the birds, the fish, the beaver, the humans, it continues to be a habitat, a place of solace, of safety, of renewal.

I tramp up the porch steps into the coffee-fragrant house, the Doctor's Office now a warm and welcoming place. The eastern sky is grey; the west hints of blue. Sunshine has been promised.

January 7, 1999

To: All Parties
From: The District Environmental Board Office
Subject: Withdrawal of Land Use Application 6G0497

On February 12, 1996, an application was filed by CMC to quarry dimensional marble and fill and rubblestone from an existing quarry site known as the Fisk Quarry.

On December 30, 1998, CMC sold its Fisk Quarry in Isle La Motte to The Lake Champlain Land Trust. Therefore, CMC is withdrawing its Act 250 Application to reopen the quarry.

Land Use Application 6G0497 shall be considered withdrawn as of the day of sale of January 1, 1999.

22. Endings & Beginnings
"Do not go where the path may lead.
Go instead where there is no path and leave a trail...."
"Ralph Waldo Emerson

August, 1927

IN AUGUST OF 1927 AN OBITUARY APPEARED IN *THE BURLING-TON FREE PRESS.* "The death of Elizabeth Hubbell Fisk of Isle La Motte, widow of Hon. Nelson W. Fisk, former Lieutenant Governor of Vermont is an irreparable loss. Mrs. Fisk was one of those persons who take so much with them when they die that their loss robs an entire community of much that enriched its life. In developing artistic handicrafts, Mrs. Fisk was a master. The products of the looms have won worldwide recognition, not as copies of what had been done, but as original contributions to creative art. Mrs. Fisk had a personality of rare charm even, charitable and generous in her judgments and quick to appreciate the good in others, sympathetic, kindly, gracious in manner, modest in achievement, beautiful in spirit." [46]

The obituary was written by Lena Hill Severance, the grandmother of my former husband, Peter Andrews, who first brought me to Isle La Motte. so many years before. It marked the end of an era for the Fisks on Isle La Motte, begun modestly shortly after the birth of the nation, rising gloriously in the nineteenth century, and ending in the twentieth century, again modestly.

It was the fossils that saved the day. There is no Vermont legislation comparable to Act 250 or Wetland legislation enabling the conservation of a geological site—even one of world fame. But it was its geological significance that enabled us, with our conservation partners, the Preservation Trust of Vermont and the Lake Champlain Land Trust, to raise funds to purchase the land. In the spring of 1999 the US Internal Revenue Service issued tax exempt status to the Isle La Motte Reef Preservation Trust, hereafter designated as a non-profit organization with 501(c)(3) status.[47] The Lake Champlain LandTrust then turned ownership over to the Isle La Motte Reef Preservation Trust as as had been previously agreed.

Finally we owned the Fisk Quarry—now to be known as the Fisk Quarry Preserve. We applied for and received a grant from the Lake Champlain Basin Program which enabled us to create a public path and viewing area as well as a kiosk which told the geological, the human, and the ecological story of the quarry in both French and English.

And then, on June 19, 1999, we held a Grand Opening of the Fisk Quarry Preserve. It was a hot day. Photos show Carol and me standing in the shade of the new kiosk in broad brimmed garden hats; Mary Jane is there along with Scott, and other Qwarriors. Paul Bruhn, Vermont State Senator Dick Mazza and Representative John LaBarge, stand in the shade of the new kiosk.

A letter of congratulations from Governor Dean was read and bagpipes sounded from the quarry cliff played by, of all people, Geoffrey Green, in kilts. After the ceremonies we adjourned to the lawn of Fisk Farm where music was played, and refreshments and general merriment was served up to all.

A dinner at nearby Ruthcliffe Lodge followed, with Paul Bruhn and the president of CMC and his wife present as honored guests. Toasts accompanied roasts. Somehow this arduous three year battle had transformed into my naive hope of three years ago: a win/win solution.

A grant from the Lake Champlain Basin Program enabled a public path and viewing area as well as a kiosk telling the geological, the human, and the ecological story of the quarry

More than twenty years have passed since we began this effort in 1995. What has happened since then? Early on, Charlotte Mehrtens strongly urged us to continue to preserve land. "Remember that the bedrock on the southern third of Isle La Motte is composed of reef layers of different ages. They show how the reef evolved over time. It is important to scientists that examples of the different ages be preserved for further research and study."

So in the year 2000, the directors of the young Isle La Motte Reef Preservation Trust agreed to try to purchase more of the reef. We knew that there was a famous site which geologists called the "Goodsell Ridge" located about a mile to the northeast of the Fisk Quarry. It was owned by Tom and Shirley LaBombard, and for many years was used for grazing dairy cows.

Tom and Shirley, without much formal education, had met up with many scientists in their pastures over the years and had learned a great deal about the reef. They guarded the fossils and anyone caught in the act of chipping away at rock to obtain samples met with their wrath. (Their young daughter had once let the air out of the tires of an intruding bus.) They were delighted that we had preserved the Fisk Quarry and suggested that we might be interested in buying some of their land as well.

In partnership with the Lake Champlain Land Trust, a fundraising campaign was begun in 2001 to purchase 81 acres of the Goodsell Ridge. Early in the process, board member Bob McEwen and I conspired to buy—without any perceptible source or promise of funds—the first ten acres of the land, on which stood a crumbling farmhouse and barn. Somehow, we thought, some kind of Visitor/Interpretive Center might be fashioned out of these impossible buildings. A local bank loaned the money and we signed the deal...with fingers crossed. And somehow found the funds.

By 2005 funds for the remaining 71 acres were raised—thanks to our conservation partner, the Lake Champlain Land Trust, whose Director Peter Espanshade and his associate Chris Boget spearheaded a successful fundraising campaign. The land was purchased in the fall of 2005 and, as with the Fisk Quarry Preserve, conservation easements co-held by the Vermont Housing and Conservation Board and the Lake Champlain Land Trust were placed on the land, protecting it in perpetuity.

With volunteer labor and some professional expertise, we restored the small farmhouse which became the Visitor and Learning Center. We developed exhibits to tell the story. Trails winding through pastures and woodlands were created by volunteers. Interpretive signage designed with the help of consulting geologists led to "Fossil Discovery Areas" and another kiosk—funded by the Lake Champlain Land Trust—was designed to tell the story of the ancient reef and its place in Earth History.

Restoring the Farmhouse:
Standing from left to right: Claude Genest, Scott Newman, Kevin Behm, Russell Coe, Betsy Howland, Donald Gibson, Martha Walton, Pam Craige.
Kneeling from left to right: Bill Howland, Kevin Walton.

In 2002 my son, Lyle, had created a video called "The Oldest Reef" to help raise funds. Now it became a valuable educational tool for visitors.

The Goodsell Ridge Preserve officially opened in 2006. Visitors walked the grassy paths to Fossil Discovery Areas; groups of children and adults crawled on hands and knees to peer at the faint outlines of ancient marine life which once inhabited the ocean. "I think I found something good," said a four year old girl staring into a solution channel--a deep crevice in a limestone mound.

The geologists were out in force. Vermont State Geologist, Larry Becker, strolled about with former State Geologist, Charles Ratté. Charlotte Mehrtens, Chair of the Geology Department at the University of Vermont, was ensconced on a rock mound talking about the food web of the ancient Chazy Reef. David Griffing, Geologist from Hartwick College in Oneonta, New York, lectured the crowd while supervising two undergraduates with surveying equipment who were mapping reef outcrops for a senior thesis.

Back in 1996 Charlotte Mehrtens wrote: "The significance of these reefs is such that they should have designation as a US rare and historically significant spot. Every avenue of preservation should be looked into here all the way up to National Monument status because they are of such significant merit."

Board member and west shore neighbor, Charles Shelley, followed up on this. After much research, Charlie decided that the most appropriate designation for the Chazy Reef would be that of National Natural Landmark. This designation had been created in 1962 by Secretary of the Interior, Stuart Udall. National Natural Landmarks are selected for their rarity, and their importance to science and education. For several years Charlie persevered, laying the groundwork for this project. He traveled extensively, contacting geologists, sharing news of our efforts. Support letters arrived from eminent professionals, from Yale, Columbia, Cornell, from the President of the Paleontological Society. "A world paleontological treasure" was a phrase that many of them used.

Charlie also worked with Charlotte Mehrtens who wrote an extensive application for the designation which was submitted, along with the many letters of support, to the Department of the Interior. In 2009, significant sites of the Chazy Fossil Reef received the designation of National Natural Landmark. In an announcement letter the Secretary of the Interior wrote:

"The Chazy Fossil Reef is significant as the oldest known occurrence of a biologically diverse fossil reef, the earliest appearance of fossil coral in a reef environment, and the first documented example of the ecological principle of faunal succession. National Natural Landmark designation recognizes this surface exposure of an Ordovician fossil reef, as an extraordinary paleontological resource."[48]

The years of the Quarry War were painful for many reasons. The concept of conservation was not as prevalent as it is now. But there was a sense of local pride in a particular piece of history: the visit of Vice President Teddy Roosevelt to Isle La Motte. In 2001, the 100 year anniversary of Roosevelt's visit, Bob McEwen of the Isle La Motte Preservation Trust—later to become president of the Isle La Motte Historical Society—spearheaded a centennial celebration with the Champlain Islands Chamber of Commerce, part of which took place at Fisk Farm where Roosevelt once spoke to a thousand Vermonters.

It was a rousing good time with a great tent set up on Fisk Farm and a Roosevelt historical interpreter (one Ted Zalewski from Boston) who appeared—wearing silk top hat and small spectacles—in an antique vehicle owned and driven by neighbor Selby Turner. Music, and general festivities harkened back to the earliest days of the twentieth century. It was, in my mind, a way to foster a conservation ethic on Isle La Motte.

Since then TR Day has become an annual tradition on Isle La Motte, now an island-wide festival celebrating the conservation of our natural, agricultural and cultural heritage.

23. Postlude

"The most beautiful thing we can experience is the mysterious.
It is the source of all true art and science."
Albert Einstein

Scientists currently agree that the universe is 13.8 billion years old. Tiny Earth is a mere 4.6 billion years of age. Compared with those inconceivable stretches of time, the almost half billion year old Chazy reef is a relatively recent development. And to walk the ancient sea beds of the Chazy Reef and to ponder what scientists refer to as Deep Time is to raise the question: "What happened before the reef was formed? And what happened afterward?"

Visitors who came to the preserves had difficulty conceiving of 480 million years. Much less the 4 billion or so years of Earth history that preceded the beginnings of this ancient reef. Could we make a timeline of Earth history?

In Princeton I met Jennifer Morgan, author of a series of children's books called *The Universe Trilogy* describing the beginnings of the Universe, the formation of Earth, and the history of life. With an unlikely degree in theology, she had become an expert in translating concepts of science into lay language, into children's language. She became a keynote speaker at Education Conferences around the country and abroad, nurturing the philosophy that education is most powerful when taught "through the lens of a deep time perspective." She became my mentor and educational consultant for the Isle La Motte Preservation Trust, helping me to overcome a lifetime aversion to and fear of science. With her help I made a primitive timeline of Earth history for our Visitor Center. "Wouldn't it be great if we could have an outdoor timeline," I said to Jennifer at one point.

It was January of 2014. I was in Princeton, the phone rang and it was Jennifer.

"I just got a call from this person in California. Actually I met him at a conference--his name is Geoff Ainscow and he's the Manager of a project called "Walk Through Time." He's wondering if I know of an organization that would be interested in displaying it. It consists of 90 panels telling the story of the 4.6 billion year history of life on Earth and is designed to be set up on a trail almost a mile long. Actually, 4,600 feet long to be exact, with every foot representing a million years. How cool is that! Anyway, he asked if I know of an organization which might have an interest in an outdoor timeline? I told him I'd call him right back."

A 4,600 foot "Walk Through Time!"
Could this be some kind of incredible dream?
How much would it cost?

The "Walk Through Time" exhibit (known as WTT) had been the inspiration and creation of scientist Sid Liebes. I learned later that he had grown up on the San Francisco Peninsula from which, "in the 1930s, I could hike forever through fields of poppies and forests of eucalyptus...The air was pure. The sounds around our house were of birds, rustling leaves of eucalyptus trees."[49]

With a Ph.D. from Stanford Dr. Liebes moved to Princeton University in the late fifties where he taught physics and researched the properties of gravity. He returned to California in the 1960s to work in the Genetics Department of the of the Human Biology Program and Computer Science Department at Stanford University and eventually, as Senior Scientist, at Hewlitt Packard. Upon his return to California he was shocked by the changes in the landscape of his boyhood. "The poppy fields and eucalyptus forests were gone. The cities of the Peninsula had merged into 50 miles of uninterrupted urbanization. The apricot orchards surrounding San Jose had succumbed to urban sprawl...I felt a tremendous sense of loss for me and for others."[50] His goal became to work "for the preservation of options for the future" and dedicated himself to environmental causes.

> "I felt that science could do a better job of providing the public with perspective: an appreciation of the enormous span of time over which life had evolved on Earth; an awareness that the sun could support life on Earth for another billion years; knowledge that man was precipitating what could rapidly become the next mass extinction; awareness that human actions today were threatening the diversity of life on Earth for 10s of millions of years into the future. I believed that if people knew they would care."[51]

A year before his retirement from Hewlitt Packard, the company offered to fund a dream long cherished by Dr. Liebes: the design and construction of an exhibit of panels describing the 4.6 billion year history of life on Earth. Through collaboration with scientists, writers and volunteers the "Walk Through Time" display--consisting of 90 large panels to be spaced along a 4,600 foot trail--was completed. The exhibit was first displayed on Earth Day,

1997, for a five day meeting of 350 HP scientists from around the world. After that it was shown all over the world—in Australia, Canada, Costa Rica, England, Germany, Mexico, Switzerland, Singapore, South Africa, and Portugal.

"My Walk Through Time was an unforgettable experience, awe-inspiring, and humbling…" wrote one well known walker, anthropologist Jane Goodall.

I learned that there were three sets of the exhibit: one in the Bay Area in San Francisco, one in Switzerland, and one currently in Grand Rapids, Michigan where it had been recently displayed at a conference. It needed only a truck and driver to haul the trailer in which the exhibit was stored back from Grand Rapids. I contacted our Board members, they gave us a green light and things began to happen. "It's a great educational opportunity," said Tony Fowler, new chair of our Education Committee and recently retired professor of geology.

ILMPT Board member, Scott Newman and his son Brock, drove out to Grand Rapids, Michigan in April of 2014, located the exhibit in its specially designed trailer, and hauled it back to Vermont in a truck loaned by Isle La Motte neighbors, Carol and Steve Stata. For two weeks in May our 4,600-foot trail was carefully created by volunteers on the Goodsell Ridge Preserve with measuring tape, mowers, clippers, and the occasional chain saw. Finally, on May 31 of 2014, Tony Fowler organized the setup of the exhibit by twenty-five enthusiastic volunteers.

The Trail begins on a grassy knoll with a sign that tells me that the 4,600 foot walk I am about to take unfolds a scientific understanding of the 4.6 billion year history of Earth. I walk 100 feet—each foot representing a million years—and come upon another panel depicting Earth at the age of 4,600 years. I read "Orbiting gas and dust come together in planetesimals which collide to build the planets and moons of our solar system." Earth, with the other planets, is being born. On and on the trail continues, through a grassy field, through cedar groves, into dense woods, then back into the sunshine, where Earth history as understood by science today, is told on colorful panels.

In the summer of 2014, some twenty years after we first heard the jackhammers in the Fisk Quarry, visitors flocked to our preserves. The "Walk Through Time" trail was trodden by many hundreds of folk, people of all ages, of varying educational backgrounds—not only from Vermont—but by visitors from many other states. Other countries. "Humbling," they wrote in our sign-in book. "Incredible." There seemed to be a hunger for this kind of information. This kind of learning. Students were breathless as they became aware of the short and fragile place of human beings in the vast reaches of time. Some educators who visited began to imagine ways of teaching not only science but indeed all subjects, through the lens of deep time.

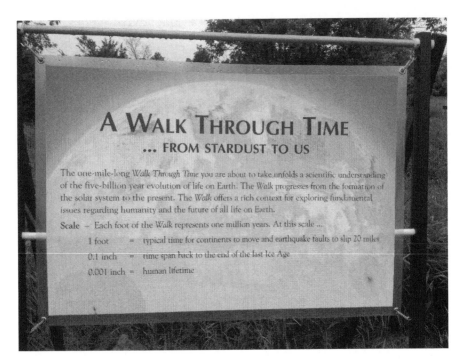

A WALK THROUGH TIME
... FROM STARDUST TO US

The one-mile-long *Walk Through Time* you are about to take unfolds a scientific understanding of the five-billion year evolution of life on Earth. The *Walk* progresses from the formation of the solar system to the present. The *Walk* offers a rich context for exploring fundamental issues regarding humanity and the future of all life on Earth.

Scale – Each foot of the *Walk* represents one million years. At this scale ...

    1 foot   = typical time for continents to move and earthquake faults to slip 20 miles

    0.1 inch = time span back to the end of the last Ice Age

    0.001 inch = human lifetime

Early in 2010, with large groups of visitors coming to the two preserves, it was clear that we would need a commodious education center, larger than what our small farmhouse could provide. After two years of studies by architects and engineers, Merrill—our master scout and builder—began, in 2012, to rehabilitate the crumbling old dairy barn on the Goodsell Ridge, a weary old structure that stood uneasily just north of the little farmhouse, our current Visitor Center.

Up on the hayloft floor he built four giant trusses which would serve to hold the barn together and then raised them up: two with the use of Tony Fowler's electric winch fastened to an old jeep, one with an antique hand winch belonging to neighbor Selby Turner, and one through magical levitation—all with an elaborate system of ropes, chains and pulleys.

"I learned how to do this stuff when I was a kid and helped my father drag logs out of his woods with his horse," said Merrill when the dust had settled. He then knocked out the hayloft floor and the ceiling of the milking parlor below, creating a great cathedral-like space.

"We call this place the 'church of the rocks,' "said a group of four men whom I met several years ago, hiking along a trail on the Goodsell Ridge Preserve. "We come here every Sunday to hike around, look at the rocks, think about them--their age, the age of the earth. It's hard to imagine--deep time and all--but when we are here it seems like a kind of holy experience."

Though we humans have lived a micro fraction of time, the school children, and the other visitors who come here, do not feel diminished by their dawning sense of Deep Time. It becomes increasingly clear that we are part of a very large story, born out of the ever-so-ancient formation of the stars; the birth of the elements. It is a science story and a sacred story and leaves us in awe as we stare at those ancient cephalopod shapes in the rock--ancestors of the intelligent squid and octopus, the stromatoporoid communities--critical builders of the reef, the coiled gastropods--taking on the universal spiral form which characterizes much of life and other phenomena of being.

In the spirit of John Muir, it was the healing and even sacred power of beauty, of nature, that fueled our journey. But with that preservation success, we gained more than we had ever imagined. To preserve this little corner of rock has been to create a place which gives rise to curiosity about the most fundamental of questions. We are happy when visitors come to look and--often--leave with a sense of awe.

Sid Liebes, creator of the Walk Through Time trail, once wrote: "I ponder...is it possible that a sense of awe and wonder, place and possibilities, can and perhaps must, become operational imperatives in guiding humanity into the future? It is not too late to transform our values and adapt our policies... None of us can predict the future. However, each of us is free to determine how we will contribute to the circumstances out of which the future will evolve."[52]

The dream goes on. Old animosities have mostly died away. I've told the story. A love of the land persists. And we remember Joe.

Fisk Quarry
by Carol Bemmels

Sometimes a great wound heals
into a work of art.

After the blasting,
the last chunk gouged from its heart,
the quarry lay still.

Something happened then.
Call it time.
Call it nature.
Call it God.
Call it rain filling a hole
or wind bearing soil.
Call it one seed at a time.

Beaver came and birds,
turtles, frogs, white-tailed deer,
Duckweed,   lichen,   Purple Aster,
Sumac, blazing red in autumn,
Blue-eyed Chicory,
Queen Anne's Lace.

Each signed its name
and the face of desolation
grew soft and lovely.

So now when people come,
like you or me,
or anyone, really,
who's known a loss—
it is possible to stand at the edge
of this great, grey hole
and find in any season:

changing color,
fresh tracks.

Linda Vaughn Fitch

Gratitude

At the end of a book you get to list the folks who have played a part in the story, who have made the journey with you. My list feels more like an expansive night sky with stars too numerous to count. I will make a rough try, however, knowing that I will be missing many. And of course the categories merge together. Qwarriors, geologists, expert witnesses, board members, and the rest...all will always be important people in my life.

I will always be grateful for:

The Qwarriors: Joe Bivins of course--brought to us by Randy Koch; Merrill Hemond who scouted the land, photographed the creatures and masterfully shaped the technical arguments both before and after Joe's death; Dan Froelich watcher of the birds and other living things; Andy Mills who mapped the water as it went over and under and through the land; Mary Jane Tiedgen (Southwitch), her husband Dave, her brother Jeff Williams and her father Carl Williams, all of whom who knew where the wild creatures lived; other neighbors--Joe and Leslie Bajorski, Elva Grant Garinther, Neil and Elaine Hanna, Ross and Phyllis Firth, John Scully, Vincent Scully, Scott Newman, Elizabeth Newman; after Joe's death Stephanie Kaplan - riding in on her bicycle (she was referred to as "Joy Rider" by Joe Bivins) if not her white horse, armed to the teeth with years of legal experience, and a passion for the land; also to the rescue Joe Kennedy, constantly applying his legal mind and training to the situation; expert witnesses Mary Kapkanis, Steve Revell, Jeff Parsons and probably others whom I have inadvertently left off this list, also provided great help toward the end of what my mother called the Quarry Crusade. Some of them have passed away including--at much too early an age--Mary Jane Tiedgen and John Scully. They live in our memories.

The Preservation Trust of Vermont and Paul Bruhn whose legendary preservation work throughout Vermont made the Fisk Quarry purchase possible; likewise the Lake Champlain Land Trust and Peter Espenshade and Chris Boget who found much of the funding for the Goodsell Ridge purchase; not to forget Karen Cady who brought our early struggles to the attention of the Lake Champlain Land Trust.

The geologists: Charles Ratté, former VT State Geologist who began the story, Charlotte Mehrtens of the University of VT who continued the story, George McGhee of Rutgers University who mobilized an international cadre of paleontologists on our behalf, Max Pitcher who did early important scientific work on the Chazy Reef, David Griffing of Harwick College who helped design some of our exhibits, Anthony Fowler of the University of Ottawa who grew up exploring the rocks on Isle La Motte and now serves on our Board of Directors, and finally, the many other geologists who have sent emails and letters of support.

The folks who have brought art and music to Fisk Farm which, for many years, have played a major role in supporting the operating budget of the Isle La Motte Preservation Trust: first Art Director, Valerie Ugro; Art Director for over a decade, Maurie Harrington; Music Director, Michael Waters who manifested two grand pianos in the restored Horse & Carriage Barn and has brought many great musicians to Isle La Motte; folk musicians Jack Harrington, Donna and Bernie Martin, Cathy Tudhope and many others.

The hardworking board members of ILMPT: As of this writing they are Betsy Howland, Bob McEwen, Charlie Shelley, Kevin Behm, Claire Durand, Tony Fowler, Kris Luce, and Scott Newman. Former Board Members include Mary Jane Tiedgen, Neil Hanna, Larry Bruce, Rabbi Michael Cohen, Tom Benson, Chuck Woessner, Dave Liloia, Charles Gurney. One also must mention volunteers David and Lee Oborne, Terry Anderson, Kathy Balutansky, Paul and Ann Germanowski, Sharon Powers, and so many others.

Charlie Shelley who, with Charlotte Mehrtens, obtained the designation of National Natural Landmark for significant sites of the Chazy Fossil Reef.

Keeper of Elizabeth Fisk's artistic legacy: Marty Turner Dale (Great niece of Elizabeth Fisk).

Educational Consultant: Jennifer Morgan, Author of "The Universe Trilogy" and a global social website--"Deep Time Journey"--bringing hundreds of children and adults into an appreciation of science and the power of deep time cosmic education; with Jennifer have come important new friends: Sid Liebes, Geoff Ainscow, and The Stiftung Drittes Millennium (Foundation for the Third Millennium) based in Zurich Switzerland, dedicated to promoting global sustainability and official owner of the "Walk Through Time" exhibit.

Dyed in the wool old friends: many of those mentioned above as well as Carol Bemmels, Claire Durand, Maureen and Selby Turner, Bill & Betsy Howland, Deborah La Porte Bremer; Pat Elmer and her husband Thomas, Claude Genest, Susan Larkin, Jean Kennedy, and many many more. New friends have enriched my understandings of all the themes in this book, particularly composer Sam Guarnaccia who tells the universe story in his great musical work "The Emergent Universe Oratorio" and his gifted wife Paula, and environmental historian Donald Hughes and his musician wife, Pam.

My in-laws: my former husband, Peter Andrews, who first brought me to Isle La Motte, a kind person and a great mathematician, and his supportive wife and my friend, Cate; Peter's family whom I will always continue to claim as my family including Peter's parents now deceased,--Edith and Emerson Andrews; my brother-in-law, Bryant Andrews; my brother-in law now deceased, Frank Andrews; my sisters-in-law, Ann and Betsy Andrews (who have supported this project in invisible and invaluable ways), my niece and nephews Sue, Chris and Kris, Kenneth, Steven and Esther along with their delightful progeny.

My family of origin beginning with my ever supportive parents now deceased, my father Lyle Fitch, who encouraged me to write and my mother, Violet Vaughn Fitch, who taught me about music and loving; my two brilliant sons, Lyle and Bruce Andrews, whose childhood explorations of the quarry contributed important information to the Quarry War; Bruce's talented wife and my daughter-in-law, Tobi; again Lyle who created the video "The Oldest Reef" which has been an invaluable educational resource for our many preserve visitors; and my Uncle Val Fitch--a scientist whose life and work which, though I will never understand it, has inspired in me the deepest respect for science.

My dear friend, partner, and editor, Donald Gibson, Professor Emeritus of English, Rutgers University, who has kept me on track and sustained and encouraged me since 1998.

My brother Devin who died in 1967 but whose loss taught me about tragedy, suffering, and, ultimately, the possibility of healing.

Synchronicity

"I do believe in an everyday sort of magic--the inexplicable connectedness we sometimes experience with places, people, works of art and the like; the eerie appropriateness of moments of synchronicity; the whispered voice, the hidden presence, when we think we're alone."

— *Charles de Lint*

Much of this tale is about synchronicity, the unexpected, unplanned coming togethernesses of people which resulted in the most unexpected of happenings. For example: after the "Walk Through Time" had been set up on the Goodsell Ridge, it occurred to me to look up some additional information about its creator, Sid Liebes. I knew only that he had been at Hewlitt Packard as a scientist, but what field of science had he been in? I went online. The following set of emails ensued:

June 24, 2014
Linda to Geoff Ainscow
Hi Geoff,

I just found a bit more online information on Sid Liebes and discovered that he had been at Princeton. Would you ask him if he knew my uncle, Val Fitch, physicist at Princeton?
Best,
Linda

July 3, 2014 -
Geoff Ainscow to Sid Liebes
Hi Sid,

When you were at Princeton did you know a professor by the name of Val Fitch? He is the uncle of Linda Fitch, who is the president of the Isle La Motte Preservation Trust, where the Walk is on display. Linda is the person responsible for organizing the placement of the Walk.
Cheers,
Geoff

Sidney Liebes to Geoff Ainscow

Congratulation, Geoff! Thanks, for sending the report on the opening. Lots of dedicated people, and beautiful setting. Small world. Not only did I know Val Fitch, we were close friends, tennis partners, and shared an office together, in the early 1960's.

One day, after he and his colleague had completed a particle physics experiment that disagreed with prevailing theory, he paced the office pondering the discrepancy.

Turning to me he asked, "Can you see what's wrong with the experiment?"

I replied that my knowledge of particle physics was not sufficient to help.

This was the experiment that they courageously concluded to publish, risking their reputations in doing so. Instead, they were granted Nobel Prizes.

Best,
Sid

Geoff Ainscow to Linda
Hi Linda

It is a small world and I think the WTT was destined to arrive at Isle La Motte.. I'm forwarding this message from Sid. He shared an office with your uncle. Amazing synchronicity.

Cheers,
Geoff

Val Fitch died on February 5, 2015

About the Author

Linda Fitch of Isle La Motte, Vermont and Princeton, New Jersey was born in Gordon, Nebraska in sandhill country. Her parents migrated to New York City where her father earned a Ph.D. in Economics at Columbia University, her mother studied music for a year at Juilliard, and where Linda first learned to walk in Riverside Park. After that her family moved to Middletown, Connecticut and then to Princeton, New Jersey. Summertime trips back to Nebraska and riding horseback on her grandfathers' ranch and farm with a host of cousins were memorable occasions which shaped her perspective.

Music was an important part of her growing up years and she studied piano with her mother, and then piano and flute at the Julius Hartt School of Music (in Hartford, CT.) She picked up folk guitar after the death of her brother and has been playing and singing ever since.

She graduated from Barnard College in New York City with a degree in history and then married a young mathematician with a Ph.D. in mathematics. They moved to Pittsburgh where he spent his career at Carnegie Mellon University. Later she received an MA from Carnegie Mellon, also in history. Peter and Linda had two sons, Lyle & Bruce.

In Pittsburgh she was a cofounder of the IMAGINARIUM, which became a nationally known arts-in-education model based in the Carnegie Museums of Art and Natural History; she also served as Vice President of the "Collaborative for the Arts in Pittsburgh Education," and Member of the Music Advisory Panel for "The Pennsylvania Council on the Arts." In the 1980s she moved back to Princeton and served as a trustee of the Symphony for United Nations in New York City working to use music and the arts as vehicles for conflict resolution, particularly in the Middle East. She also served as President of the Board of LIFT in Trenton, NJ, a nonprofit organization which focused on the issues of teen pregnancy and poverty.

She has conducted workshops in communication, creativity and change in such corporate, educational and clinical settings as Bell Labs, AT&T, the Pennsylvania Department of Education, and the General Hospital of Naples Florida.

In the 1990s, quite by accident, she found herself thrust into the areas of conservation and paleontology and has spent the subsequent years integrating that work with her interest in the arts, humanities and education. She is currently a resident of Vermont, living during the winter in Princeton, NJ.

The Qwarriors

Endnotes

1 Robert Dalrymple, *Letter to the Author,* 28, December 2003. TS.

2 Allen S. Stratton, *The History of the Town of Isle La Motte,* (North Hero, VT A.S. Stratton 1984) 117-125.

3 Ibid. p.118.

4 Ira Hill, "History of the Town of Isle La Mott, *Gazeteer of Vermont,* 1849 http://www.rootsweb.ancestry.com/-vermont/GrandIsleIsleLaMotte.html. Latest date of access Feb 10, 2015.

5 Nigel Copsey, *Report of Works Carried Out.* June 2004. Personal Communication.

6 Allen Stratton, *The History of the Town of Isle La Motte,* North Hero. VT A.S. Stratton, 1984.

7 Christopher Graff, "Arthur Gibb, VT. Legislator, Pioneer of Environmental Law," *The Boston Globe,* November 5, 2005. http://www.boston.com/news/globe/obituaries/articles/2005/11/05/arthur_gibb_97_vt_le gislator_pioneer_of_environmental_law/ Latest date of access February 10, 2015.

8 Hill, Ira. "History of the Town of Isle La Mott," *Gazeteer of Vermont,* 1849 http://www.rootsweb.ancestry.com/-vermont/GrandIsleIsleLaMotte.html. Latest date of access February 10, 2015.

9 Attributed to Scott Newman, Historic Preservationist.

10 Allen S. Stratton, *The History of the Town of Isle La Motte* (North Hero, VT A.S. Stratton 1984) 117-125.

11 Elizabeth Fisk's great niece, Martha Turner Dale, has made it her life's work to collect, preserve, and educate about the Elizabeth Fisk weavings. (http://fisklooms.org). Latest date of access February 10,2015.

12 George Perkins Marsh, *Man and Nature* (New York: Charles Scribner & Co., 1867) Kindle version. Retrieved from Amazon.com.

13 Theodore Roosevelt, "John Muir:An Appreciation," *Outlook*, vol 109 pp.27,28 January 16, 1915. http://vault.sierraclub.org/john_muir_exhibit/life/appreciation_by_roosevelt.aspx). Latest date of access Feb 10, 2015. January 16, 1915

14 John Muir, *The story of my Childhood and Youth*, (Boston & New York: Houghton Mifflin Company. 1913 Riverside Press Cambridge) Kindle version. Retrieved from Amazon.com.

15 Theodore Roosevelt, *John Muir: An Appreciation. Outlook*, vol 109 pp.27, 28 January 16, 1915. http://vault.sierraclub.org/john_muir_exhibit/life/appreciation_by_roosevelt.aspx). Latest date of access Feb 10, 2015.

16 Author Unknown, "*A Pal of Presidents,*" *Burlington Free Press, 1986).*

[17] These offices were destroyed by "Hurricane Irene" in 2011 but are being rebuilt at the time of this writing.

[17] Emporia State University, Richard O. Sleezer, History of Wetland Soils in the United States:Wetland Environments. http://academic.emporia.edu/aberjame/wetland/soils/soils1.htm).

[19] Ibid. p19.

[20] (US Department of the Interior, "ScrubShrubWetland," https://dnr.state.il.us/wetlands/scrub-shrub.htm) Latest date of access Feb 10, 2015.

[21] Ann Chapman, "Nineteenth Century Trends in American Conservation," (http://www.nps.gov/nr/travel/massachusetts_conservation/Nineteenth_Century_Trends_in_%20American_Conservation.html) Latest date of access Feb 10, 2015.

[22] Doris Kearns Goodwin, The Bully Pulpit, (New York, London: Simon Schuster, 2013) p81.

[23] National Park Service, "The Works of Theodore Roosevelt: Outdoor pastimes of an American Hunter, http://www.nps.gov/thro/historyculture/theodore-roosevelt-quotes.htm) Latest date of access Feb 10 2015.

[24] Goodwin, Doris Kearns. The Bully Pulpit (New York, London: Simon Schuster, 2013 pg 259.

[25] IBID A general discussion of this phase of Roosevelt's career can be found in Chapter 9.

[26] Theodore Roosevelt, Speech on the occasion of the Fish and Game League Annual Meeting, Isle La Motte (The Burlington Free Press, September 7, 1901).

[27] The reporter undoubtedly meant "the Adirondack" Mountains.

[28] http://en.wikipedia.org/wiki/History_of_the_National_Park_Service.

[29] J.B. Burnham, "Vermont League Outing," Forest and Stream 14 September 1901 v57n11;pp 208-208.

[30] The University of Montana, "Gifford Pinchot: America's First Forester". http://www.wilderness.net/NWPS/Pinchot. Latest date of access Feb 11, 2015

[31] From Breaking New Ground, Washington, D.C.: Island Press, 1998, page 27.) http://en.wikipedia.org/wiki/Sustainable_forest_management.

[32] From a draft manual on Act 250 written by Don Avery, a close friend of Joe Bivins and a member of the Citizens' Participation Network.

[33] This effort has begun to fall out of favor with conservationists increasingly concerned about water shortages and adverse impact of irrigated agriculture.

[34] American Antiquities Act of 1906.www.cr.nps.gov/local-law/anti1906.htm.

35 Quote from Theodore Roosevelt on the occasion of establishing the American Antiquities Act. http://www.theodorerooseveltcenter.org/Blog/2012/January/11-Preserving-the-Grand-Canyon.aspx. Last date of access Feb 17. 2015.

36 "Rip rap is made from a variety of rock types, commonly granite or limestone, and occasionally concrete rubble from building and paving demolition. It can be used on any waterway or water containment where there is potential for water erosion." (http://en.wikipedia.org).

37 JohnMuir, Hetch Hetchy Valley, *The Yosemite Chapter 16* http://www.sierraclub.org/john_muir_exhibit/writings/the_yosemite/chapter_16.aspx) Last date of access, February 10, 2015.

38 Gifford Pinchot, *Hetch Hetchy* (https://facultystaff.richmond.edu/~sbrash/ES%20201/Readings/Readings.pdf).

39 IBID

40 Timothy Egan, *The Big Burn*. New York, (Houghton Mifflin Harcourt Publishing Company, Boston, New York, 2009). Kindle Edition. Retrieved from Amazon.com.

41 Betty Atwood, "Elizabeth Fisk, Early 20th Century Vermont Weaver," *Handweaver and Craftsmen*, Summer 1968.

42 IBID.

43 PBS The "National Parks:America's Best Idea, John Muir" http://www.pbs.org/nationalparks/people/historical/muir/.

44 Sierra Club,Theodore Roosevelt, "John Muir: An Appreciation," *Outlook*, vol 109 pp.27,28 January 16, 1915. http://vault.sierraclub.org/john_muir_exhibit/life/appreciation_by_roosevelt.aspx). Last date of access Feb 10, 2015.

45 IBID.

46 Lena Hill Severance, "Isle La Motte Woman Pays Tribute to Life of Mrs. N.W. Fisk," *Burlington Free Press*, August 22, 1927.

47 In 2003 the Board decided to change the name of the organization to the Isle La Motte Preservation Trust, giving it greater scope for conservation activity on Isle La Motte.

48 Dirk Kempthorne, Letter to Author. 16, Jan. 2009.

49 Sid Liebes, Walk Through Time" (Remarks at the State of the World Forum. San Francisco, CA. 5, November 1997.

50 IBID.

51 IBID.